THE

POSTMODERN

ORGANIZATION

Mastering
the Art
of Irreversible
Change

WILLIAM BERGQUIST

THE

POSTMODERN

ORGANIZATION

Mastering
the Art
of Irreversible
Change

Jossey-Bass Publishers • San Francisco

Substantial discounts on bulk quantities of Jossey-Bass books are available to corporations, professional associations, and other organizations. For details and discount information, contact the special sales department at Jossey-Bass Inc., Publishers. (415) 433-1740; Fax (415) 433-0499.

For sales outside the United States, contact Maxwell Macmillan International Publishing Group, 866 Third Avenue, New York, New York 10022.

Manufactured in the United States of America

The paper used in this book is acid-free and meets the State of California requirements for recycled paper (50 percent recycled waste, including 10 percent postconsumer waste), which are the strictest guidelines for recycled paper currently in use in the United States.

Library of Congress Cataloging-in-Publication Data

Bergquist, William H.
    The Postmodern organization : mastering the art of irreversible change / William Bergquist. — 1st ed.
      p.   cm. — (The Jossey-Bass management series)
    Includes bibliographical references and index.
    ISBN 1-55542-533-X
    1. Organizational change. I. Title. II. Series.
HD58.8.B473   1993
658.4'063—dc20
                                            92-43606
                                              CIP

FIRST EDITION
HB Printing   10 9 8 7 6 5 4 3 2 1   *Code 9335*

The Jossey-Bass
Management
Series

Contents

ix

Preface

Prophets, poets, and social critics have declared that the modern world is dying or already dead. A new world has not yet emerged to take its place. We appear to be living and working on the edge of a new era. We define everything by what it used to be (postindustrial, postcapitalist, post-Marxist, post–cold war) but we do not yet know what it will become.

The Postmodern Organization is devoted in part to an examination of contemporary organizations as they hover at the edge of the postmodern era. I have taken the stance of an observer who has lived through the later stages of the modern era and is living through the early stages of the newly emerging era. I assume that the modern era has ended, although many vestiges of it surround us and have an impact on our daily lives. I speak of both the premodern and modern eras in the past tense and use the present and future tenses to speak of the postmodern era. From this vantage point, I examine the characteristics of postmodern organizational forms and dynamics and compare them to those of organizations as they functioned in the premodern and modern worlds and continue to function in the hybrid reality of our emerging postmodern world.

I also examine the postmodern threshold from another perspective: perhaps this transitional era in which we now live is in fact *the* new world rather than merely a way station to a new world that has not yet been born. We may now be living not in the age of anxiety but rather in an age of "edginess," poised on the boundary between order and chaos. Obviously, for many years organizations have been described primarily as bringing order into the world. Particularly during the modern era, organizations were praised for the systematic, bureaucratic way in which human labor and machines were brought together to accomplish a predefined task. Organizations have long epitomized order. Yet contemporary organizations are also sources and victims of substantial disorder and chaos. Many organizations that could be labeled postmodern are poised on the brink of chaos—not chaos as it is commonly defined, as anarchy or complete disorganization, but according to its emerging use (see Gleick, 1987; Briggs and Peat, 1989), as a state of unpredictability and complexity.

The premodern era was characterized by the predominance of small organizations with simple structures, unclear (and often unnecessary) missions and boundaries, and paternal or charismatic leadership. Growth was either nonexistent or organic. (Many premodern organizations were devoted to agriculture or crafts.) Communication in premodern organizations was primarily oral and face-to-face; land and reputation were the primary forms of capital; and workers provided manual labor, primarily in exchange for food, shelter, and security.

By contrast, the modern organization was large and complex; growth was a primary criterion of success. Typically, the mission of modern organizations was unclear, though boundaries were usually quite clear. Leadership was based on the systematic application of sound management principles, with communication occurring primarily through formal, written documents (memoranda, legal documents, letters). Money, buildings, and machines were the primary forms of capital in the modern era. Labor was compensated through formal wage and salary structures.

The postmodern organization is a combination of the premodern and the modern organization, yet it has certain distinctive features—notably, an emphasis on small-to-moderate size and complexity and adoption of flexible structures and modes of interinstitutional cooperation to meet turbulent organizational and environmental conditions. Clarity of mission is emphasized, in part to compensate for the increasingly diffuse boundaries in these institutions. While management is still critical in the postmodern organization, leadership is often defined as something quite different from management. Increasingly, postmodern leaders are effective in specific settings at specific times, and their reign is often short and turbulent. Communication in the postmodern organization tends to be oral (as in premodern times), although often electronically mediated rather than face-to-face and based on temporary rather than long-term relationships. Capital in the postmodern organization takes the form of information and expertise, and knowledge workers are often much more influential and expect more intrinsic satisfaction from their work than did workers in either the premodern or the modern organization.

What is it like to live and work in a postmodern organization? Living on the edge is certainly difficult, given the many troubling ambiguities and the demand for new skills and attitudes that characterize the edge. It is also, however, exciting and addicting. Living on the edge is a "threshold" experience (Turner, 1969), a "flow" experience (Csikszentmihalyi, 1975, 1990), that brings us into a special realm free (at least temporarily) of both boredom and anxiety. We often gain a much clearer sense of ourselves when we find ourselves at the edge of a new era in our personal lives or in our society. At the edge we often must make critical decisions regarding what we stand for and what we want in life. The edge is a boundary between two or more different systems or cultures. It is at the boundary of any system that we find maximum information exchange and maximum unpredictability, for the edge is where a system is conducting transactions with the outside world.

I offer a third perspective in this book. The seemingly complex and chaotic nature of contemporary, postmodern organizations may be neither a transitional state nor a new, permanent state of affairs; instead, the growing emphasis on postmodernism in contemporary organizations (see, for example, Clegg, 1990) may simply be part of our growing awareness of and insight into the ways in which organizations have always run in our world—or at least the ways in which they have operated for the past two centuries. Organizations may have always been straddling the border between order and chaos. Perhaps, as some systems theorists claim, the primary function of any organization (or any human enterprise, for that matter) is to snatch structure and order from the jaws of chaos, to reverse the course of what systems theorists call entropy—the tendency of all systems to move toward disorder or chaos. Many systems in our world can be best described as entities that hover on the edge or move back and forth between the states of order and chaos.

In preparing this exploration of the postmodern organization, I have made use of three primary sources. First, I have drawn on my own twenty-five years of experience as an organizational consultant to more than five hundred corporations, human service agencies, educational institutions, and churches, along with my ten years of experience as an administrator in an interstate educational agency and as president of an independent graduate school. Second, I have benefited greatly from the insights offered by mature graduate students in both psychology and management programs. I have taught courses on the postmodern organization for the past eight years and have learned much from my interaction with students and from the many term papers and case studies that they have prepared on this topic. Third, I build on my extensive reading in the fields of psychology, management, and social history, including, specifically, reading of books and articles on postmodern thought and chaos theory.

Overview of Contents

The book is divided into three parts, each of which examines a variety of organizational issues from a different vantage point. In

Part One, I look generally at the newly emerging perspectives on organizational life. In Chapter One, I borrow from the work of contemporary chaos theorists and present the major thesis of this book: that the multiple changes occurring in many contemporary organizations are not reversible. We will see no return to the old order. Rather, the postmodern condition and emerging perspectives will, like fire, consume and transform the old order and the modern-day operations of organizations. Our job, as those who live and work in these organizations, is to tend the fires of the emerging postmodern world. In Chapter Two, I introduce several hallmarks of the postmodern condition, as articulated by not only chaos theorists but also by literary critics, social historians, and artists in many different fields. This book represents one of the first attempts to blend diverse perspectives from the sciences, arts, and humanities and to apply these perspectives to our understanding of contemporary organizations.

In Part Two, I examine the central characteristics of the postmodern world and the organizations that now exist or will exist in such a world. I assess differences in the ways organizations operate in the premodern, modern, and postmodern eras, and the ways in which the modern and premodern structures and dynamics of organizations persist and thrive in the emerging postmodern world. I conduct this systematic examination by focusing on five dimensions of organizational life: size and complexity (Chapter Three), mission and boundaries (Chapter Four), leadership (Chapter Five), communication (Chapter Six), and capital and worker values (Chapter Seven).

Part Three includes an examination of four different models of the postmodern organization. The *hybrid organization* model (Chapter Eight) focuses on the diversity of forms and dynamics that are found in the postmodern organization. The *cyclical organization* model (Chapter Nine) examines the interplay between order and chaos within organizations as they move through both predictable and unpredictable changes. The *intersect organization* model (Chapter Ten) focuses on the troubling ambiguities in postmodern organizations that reflect traditional divisions between public and private, profit and nonprofit, and large and small institutions in our society. The *turbulent organization* model (Chapter Eleven) illustrates the complex interplay between change, stability, and stagnation in postmodern institutions. Irreversible processes of change are described and a new metaphor of organizational functioning is introduced to define the dynamics of postmodern organizations as a journey across a tilted, warped plane. The four alternative models, and the postmodern perspectives that underlie them, can serve as critical elements in the formulation of new theories of organizational life in the coming decade and in the preparation for strategies for tending organizational fires in our postmodern world.

Acknowledgments

In preparing this book, I have relied heavily on the generosity of my friends, colleagues, students, and family, who provided me with an abundance of ideas, support, and understanding as I completed this ambitious project. I wish first of all to thank my mature and accomplished graduate students in management, psychology, and higher education from the United States, Canada, and Asia. They have provided this book with a "mid-management" perspective on postmodernism in their own organizations. I believe that their perspectives are more accurate and up-to-date than are those from the top of the organization (on which some other books about contemporary organizational life have tended to rely). Because my students are experienced professionals (usually in their thirties, forties, or fifties) who continue to manage organizations while attending school, they artfully blended theory and practice in their written and oral comments on the concepts presented in this book. Their contributions are evident throughout. However, because these people come from the middle of the organization rather than the top, they must often remain anonymous. They know who they are and know of their specific contributions to this book (since they have given me permission to use their case material). I wish to thank all of them for their wisdom and enthusiasm.

I am particularly indebted to two people for many of the ideas contained in this book—although I take credit for my misuse or unique use of the concepts they have tried to teach me. I wish especially to thank Randy Badler for his insights and suggestions regarding postmodernism, and Ouisue Packard for her remarks and insights concerning chaos theory. I hope someday to write books with each of these wonderful scholar-practitioners that will expand on the ideas contained in this book. Two other colleagues were very influential in my early thinking on the topic: David Halliburton, who told me about alternative approaches to the study of systems, and Alan Briskin, who discussed alternative approaches to the study of control and authority. Ping-Chi Mao and April Chi offered me the opportunity to learn from knowledgeable colleagues in Asia, and Diane Morrison afforded me a similar opportunity in western Canada. My staff at the Professional School of Psychology (in particular, Nancy Barber, Richard Weiser, and Eunice Kelly) have given me the chance to write this book while serving as president of their institution. Without their extraordinary competence and commitment, I would have been unable to find the time to complete this task.

Finally, I wish to express my deep love and respect for my wife, Kathleen O'Donnell, who has been an exceptional source of support for more than a dozen years. My son, Jason, my daughter, Katy, and my daughter-in-law, Marybeth, provide a focal point for my life and work. They have taught me a great deal about postmodernism and life in general through their expression of love and through our conversations—what a joy to witness the maturing of your own child's mind! Because this book is about the future as well as the present, I wish to dedicate it to my two young granddaughters, Alicia and Julia, who will be living in the postmodern world that is now unfolding. I wish them a safe and enlightening journey through the coming century and will try to tend carefully the fires so that they are still burning when Alicia and Julia assume their role as citizens in this remarkable new world.

San Francisco, California William Bergquist
February 1993

The Author

William Bergquist is president of
of the Professional School of Psychology in San Francisco and in
Sacramento, California. He received his B.A. degree (1962) in psychology from Occidental College in Los Angeles and his M.A.
(1963) and Ph.D. (1969) degrees in psychology from the University
of Oregon.

During the course of his career, Bergquist has served as consultant to more than five hundred corporations, human service
agencies, governmental bodies, and educational institutions in such
areas as program design, human resource development, problem-

solving, team building, and strategic planning. He has authored or coauthored more than a dozen books, including *The Four Cultures of the Academy* (1992), *Developing Human and Organizational Resources* (1993), and *In Our Fifties* (1993, with Greenberg and Klaum).

THE

POSTMODERN

ORGANIZATION

Mastering
the Art
of Irreversible
Change

Part One

Farewell to the Old Order

Chapter 1

From the Pendulum to the Fire: Coming to Terms with Irreversible Change

If Western Civilization does go down, irrevocably, the last figures to be seen above the floodwaters will have pencil and notebook in hand, as they busily conduct an investigation of what is happening. No. We need to understand our ailing visions in order to know what to reject and what to accept in them, but all our study is only a preliminary clearing of the decks for the urgent vision-work of creating tomorrow. Self-analysis is only meaningful if it liberates us to choose our own destiny. Man has the capacity to dream finer dreams than he has ever succeeded in dreaming. He has the capacity to build a finer society than he has ever succeeded in building. We have always known this. Must this knowledge paralyze us? Here lies the real challenge! There are among us even now dreamers and builders ready to repeat the age-old process of splitting the atom of time, to release the Western world from its too-long imprisonment in the present. Then man will once again be free to "seek the city which is to come."

Fred Polak, *The Image of the Future*

Contemporary organizational theory—for that matter, most organizational theory of the past century—is built on a solid, mechanistic foundation. Organizations operate like other systems; they import resources from the outside (such as raw materials, employees, capital, sales orders, and customers), effect some sort of transformation on them (such as converting iron to automobiles or untrained children to properly educated citizens), and export the transformed products to other organizations located in the external world. Under the best of circumstances, organizations operate like a carefully designed and crafted Swiss watch. At other times, unfortunately, organizations appear ill-

3

managed and ill-equipped to deal with a highly turbulent world. Nevertheless, even under conditions of turbulence, we expect contemporary organizations to somehow come to terms with this external world, and we speak of searching for equilibrium and homeostasis in a volatile environment.

The mechanistic organization, in essence, runs like a pendulum, which epitomizes elegance and simplicity in motion. We can disrupt the course of the pendulum by giving it an added push or by bumping into it and slowing it down. In either case, the pendulum will adjust its course and continue swinging back and forth at a greater or lesser magnitude. The pendulum, in modern systems theory terms, always returns to a homeostatic balance, retaining its basic form or pathway.

According to many contemporary theorists, organizations are homeostatic in nature. They tend to return to their previous form and function after disruptions and interferences. While the contemporary organization may seem to be chaotic and in disarray, we are merely witnessing a long-term process of homeostatic readjustment, with an ultimate return to a former state or style of functioning.

Fire and Second-Order Change in Organizations

Is this mechanistic analogy to the pendulum still accurate for contemporary organizations? Was it ever very accurate, for that matter? Ilya Prigogine, a Nobel Prize–winning scientist, suggests that many processes in nature do not work mechanistically—as much as scientists throughout the ages have wanted the world to resemble the orderly pendulum or Swiss watch (Prigogine and Stengers, 1984). Rather, many processes of the world more likely resemble the phenomenon we call fire.

Fire is an enduring problem in the history of science. Prigogine (Prigogine and Stengers, 1984) notes that modern scientists, in an effort to create a coherent mechanistic model of the world, have tended to ignore the complex, transformative processes of fire, concentrating on only one of its properties: the capacity to generate heat. Fire became a heat-producing machine for scientists and was thus treated in a mechanistic manner.

Fire, however, has many fascinating properties. Most important, it is an irreversible process: it consumes something that cannot be reconstructed. Homes lost in a fire can never be unburned; a community destroyed by fire can never be readjusted. There is only the construction of new homes and a new community, which will never exactly replicate the old homes or community. Many other processes of change and transformation are similarly irreversible. Avalanches can never be undone, nor can Pandora's box ever be closed once the lid is opened and the evil spirits have escaped.

The process of change in organizations often operates like fire. We blurt out organizational truths in moments of frustration or anger and can never cover them up again. We tentatively consider a change in organizational structure, but the word gets out and we are soon stuck with the change whether we like it or not. Equilibrium has been disturbed, chaos often follows, and we ourselves are not the same as we were before. Time moves in one direction and cannot be reversed.

A second remarkable characteristic of fire is its ephemeral nature. It is all process and not much substance. As Prigogine notes, the Newtonian sciences concentrated on substances and the ways in which various forces operated on various substances. The Newtonian world was governed by a "science of being." Fire, by contrast, is a "science of becoming" (Prigogine and Stengers, 1984, p. 209). A science of being, argues Prigogine, focuses on the states of a system, whereas a science of becoming focuses on temporal changes—such as the flickering of a flame. Fire demands a focus not on the outcomes of a process but rather on the nature of the process itself.

Much as children focus on their process of drawing when showing their parents a picture they have made, so must we focus on organizational processes, for example, ways in which decisions are made in organizations or styles used to manage employees, rather than focusing on the final decisions that are made or the relative success of an employee's performance. Unfortunately, organizational processes (like fires) are elusive. They are hard to measure and even harder to document in terms of their ultimate impact on an organization.

Pendulums operate in a quite different manner from fires. First of all, the movement of a pendulum is quite predictable, whereas that of fire is unpredictable (as in the case of most dynamic systems). Once we know the initial parameters of the pendulum (length of stem, force applied when pendulum is first pushed in a specific direction, and so forth), we can predict virtually everything of importance about this mechanistic and relatively closed system. Even without any initial information, we can readily predict the future movement of the pendulum after observing its trajectory once or twice.

A second important feature of the pendulum—one that makes it a particular favorite of many modern scientists—is its primary connection to one of the central building blocks of Newtonian science: gravity. While fire seems to defy or at least be indifferent to gravity, flickering about apparently weightless and formless, our noble pendulum provides clear evidence that gravity is present and that it operates in a uniform and predictable manner on objects of substance. The pendulum is a tool that is readily transformed into a technology (for example, the Swiss watch), based on its dependability and conceptual accessibility. Fire, by contrast, can burn and rage uncontrolled. Once started, fires tend to take on a life of their own, seemingly defying the laws of entropy. Pendulums are domestic and obey the laws of entropy. They stop when they receive inadequate attention and never rage out of control.

A third feature of the pendulum is the reversibility of its process. The pendulum swings back and forth, repeatedly moving back to a space that it occupied a short time before. The pendulum, like many mechanistic systems, frequently undoes what has already been done in order for the system to remain in equilibrium and in operation. A pendulum that swung in only one direction (to but not fro) would soon be replaced by one that works properly.

Organizations that operate like pendulums seem to be everywhere (though they are becoming less common). An organization shifts in one direction, then soon corrects itself and shifts back in the opposite direction. Large inventories are soon corrected by a drop in production orders. Later, production orders are increased to make up for a drop in inventory. In organizations that resemble pendulums, homeostasis is always preserved—eventually. The organization keeps returning to an ideal or at least minimally acceptable state. Homeorhesis (a Greek word referring to the tendency to return to a common pathway or style) is also preserved. The organization monitors, reviews, and readjusts its mode of operation in order to return to a desired path, style, or strategy.

Gregory Bateson (1979), the exceptional biologist and anthropologist, speaks of this process as "first-order" change. In essence, a first-order change occurs when people in an organization do more of something that they are already doing or less of something that they are already doing as a way of returning to some desired state of being (homeostasis). We spend more money on a computer system in order to reduce our customer response time to a former level. We reduce the cost of a specific product in order to restore our competitive edge in the marketplace. We pay our employees higher wages in order to bring back high-level morale and productivity to the company. First-order changes are always reversible because we can go back to the drawing board and repeatedly readjust our change effort, using feedback systems that provide us with information about how we are performing relative to our standard or goal.

Bateson identifies "second-order" change as a process that is irreversible. A second-order change occurs when we decide to (or are forced to) do something different from what we have done before, rather than just doing more or less of what we have already been doing. A second-order change occurs when an organization chooses to provide a new kind of compensation, rather than merely increasing or decreasing current levels and rates of compensation. Rather than paying more money or less money, I pay my employees with something other than money (for example, stock in the company, greater autonomy, or a new and more thoughtful mode of personal recognition and appreciation). Second-order change happens when I choose not to increase or decrease my rate of communication with my subordinates (first-order change), but rather to communicate something different to my subordinates from what I have ever communicated to them before. In other words, rather than talking more or talking less about something, I talk about something different.

In the case of any second-order change, there is a choice point when an organization begins to move in a new direction. Once this choice point (what systems theorists call the point of "bifurcation" and what poets call the "fork in the road"), is traversed, there is no turning back. Once the fire has begun, one cannot unburn what has already been consumed. One can extinguish the fire, but a certain amount of damage has already been done and a certain amount of warmth has already been generated. Once I have changed the way in which I compensate my employees, there is no turning back (as many leaders have found in their unionized organizations).

In summary, the idea of reversibility and irreversibility of organizational change relates directly to the concepts of pendulums and fires, and first- and second-order change. Just as some changes are first order and others are second order, and some look like the period adjustment of a pendulum while others look like fire, so it is the case that some changes appear to be reversible and others are irreversible. Those organizational change processes that are reversible involve the restoration of balance or style. They typically are first order in nature and resemble the dynamics of a pendulum. Other organizational change processes are irreversible. They bring about transformation and parallel the combustive processes of fire, rather than the mechanical processes of the pendulum. Second-order change is typically associated with these irreversible processes of combustion.

Throughout this book, I explore the nature of irreversible, second-order changes in our emerging postmodern world. The implications of organizational irreversibility are profound, for major problems often emerge when organizational fires are mistaken for organizational pendulums. The 1991 Soviet coup, for instance, appears to exemplify an irreversible, combustible form of change. Whereas the coup leaders thought that the Soviet Union would continue to operate as a pendulum, with each new group of leaders restoring the government to its previous state, the people on the streets saw an opportunity to kindle a fire—a second-order change. Their new order of things was not one of restoration, but rather one of transformation. Whatever happens in the old Soviet Union, there will never be a return to the prior order. The toothpaste can't be shoved back into the tube. The story cannot be untold.

Poised on the Edge of Order and Chaos

In a recent article, Stuart Kauffman (1991) introduces a new concept of chaos and order. He describes three different categories—or states—in which many systems (perhaps even organizations) can be placed. One of these states is highly ordered and structured. Kauffman uses an analogy between this state and the solid state that water takes when it is frozen. A second state is highly chaotic and disorderly. Kauffman equates this state with the gaseous form water takes when it is evaporating. The third (most interesting) state is one of transition between order and chaos, which Kauffman identifies with the liquid state of water (though he notes that true liquids are not transitory in nature but are instead a distinct form of matter). The differentiation between solid, gaseous, and liquid networks can be of significant value in setting the context for any discussion of postmodernism in organizations—and, in particular, the irreversibility of many organizational processes. We must look not only at ordered networks (the so-called solid state) and at chaotic networks (the so-called gaseous state) but also at liquid networks that hover on the brink of chaos if we are to understand and influence our unique postmodern institutions.

The third (liquid) state holds particularly great potential when we examine and seek to understand confusing and often elusive organizational phenomena such as mission, leadership, and communication. Turbulent rivers, avalanches, shifting weather patterns, and other conditions that move between order and chaos typify the liquid state. Liquid systems contain chaotic elements as well as elements of stability. There are both quiet pools and swirling eddies in a turbulent river; mountain avalanches consist not only of rapidly moving volumes of snow but also of stable snowpacks; stable and chaotic weather patterns intermingle to form overall climatic patterns on our planets. The liquid state is characterized by edges and shifting boundaries. A liquid, edgy state is filled with the potential for learning.

How is a liquid state formed? At certain points in the life of solid-state systems, the system reaches a supercritical state and can no longer adjust to additional change or variation in pattern. The snowpack grows larger with each additional snowflake. At some critical point, the snowpack can no longer grow larger. At this point, the system becomes fluid and an avalanche occurs. Once the avalanche has stopped, the snowpack (now further down the hill) assumes a new form (as a function of the landscape at this location on the hill) and is once again stable. The system (snowpack) can once again adjust to the addition of a few changes or alterations in pattern (additional snowflakes).

I suggest that most organizations exist in the liquid state, poised on the edge of chaos. Furthermore, organizations are mechanisms that can learn and adjust (through first-order change). Yet, at a supercritical stage, organizations can no longer adjust; they can no longer accept even one additional change or one additional crisis. An avalanche begins, and the organization changes in a profound manner (a second-order change). The theory of self-organized criticality (Bak and Chen, 1991), or weak chaos, suggests that small events (first-order changes), such as a shift in leadership, will usually produce only minor alterations in the structure and dynamics of the organization (the snowpack will grow a bit wider or a bit deeper with each new snowflake). Sometimes, however, a change in leadership will create a major second-order alteration (an avalanche). Furthermore, while the outcomes are dramatically different, Bak and Chen propose that the same processes initiate both the minor and major changes and that the onset of the major event cannot be predicted—in part because the same process brings about both outcomes (one snowflake will add to the snowpack, while a second snowflake will precipitate an avalanche).

The liquid state and the edge are places of leadership and innovation ("the leading edge"). They are settings where things get done, often in the context of a very challenging and exhausting "white water" environment (Vaill, 1989; Quehl, 1991). Edges have no substance; they come to a point and then disappear. Perhaps this is what the new postmodern edginess—what Milan Kundera (1984) calls "the unbearable lightness of being"—is all about.

We must learn how to live and work in this new world of edges. Perhaps we need to listen to the architects and prophets of postmodernism, for they may provide some valuable clues as to how this world might best be faced. These architects and prophets come in many different forms: deconstructionists, feminists, chaos theorists, structuralists. This book is devoted, in part, to the examination of these postmodernists as they might help inform and revise our assumptions about the nature, purpose, and dynamics of the organizations in which we live and work.

I propose that we are poised on the edge of order and chaos in our contemporary organizations—that an avalanche has already taken place and the new form of the snowpack is already defined (though obviously some major adjustments are still occurring as the snowpack settles into the new landscape). We may have entered a new, distinct, and long-lasting postmodern era that in many ways—like the avalanche—is irreversible. Alternatively, we may be living in a short-term transitional period, having left the modern era forever; the avalanche, in other words, is now under way and we are living in it. If this is the case, then we have not yet settled into a new era but are instead living temporarily in an intermediate stage on the edge of something that we cannot yet know, let alone describe.

Regardless of which perspective one wishes to take, the process seems to be irreversible. While the past fifty years might best be described as an era of adjustment (the modern-day organizational pendulum), we are now entering an era of fire, during which old organizational forms, structures, and processes will be consumed and new forms, structures, and processes will emerge, like the phoenix, from the ashes of firey consumption. This new era, however, will not be composed entirely of new organizational elements; rather, it will offer a blend of very old, premodern elements of our society, modern-day elements of our society (as exemplified by many organizations that reached their zenith during the second half of the twentieth century), and newly emerging elements that bear little similarity to either their premodern or modern-day precursors.

Poised on the Edge of Postmodernism

We are currently poised on the edge of a newly emerging, complex world that many social observers have labeled *postmodern*. This is a particularly exciting and challenging time, for the edges of large social systems have always been the primary source of activity and information in defining the nature of cultures and societies. We can best understand an organization—or any other large or small social system—by examining its edges and the ways it interacts with other components of its environment. We should consider the "edginess" of the emerging postmodern era to be not simply a restatement of the modern-day "age of anxiety" but rather as a sign of the potential that confronts us in our information-rich world.

Postmodernists encourage us to identify differences that truly make a difference in our world. We must discard that which is superficially interesting but transitory and determine that which we individually and collectively should attend to at any point in time. Information derived from the identification of differences becomes critical to any leader or manager in a postmodern organization. Many organizational theorists are coming to recognize the importance of detecting change and difference. When change and differences are very gradual or when they are noticed after considerable delay, it is often too late to respond to them, leaving the organization in an exceptionally vulnerable position. We have only to look at the American auto industry or, more broadly, the world's ecology to appreciate the devastating effect of delayed recognition of a problematic change. The need for sensitivity to change and to differences-that-make-a-difference offers a considerable challenge for many men and women in postmodern organizations, given that we have been trained and rewarded primarily for noticing and encouraging nondifferences (that is, conformity to preestablished standards). In this book, I focus on differences that I believe do make a difference. These are differences not only in terms of premodern, modern, and postmodern elements of contemporary organizations but also in terms of alternative perspectives in examining the essential nature and purpose of all organizations at any point in time.

We also find the edges of postmodernism in the complex interplay between order and chaos. Everywhere we look in contemporary organizational life, we find order and chaos existing side by side. Sometimes organizations seem to make sense. The policies and procedures look right (at least on paper), and things seem to be moving along in a predictable manner. At other times, everything seems to be fragmented and chaotic. Nothing makes any sense in the organization, and one wonders if the center can hold. Postmodern theorists (especially those who are studying chaotic systems) suggest that these seemingly contradictory observations are actually a result of examining the organization at different levels (a spatial perspective) and at different points in its history (a temporal perspective).

Organizations (like virtually all other systems) contain layers and moments of both chaos and order. When confronted with a seemingly chaotic and unpredictable organization, we have only to move up one level (to greater abstraction) or down one level (to greater specificity) if we wish to find order. Alternatively, we have only to move backward or forward in time to find either order or chaos. For instance, the behavior of members of a specific department may make more sense if we examine the overall dynamics of the department, rather than just looking at their individual behavior. Organizational theorists now tell us about the deskilling of personnel that often occurs in organizations and the ways in which this deskilling contributes to stability. We have only to look back through the history of the organization and its culture to understand the orderly nature of and reason for this deskilling.

Similarly, we can move up or down levels of analysis to find chaos in an organization that seems to be orderly. The operation of a ballet or theater company, for example, may look very orderly from the rather limited perspective of a member of the audience. At a higher level, however, everything may look quite chaotic (inadequate funding, props that never arrive, recalcitrant performers), just as at the level of the individual performer we will find stage fright, confusion, rivalry, and other forms of "nonrational" and chaotic behavior that are never seen by the appreciative audience. Certainly, in many large organizations, the customers (and perhaps even corporate board members) are never allowed to witness such pervasive chaos.

Leaders of this edgy postmodern world must somehow navigate a turbulent "white water" environment, one filled with unpredictability and requiring both short-term survival tactics and long-term strategies based on broad visions and deeply embedded values. Leaders must be sources of integration in postmodern organizations. They perform this integrative role through the creation and sustenance of community and through acting in the role of servant to those with whom they work. The notions of community and servanthood, in turn, lead us away from the traditional (both premodern and modern) notions of a society based on dominance to a society based on partnership and collaboration—styles of leadership more commonly found among women than among men. This model of leadership calls into question much of the traditional managerial training of leaders and many of the motives that guide men and women to seek positions of leadership in our society.

While organizational transformations during the postmodern era may often seem thunderous, individual men and women during this period will come silently into the world of personal transformation. Postmodern conditions usually require small steps toward renewal rather than elaborate plans. These conditions also require a shift to different levels of understanding and modes of learning. In the modern world, boundaries (and identities defined by roles and rules) serve as containers of anxiety. In the postmodern world, we must look to an inner sense of self and to an outer structure of support and community for shelter, stability, and insight in an edgy and turbulent world.

In the postmodern world, we must find commitment within the context of faith and doubt. We must discover ways to make commitments and take action, while keeping a relativistic stance in a world that no longer allows for simple values or answers or for a stable ground of reference. We must often look to that which is old and that with which we disagree to find the balance and the kernel of truth we need to navigate successfully in our turbulent and confusing postmodern world. We return to the wisdom found in virtually all premodern cultures concerning the facade of progress and the ephemeral nature of planning. While standing on the edge of a postmodern world, we must discover wisdom in the patience and persistence of premodern man. We must return to premodern perspectives regarding the sacred nature of human organizations and once again listen to enlightening stories regarding our own human history and destiny. Only in this way can we successfully tend the complex and irreversible fires of the postmodern world.

Chapter 2

Postmodern Thought in a Nutshell: Where Art and Science Come Together

I cannot remember exactly when I first encountered the term postmodernism. I probably reacted to it in much the same way as I did to the various other "isms" that have come and gone over the past couple of decades, hoping that it would disappear under the weight of its own incoherence or simply lose its allure as a fashionable set of "new ideas."

But it seemed as if the clamor of postmodernist arguments increased rather than diminished with time. Once connected with poststructuralism, postindustrialism, and a whole arsenal of other "new ideas," postmodernism appeared more and more as a powerful configuration of new sentiments and thoughts.

David Harvey, *The Condition of Postmodernity*

The postmodern world is in the midst of being born. It does not yet have clear definition, other than its origins in and difference from the modern era. Hence the term *postmodern:* the concept is still defined with reference to its mother (modernism) rather than reflecting a free and independent movement or set of ideas and images with its own distinctive name. In many ways, postmodernism is a fad—and is at the same time about fads. Even though postmodernism is characterized by superficial, facile, and often internally contradictory analyses, it must not be dismissed, for these analyses offer insightful and valuable (even essential) perspectives on and critiques of an emerging era: "The postmodern moment had arrived and perplexed intellectuals, artists, and cultural entrepreneurs wondered whether they should get on the bandwagon and join the carnival, or sit on the sidelines until the new fad disappeared into the whirl of cultural fashion. Yet postmodernism refused to go away. . . . At first, there was no clear sense as to what constituted postmodernism, when it arrived, what it meant, and what effects it was having and would be likely to have in the future. Eventually, more systematic and sustained discussion took place" (Kellner, 1989, p. 2).

In the postmodern camp, there is neither interest in the systematic building of theory (through what Thomas Kuhn, 1962, calls "normal science") nor in a warfare between competing paradigms (what Kuhn calls "scientific revolutions"). Rather, everything is preparadigmatic. Tom Peters acknowledges that in the early 1980s he knew something about how organizations achieved excellence (Peters and Waterman, 1982). By the late 1980s, he discovered that he had been mistaken. Many of the "excellent" organizations of the early 1980s had become troubled institutions by the late 1980s. Other theorists and social observers have been similarly humbled by the extraordinary events of the 1980s and early 1990s. They simply haven't been as forthcoming (or opportunistic) as Tom Peters. "Postmodernism at its deepest level," notes Andreas Huyssen (1987, p. 217), "represents not just another crisis within the perpetual cycle of boom and bust, exhaustion and renewal, which has characterized the trajectory of modernist culture." Rather, the postmodern condition "represents a new type of crisis of that modernist culture itself."

If postmodernism is to provide a solid base for useful social analysis and if it is to contribute to the formulation of a new theory of organizations, then it must move beyond the status of fad and find roots in the soil of history and precedent. The origins of postmodernism can be traced to many different sources, ranging from the Marxist-based analyses of Frederick Jameson (1991) to the more conservative observations and predictions of Peter Drucker (1989), from Cristo's art-as-event performances to Peter Vaill's (1989) spiritual leadership. To trace the origins of postmodernism is to review the cultural history of twentieth-century America and possibly of our entire contemporary world. Since this task is impossible given the scope of this book (or virtually any other book), I will focus briefly in this chapter on four different sources of postmodernism. While none of these sources relate directly to organizational life, they all help to set the stage for our analyses of organizations, which consume our attention in the remaining chapters of this book. Readers already well versed in the various properties of postmodernism (and chaos theory) may wish to move directly to Chapter Three, where the application of these concepts begins.

A first source of postmodernism is the intellectual debates and dialogues in Europe (primarily in France) regarding structuralism, poststructuralism, deconstruction, postcapitalism, critical theory, and feminism. Much of this work is very difficult to understand, let alone summarize or typify. Some say it is difficult because the ideas are subtle, elusive, and complex. Others say it is difficult because the authors purposefully make their points in obscure or convoluted manners.

The second source of postmodern thought is the much more accessible (some would say popularized) critique of contemporary art forms (particularly architecture, literature, and painting) and contemporary life-styles (for example, advertising, fashion, and the colloquial use of language). This line of thought relates to many of the critiques offered by the first source, in particular those involving deconstructionist and feminist reinterpretations of cultural history. Some of the clearest, and most controversial, writers in this feminist tradition are those who study and write about alternative versions of world (especially Western) history (for example, Eisler, 1987) and alternative ways of knowing (for example, Gilligan, 1982; Belenky and others, 1986).

A third source is social analysis of the workplace and economy, as represented by the work of Daniel Bell (1976), who first coined the phrase "post-industrial era," and Peter Drucker, notably in his recent book, *The New Realities* (1989). Popular books written by Naisbitt (1984) and Toffler (1971, 1980) also have contributed, as has Tom Peters (particularly in *Thriving on Chaos*, 1987), who accurately portrays the inadequacies of the current response to postmodern conditions. Finally, postmodernism is beholden, in a somewhat more indirect manner, to work in the physical sciences that is usually labeled *chaos theory*. This work has been made accessible to the lay public through the journalistic writing of James Gleick

(1987) and the more technical, but nevertheless fascinating, writing of Ilya Prigogine (Prigogine and Stengers, 1984).

In the remainder of this chapter, I briefly summarize the contributions made by each of these four sources, thereby setting the stage for our subsequent discussion of the postmodern characteristics of contemporary organizations. I specifically focus on four themes often associated with postmodernism and briefly indicate how one or more of the four postmodern sources have contributed to the elucidation of each theme.

Objectivism Versus Constructivism

Two different perspectives compete in the postmodern era. They may be as important in the postmodern world as the liberal versus conservative distinction has been in the modern world. These two views, in fact, are often inaccurately equated with liberalism and conservatism. Advocates for *objectivism,* on the one hand, assume that there is a reality out there that we can know and articulate. There are universal truths—or at least universal principles—that can be applied to the improvement of the human condition, resolution of human conflicts, restoration of human rights, or even to the construction of a global order and community.

Advocates for *constructivism,* on the other hand, believe that we construct our own social realities, based in large part on the traditions and needs of the culture and socioeconomic context in which we find ourselves. There are no universal truths or principles, nor are there any global models of justice or order that can be applied in all settings, at all times, with all people. There are rather specific communities that espouse their own unique ways of knowing. Furthermore, these ways of knowing may themselves change over time and in differing situations.

These two perspectives do not simply involve different belief systems. They encompass different notions about the very nature of a belief system and in this sense are profoundly different from one another. While the objectivist perspective was prevalent during the modern era, the constructivist perspective is a recent, postmodern phenomenon. The emergence of the constructivist perspective represents a revolutionary change in the true sense of the term. Mark

Edmundson (1989, p. 63) addresses this revolution in his analysis of Salman Rushdie's *The Satanic Verses.*

> One might think of postmodernism—in its negative or demystifying phase—as trying to get done what its practitioners sensed modernism had failed to do; that is, to purge the world of superstition in every form. Major modern thinkers such as Marx and Freud strove to come up with ways of conceiving of life as lived in the West that would be genuinely post-religious. Both of them practiced and promoted what Paul Ricoeur has called "the hermeneutics of suspicion." Nothing, their work taught, could be taken at face value. Readers of Marx and Freud became attuned to the masking of class conflict and the suppression of erotic desires. "Civilization" had much to hide. In fact, civilization sometimes seemed to be nothing more than a series of linked strategies for concealment. The analysis of Marx and Freud—and of those whose writings have been informed by their thought—struck through the pasteboard mask of civilization to find a universe of suppressed truths.

Edmundson (1989, p. 63) goes on to note, however, that the modernist thinkers and critics still left the door open for a new secular transcendent order: "But the problem with this modern tendency to disenchant the world was that it turned the old religious drive upside down. The traditional man of faith seeks transcendence. He wants contact with God, the One, the Truth. The modern thinker, inspired by Marx and Freud, found truth in repressed or hidden impulses, but he *found truth* nonetheless. Similarly, modern artists and critics found organic cohesion, autonomy—a form of truth, perhaps—in the grand works, works like Joyce's *Ulysses* or Eliot's *The Waste Land*."

Thus, according to Edmundson, the central challenge for a postmodernist is to retain a healthy skepticism about all purported truths—including the "truths" offered by the postmodernists themselves:

The postmodern man sees religious residues in *any* way of thinking that affirms the Truth. He reads the modern period as the time when transcendentalism gave way, yes, but to a kind of thinking that sought to penetrate the depths, there to find bedrock reality. The spirit of the . . . postmodern movement in the arts, literary criticism, and philosophy might, assuming one were determined to shrink it to bumper-sticker size, be expressed like this: "If you want to be genuinely secular, then give up on transcendence in every form." Or, if your bumper's too small for that: "Accept no substitutes—for God." In other words, don't replace the deity with some other idol, like scientific truth, the self, the destiny of America, or what have you. And (front bumper) "Don't turn your postmodernism into a faith. Don't get pious about your impiety" [1989, p. 63].

As a result of this postmodern commitment to the shattering of epistemological icons, the traditional distinction between liberal and conservative breaks down. While the capitalist and communist offer quite different versions about what the world is like and what it should be like, they both begin with the assumption that there is a reality they can describe and assess with greater or lesser fidelity and that there are stable standards and values against which one can test alternative futures. Many of the postmodernists place a curse on both of these houses.

According to the constructivists, we must construct models of social reality and social value that are fluid, or at least flexible, and open to new data and to social conditions that change in rapid and unpredictable fashion. The postmodernist (and Marxist) Frederick Jameson (1991, p. 198) disagrees with Daniel Bell's assessment that ideology (in particular, liberal ideology) is dead because of improved social conditions in society; he does agree (for alternative reasons) that postmodernism has brought about "the end of ideology."

As with so much else, it is an old 1950s acquaintance, "the end of ideology," which has in the postmodern returned with a new and unexpected kind of plausibility. But ideology is now over, not because class struggle has ended and no one has anything class-ideological to fight about, but rather because the fate of "ideology" in this particular sense can be understood to mean that conscious ideologies and political opinions, particular thought systems along with the official philosophical ones which laid claim to a greater universality—the whole realm of consciousness, argument, and the very appearance of persuasion itself (or of reasoned dissent)—has ceased to be functional in perpetuating and reproducing the system.

Social psychologist Milton Rokeach (1960) provided insight regarding this new way of thinking about social and political models of society. Rokeach pointed out that in certain important ways, the far left and the far right tend to think alike. They search for absolutes and often portray their adversaries in what William Perry (1970) later described as a "dualistic" framework: either you agree with me or you disagree with me. Either you are right or I am right. Which is it? Both liberals and conservatives often believe that their own models of social justice and governance can be applied throughout the world (with a few adjustments for culture). They are both missionary in their zeal for dissemination of the truths they hold. The dualistic frameworks of both conservatives and liberals no longer hold up. The world is changing to a more constructivist perspective, particularly with regard to its most prized fictions—such as freedom. "Man's freedom is a fabricated freedom and he pays a price for it. He must at all times defend the utter fragility of his delicately constituted fiction, deny its artificiality. . . . Man's fictions are not superfluous creations that could be 'put aside' so that the 'more serious' business of life could continue" (Becker, 1971, p. 139).
Elaboration of the new, constructivist perspective has been accelerated by several contemporary social scientists who have written about the "social construction of reality"—notably Berger and Luckmann (1967)—and by feminists who have written about unique ways many women and some men become knowledgeable

about their world (Gilligan, 1982; Belenky and others, 1986). The new constructivism has also been aided by the emergence of a critical perspective on absolute knowledge in the physical sciences, culminating in the establishment of chaos theory. Something as simple as the measurement of length and circumference is subject to debate and the particular interest and purpose of the person doing the measurement (Gleick, 1987), in addition to the effect the measurer has on the phenomenon being measured (the so-called Heisenberg Principle).

One of the earliest and most articulate scientific spokespersons for this constructivist perspective was Michael Polanyi (1969), who wrote of the problem associated with the act of "attending to" and "attending from" any phenomenon. We can never attend to that from which we are attending. The base of our perception must always remain hidden from our perception; otherwise, we will be perceiving this base from yet another base. Thus, there is the danger of infinite regression among the social constructivists: the relativistic "social construction of reality" may itself be a social construction; Thomas Kunn's observation about paradigms may itself be a social scientific paradigm of history that will soon be overturned by yet another paradigm; Michel Foucault's critique regarding the social/political origins of knowledge must itself be placed in a social/political context.

The Polanyi dilemma becomes particularly poignant when considering, as the French psychoanalyst Lacon did, the act of self-reflection. When one is attending to oneself in a mirror, one is attending back (in Polanyi's terms) to that from which one attends. Similarly, in psychoanalysis (or in any organization's attempt to study and understand itself), the subject is observing himself or herself in the mirror. Yet, the base from which one is attending can never be the subject of analysis, unless the base itself is changed. If the base is changed, then the new base will still remain elusive and incapable of simultaneous review.

Thus, an organization that brings in an outside consultant to study its culture will be subject to the particular perspectives (including distortions) of the consultant's own culture. To turn around and study the consultant's culture in order to gain a better perspective on the consultant's report would require the hiring of yet another consultant to study the first consultant—or would require that the client organization study the consultant's culture. The first approach would lead to infinite external regression (a consultant for the consultant for the consultant, ad infinitum); the second would lead to a never-ending internal regression (like looking at mirror images of mirror images of mirror images, ad infinitum). Hence, according to the constructivists, one can never obtain an objective assessment of an institution, even with the help of a skilled and honest external consultant.

Language Is Itself Reality

According to Huyssen (1987, p. 179), the postmodern world is a bit "softer" than the modern world. It is less a world of facts and figures and more a world of story and performance. We are moving from a modern world that was primarily mediated by visual communication (descriptive writing, television, and movies) to a postmodern world that is once again (as in the premodern world) mediated primarily by auditory communication (speech and narrative writing). We are moving from a world that uses metaphors of sight ("having a vision of a future world," "imagining an alternative") to one using metaphors of speech ("finding one's voice," "telling one's own story"). According to the postmodernist voices of the literary critics who do deconstruction, language gains primacy in the understanding of any text (be it literature, history, or philosophy). Rather than (to use Polanyi's term) attending *from* the language used in any text, the deconstructionists attend *to* the language, thereby making language much more visible than is typically the case in other forms of literary criticism. Deconstructionists (led by Derrida) believe that the language used in a text is itself the reality, rather than being the means by which some other reality (for example, the reality of history or the reality of a literary figure) is described.

A shift from objectivity and vision to subjectivity and voice is prevalent in our postmodern world. In its embracing of a constructivistic notion of reality, postmodernism takes a significant step in positing that language—or more generally, the use of symbols and signs—is not simply a vehicle for commenting on the reality that underlies and is the reference point for this language. This stance is opposed to an objectivist view, which is based on the assumption that there is a constant reality to which one can refer (through the use of language and other symbol/sign systems). If reality is a social construction, then the language being used to describe this elusive and changing reality is itself a major source of this social construction.

The postmodernists often take this analysis one step further by proposing that language is itself the primary reality in our daily life experiences. Language begins to assume its own reality, much as money, credit cards, electronic transfers, options, and so forth are perceived as reality. Language, like money, ceases to be an abstract sign that substitutes for the real things of value. Money used to be a substitute for gold or property; now, it is itself important. Similarly, language used to substitute for that which it denoted. Now it is important in and of itself.

In our large and complex postmodern world we are often distant from many of the most important events that affect our lives: war, the death of significant others, the use of our money by the government (taxation). Living in a global community, we no longer have direct experience of, or influence over, many of the things that were accessible when we lived in much smaller and more directly experienced communities. As a result, we often talk about things rather than actually experiencing them. We listen to a lecture on Asian art rather than actually seeing the art. Language itself becomes the shared experience. Conversation itself becomes the reality. This may have always been the case, to some extent. Language and conversation may have always played a central role in our society. Who we are—our sense of self—may have always been conveyed by the stories that we tell about ourselves. We may only be returning to a sense of reality inherent in the premodern world.

Perhaps our stories about self themselves constitute our sense of self. This means that my stories about childhood, about major adult accomplishments, and about difficult life-long disappointments may be the basic building blocks of my self-image—whether or not they are accurate. Not only are we influenced by a broad *social* construction of reality—conveyed through the stories of the society in which we find ourselves—but also by a more narrowly based *personal* construction of reality, which is conveyed through our stories about ourself (and perhaps through stories that we inherit about our own family and immediate community.)

One of the major implications of this notion of language as reality is that language—and therefore reality—is ephemeral. Once we have spoken, the reality that was created when we spoke is no longer present. Even if we say the same words, they are spoken in a different context and therefore have a somewhat different meaning. Thus, even when our speaking comes in the form of written words or in the form of other images (visual, tactile, and so on), these words or images will have different meaning depending on who hears them, the setting in which the communication takes place, and the words or images that have preceded and will follow these efforts at communication. From this perspective, therefore, reality is a shifting phenomenon subject to change and uncertainty.

Globalization and Segmentalism

According to the postmodernists, our world is becoming progressively more global, while at the same time becoming progressively more segmented and differentiated. Though many of the postmodernist theorists spoke of this contradictory trend in our world at least ten to fifteen years ago, it is remarkable how contemporary this perspective seems to be, given the developments in Europe (and elsewhere in the world) over the past five years. While European countries are moving, in a globalizing manner, toward a unified common market and community, we also see movement (particularly in Eastern Europe) toward increased nationalism and factionalism among specific national, ethnic, and racial groups. From one perspective, globalism thrives. We are increasingly successful in saying a few things that are universal for all people. Walter Truett Anderson (1990, pp. 21–22) suggests that the following "ordinary ideas" are held by most people in the world (or at least in the Western world):

- That there is a human species, all of its members biologically capable of interbreeding with all the others, but not with members of different species.

- That the world is divided up into nation-states.
- That there are such things as atomic weapons, and that a global atomic war is possible.
- That there are many different religions, and that some people do not take any of them very seriously.
- That societies change and keep changing.

Communality arises in part from shared experiences, which in turn are the product of the electronically mediated "global community" of which Marshall McLuhan (1964) spoke prophetically over twenty-five years ago. We can create world-encompassing computer-based models that predict the flow of resources, the growth of population, and the destruction of our ecology with frightening accuracy (Meadows and others, 1972). Similarly, we can now trace worldwide trends in fashion, movies, and so on. This point is vividly confirmed in the specter of a young man in China or a young woman in Iraq wearing a T-shirt with a picture of an American sports hero or cartoon character. These young people are trying to defy U.S. society while expressing its culture and values. We now have global life-styles and many more "inter-sect" cultures that readily borrow from many different societies and social values. The bohemian, international society of Paris during the 1920s is replicated in the 1990s, in settings ranging from Hong Kong and Singapore to London and now even Moscow.

At a much deeper level, there is even the possibility (or is it only a hope?) that the Eastern and Western worlds are beginning to come together. There is a growing awareness in at least some Western countries that "cultures, non-European, non-Western cultures must be met by means other than conquest and domination" (Huyssen, 1987, p. 220). In the non-Western world, there is growing recognition that issues of ecology and the environment are not just capitalistic or imperialistic artifacts, nor primarily a matter of politics. There is a deepening sense that the ecological perspective itself offers a penetrating critique of the modern world, a world the Eastern world both wants and does not want to embrace.

From a quite different perspective, the world seems to be highly segmented. We are becoming increasingly less successful in saying much that is generally valid about even our local communities or nation, let alone the world. We are confronted with discrepancies, diversity, and unpredictability. Huyssen (1987, p. 187) describes an "appropriation of local venaculars and regional traditions" in postmodern societies. Robert Bellah and his colleagues (Bellah and others, 1985) write about new forms of community in the United States. In the modern world, men, women, and children lived in small, geographically contained communities (villages, towns, small cities). According to Bellah and his colleagues, they now find postmodern community in "life-style enclaves." These enclaves are composed of people who usually don't live near each other (except in the case of enclaves that are age related, such as singles-oriented condos or retirement communities). Rather, members of the enclave, according to Bellah, have something in common that brings them together on occasion. These life-style enclaves may be found in Porsche-owner clubs or among those who regularly attend specific sporting events. They are also found among churchgoers and those who attend fashionable night clubs. Regardless of the type, enclaves contribute to the diversity and ultimately the unpredictability of the larger social system.

Physical scientists describe diverse and unpredictable systems as chaotic, in the sense that behavior inside each system and between systems is neither predictable nor readily described. While computer models have been highly successful in predicting and describing the general trends in our postmodern world (Meadows and others, 1972), they have not been very successful at predicting the precise impact of global events (such as the availability of food or temperature changes) on specific geographic regions or societies in the world. Global computer-based models have now generally been replaced by models that acknowledge broad worldwide dynamics, while also recognizing that each of these dynamics plays out somewhat differently and at a different rate in each of several geographic regions of the world (Mesarovic and Pestel, 1974). While Meadows and her colleagues attempted to build a unified, world-based model of various ecological dynamics, Mesarovic and Pestel described and modeled a world in which subsystems offer their own distinctive, "self-organizing" dynamics (Loye and Eisler, 1987, p. 59).

Similarly, we have been unsuccessful in using global models to predict weather. We are not much better at making predictions than we were ten years ago (Gleick, 1987). Specific, localized aberrations or "rogue events" (what chaos theorists call the "butterfly effect") that can neither be predicted nor adequately described apparently have a major influence on the weather in parts of the world remote from the events. In North America, we have seen the influence of El Niño (a change in the circulation of Pacific ocean currents, occurring every four to seven years), much as we have seen the impact the invasion of a very small country (Kuwait) had on the entire world community. Are there many El Niños that directly affect our daily lives? Are there other influential events that are far removed and unknown (and perhaps unknowable) to us? Perhaps we live with the contradiction between globalism and localism in many aspects of our daily lives.

Fragmented and Inconsistent Images

In a newspaper article entitled "Hip Deep in Post-Modernism," Todd Gitlin (1988) describes the blurring and juxtaposition of forms, moods, stances, and cultural levels in the postmodern world. According to Gitlin, we have moved into a form of global capitalism (perhaps better labeled postcapitalism) that requires high levels of consumption, which in turn requires "ceaseless transformation in style, a connoisseurship of surface, an emphasis on packaging and reproducibility" (p. 35). A widely seen bumper sticker—"The one who dies with the most toys wins"—illustrates this point.

Frederick Jameson (1991, p. 25) similarly speaks of the "heaps of fragments" in the production of postmodern culture, although he later declares that "The description of postmodernism [is] something for which the word fragmentation remains much too weak and primitive a term . . . particularly since it is now no longer a matter of the breakup of some preexisting older organic totality, but rather the emergence of the multiple in new and unexpected ways, unrelated strings of events, types of discourse, modes of classification, and compartments of reality."

In the postmodern world, we find hand-me-down scraps of culture and images from the modern and even premodern eras, according to Jameson. These remnants are inextricably interwoven with new and surprising cultural elements to produce fragmented and inconsistent images of our time. Such a world tends to deny the continuity of tradition and underminds the certainty of specific social constructions of reality. History, according to both Jameson and Gitlin, has been ruptured. We live in an era that need pay little attention to the past, for as Jameson (1991, p. 36) has observed, over half the people who have ever lived on earth are still alive; "the present is thus like some new thriving and developing nation-state, whose numbers and prosperity make it an unexpected rival for the old traditional ones." Yet, in spite of the absence of any postmodern attention to the lessons that might be learned from the past—from history—the postmodern era is defined primarily by what it isn't and by what it used to be. According to Gitlin, we are now experiencing our world as an aftermath. In the United States, we label our era as post-60s, post–Viet Nam, post–New Left, post-hippie, post-Watergate, post-Marxist. Jameson (1991) believes that we live in a new world of "historicism." Rather than there being a careful analysis of past historical events and careful planning for future events based on this analysis, there is a replication of the past in the nostalgic touches on buildings and furniture, in the proliferation of museums, and in the recreation of past settings (Disneyland and other theme parks).

Rather than learning from the past, we replicate it and pretend that nothing has changed or that there is no hope for the future anyway—hence, a regressive, sedating appeal to the past. Fifty thousand men and women gather each August in Pebble Beach, California, to show off, admire, race, buy, sell, and talk about old cars (Flint, 1991, p. 196). While malls lose business, consumers flock to informal markets and bazaars from the past that feature everything from potatoes to fur coats. The 1960s in particular, according to Jameson, exploded our American belief in progress, in the linear order of things, and in moral clarity. We look for truth in our search for the "real" past, yet find the past revealed in distorted and confusing manner through the postmodern mixture of premodern, modern, and postmodern cultures. Huyssen (1987, p. 196) similarly notes, specifically with regard to the arts, that "all modernist and avant-garde techniques, forms and images are now stored for instant recall in the computerized memory banks of our culture. But the same memory also stores all of pre-modernist art as well as the genres, codes and image worlds of popular cultures and modern mass culture."

Huyssen speaks of a cultural anesthesia that protects us from the abyss and uncertainty that undergird (or fail to undergird) our society. We collectively dull our senses with variety because the underneath hurts too much. We become "couch potatoes," mainlining our television while simultaneously mocking it. Everything appears to have already been done in some form or other in our postmodern world. Culture becomes a process of recycling. We have gradually begun to embrace a much more Eastern sense about time as a cyclical notion. Instead of believing in progress, we believe in a world that replicates itself again and again—hence the use and distortion of the past and history. Everything in the fragmented postmodern world is seen as a faint resemblance of reality, a private vision that knows no public substance. We are living in an era of edginess with an accompanying sense of unreality and an "unbearable lightness of being" (Kundera, 1984). This edginess may in turn lead to disengagement and dissociation.

Postmodernists are enthralled with the superficial and trendy. Television, the primary conveyer of postmodern culture, knows only the present tense; there are no beginnings or ends, only sound bits and isolated images. Newly constructed buildings offer additional examples of the postmodern emphasis on surfaces. While they provide interesting surfaces of varying texture, they also tend to be constructed without any apparent underlying theme or order (Jameson, 1991). The computerized goggles and gloves used in "virtual reality" machines can make a Boeing engineer or executive think and feel as if he or she were actually flying a plane or hooking two molecules together (Bylinsky, 1991a, p. 138). These machines convey the sense of depth, yet like holographic devices, they actually replicate only the surface, never the depth of the experience. We are tricked into believing that we have experienced depth or virtual reality when in fact we have seen only the surface. While the three-dimensional glasses of the later stages of the modern era never really captured our imagination, the virtual reality of computerized gloves, holographic images, a replicated mainstreet in Disneyland, or, for that matter, a new corporate emphasis on "the core values of our organization" lure us into belief and eventually produce a state of confusion about what is real and what is phony.

In the postmodern world, fragmented visions are coupled with fragmented attention. Fred Wydler, an astute, high-tech manager who works in a large high-tech company, speaks of the fragmentation and superficiality of his own company as it tries to change "from the environment of farmers market through industrialization and standardization back into postmodernism while preserving industrial-age pricing. We are doing this in [an] industry which is not nearly as flexible in terms of manufacturing as we would like to be. We are doing this by means of superficial measures which are barely deep enough as to not appear as a subterfuge but which are successful with our customers."

While Gitlin (1988) believes that postmodern fragmentation is global in scope and character, he also believes it is particularly prevalent in the United States. He writes of "American eclecticism" and notes the lack of a distinctive American culture. A federation of cultures (the American "variety show") has emerged in the United States, bolstered by a sense that "anything goes." Postmodern terms and concepts are defined by lists of examples rather than by any formal definition. According to Gitlin, the postmodern world in the United States consists of shopping malls, suburban strips, Disneyland, the Isuzu "He's Lying" commercial, MTV, David Letterman, Hyatt Regency hotels, Doctorow, Foucault, Lacan, Derrida, Baudrillard, and remote control–equipped viewers "grazing" around the television dial. American postmodernism is Tom Peter's description of a manufacturing firm that is able to change its product line every four hours with the assistance of computers and robotics. Nothing remains the same for very long, and what does remain must reside alongside things that are very old, very new, or short-lived. The rest of the world is following in the footsteps of the United States and will soon be just as fragmented and inconsistent.

The State of Postmodern Theory and Analysis

The inconsistency and fragmentation of the postmodern world make it very difficult to build a coherent theory or to recommend specific strategies or courses of action in response to these new societal conditions. Each of the pressing themes of postmodernism (constructivism, language as reality, globalism, and segmentalism) contribute to an even more basic theme that often makes the very analysis of the postmodern condition particularly difficult. In essence, it is virtually impossible to make a definitive statement about our contemporary world because this world is filled with contradictions and discrepancies. We are living in a world that is simultaneously premodern, modern, and postmodern. For every new phenomenon that can be identified as postmodern, we can find another phenomenon that is clearly modern or even premodern.

Ironically, all of these diverse phenomena provide evidence of the universal presence of a postmodern world. The inconsistencies of the hypothesized postmodern era allow the postmodern analyst to never be proven wrong. Any data (other than absolute uniformity, which will never be the case) fit into the postmodern model, for the more discrepant the data, the more confirming these data are of the postmodern hypothesis. Show me evidence of modernism and I will declare it amenable to my postmodern analysis. Show me premodern styles and forms, and I will be equally convinced that my postmodern hypothesis is correct. As in the case of a Freudian analysis of dreams, all evidence can be used in a way that confirms the initial hypothesis. Thus, in some ways, the world picture conveyed by postmodernists can't be disproven, for contradictory evidence is itself part of the postmodern premise.

The postulation of a fragmented and inconsistent postmodern world, however, seems to be more than just a semantic or intellectual ploy to avoid any disproof of the postmodern perspective. There is ample evidence to suggest that this is a central (if not *the* central) characteristic of our contemporary world. The postmodern world is filled with fragmented and incoherent images of the future, as well as fragmented images of art, politics, and the sciences. This is most concretely and perhaps clearly exemplified in the calvacade of events that many of us experience as we transact our daily work. Several days ago, for instance, I was walking down a street in an American city and passed a man with a flower in his lapel, who was tap-dancing and encouraging each of us passing by to "smile and be happy." A second man, twenty feet beyond the tap dancer, wore a sandwich board on his back that solemnly declared that human-kind and the American government were irredeemably corrupt and that our world was about to come to an end.

These two messages were received in a very confusing con-text. Wealthy businesspeople were walking rapidly past other men, women, and children in torn clothes who were begging for money. Newspaper headlines spoke of candidates no one wants to elect and of gross mismanagement of public and corporate funds. Yet, it was a beautiful day. The air was fresh because pollution control stan-dards were beginning to work; a nearby park had been successfully restored by concerned citizens. Should I be happy? Should I be sad? Should I be angry? Is the world (at least, as we know it) coming to an end? How did we ever come to a state where there is such a discrepancy in the living conditions of American citizens? These fragmented and contradictory images must either be ignored, on a daily basis, or somehow comprehended in a manner that makes sense to me and my fellow city dwellers.

The fragmented and inconsistent image is also exemplified in the emergence of postmodern architecture. Whereas modern ar-chitecture tended to stress uniformity and order, postmodern archi-tects have emphasized diversity and complexity. Postmodern buildings in many cities blend classic greco-roman columns and cornices with clean modern lines and neobaroque bric-a-brac. Rough cement slabs are placed next to smooth marble walls and wood-inlaid ceilings. Water spills out over highly abstract brass forms, while tourists and workers on lunch break sit on nineteenth-century New England–style wrought iron benches, watching brightly colored balls roll through plastic tubes in order to set off quarter-hour chimes or bang against Japanese-style resonant wood blocks. Corporations throughout the United States, such as Nike and Trivona, have built postmodern facilities in suburban areas that include lakes, beautiful grounds laced with walking and jog-ging trails, fitness centers, and gourmet lunchrooms, usually inter-mixed with rather sterile-looking concrete buildings filled with confining cubicles and mauve or gray-colored modularized furnish-ings. Optimistically, we are told (Alpert, 1991, pp. 141–142) that a new era of more user-friendly office buildings has come: "Unlike most office parks built in the past three decades—anonymous-

looking blocks of steel and glass, many of them Darth Vader black—
the new suburban complexes will be designed on a smaller, more
human, even homey, scale. Often they will resemble farms or college campuses."

The people who fill these urban and suburban buildings are
diverse with regard to gender, age, nationality, and physical challenges, as are their customers. Members of the organization even
participate in a variety of premodern celebrations: companywide
Christmas and Hanukkah gift giving, Fourth of July picnics, and
departmental birthday parties. Yet, in true postmodern fashion, one
wonders to what extent the premodern celebrations are a bit phony
and, even more important, to what extent there really are postmodern equity and equal access for these people to the career opportunities of this organization. A postmodern canopy of diversity often
seems to be draped over a very modern and Waspish culture of
privilege and discrimination.

At an even deeper level, one wonders if this fragmentation
and inconsistency—and the accompanying edginess—are temporary. Does postmodernism suggest that we are in a major transition
between a modern society and some new society that has not yet
become clear or at least been properly named? Alternatively, is the
postmodern world in which we now live a long-lasting phenomenon? We may be moving into a fragmented world that will not
readily change. We may never (at least in our lifetime) be able to
return to a world of greater simplicity. Regional or national coherence and consistency may be nostalgic remnants of the past.

The implications of a long-lasting fragmented and inconsistent society are great. Remarkable futurist Fred Polak (1972) proposed several decades ago that the continuation of any society
depends in large part on the presence in the society of a sustaining
and motivating image of its own collective future. For instance,
European communities thrived for many centuries under a clearly
articulated, Christian-based image of personal and collective salvation. Similarly, many Asian countries have been guided for centuries by a coherent set of propositions about the nature of the world
and society that were offered by Confucious (or Buddha). According
to Polak, when a society has lost an image of its future, then this
society will soon crumble, and a new society will rise in its place

that does have a clear and guiding sense of some collective future. Polak assembled an impressive collection of historical facts and figures to buttress his argument.

If Polak is correct, one wonders about the survival of our fragmented and inconsistent postmodern societies. Where do we find the clear and coherent images to guide us in preparing for our own collective future? Will we lose our way and our vitality at this critical point in our history? Perhaps Polak is only partially correct. We may find that many small, microcommunities will form, each with its own image of the future and its own sustaining vision of the proper order for society. If this is the case, then the question shifts slightly: can our world continue to exist in such a fragmented state? What will prevent these microcommunities from constant conflict regarding the validity and universality of their different visions? To what extent is the recent Persian Gulf War a preliminary vision of a neofeudal world to come?

Any easy answers to the questions posed by Polak diminish the importance and profundity of his analysis. I will not, therefore, attempt to provide these kinds of answers. What I offer in this book are several preliminary suggestions concerning how our postmodern world will play out in organizational settings and what actions we might take to address these problems of fragmentation and potential dissolution. These matters are not easy to assimilate, as one of my students has candidly noted:

> For me, as well as most present generation managers, postmodern theory has a rather disconcerting feel to it. We have been schooled in modern theories that are strongly grounded in systems approaches, scientific methods, and the benefits of increasing efficiency. Postmodern theory, though not invalidating these concepts, holds that they are only part of the solution to the social and economic work that organizations are formed to do. The modern manager sees systems as the ultimate tool for making sense out of chaos. The postmodern manager sees chaos as what is to be managed and systems, though very useful, as merely one aspect

of the chaotic environment. To the postmodern manager chaos is not bad. It is what is.

If this book makes a valuable contribution to our new dialogues about postmodernism, it will help find the order that underlies much of the chaos in contemporary organizations. If this book is intellectually honest, it will also help expose and analyze the chaos that inevitably underlies much of the apparent order in contemporary organizations. We turn in the next section of this book to such an analysis.

Part Two

Timeless Challenges Facing the Postmodern Organization

Chapter 3

Size and Complexity: Can the Center Hold?

[My organization's] strategy over the last four years seems to resemble a living organism more than it does a corporate entity. There seems to be very little planning or forethought for the organization structure. The structure that exists today at [my company] seems to be more the result of reacting against unforeseen circumstances like an animal out in the wild.

Mid-level manager in a high-tech firm

We are now in a world where the central question for many organizations is, can the center hold? Will we be able to keep things together in the large and complex institutions that dominate our collective lives? At the heart of this question is the dilemma of size and complexity itself. In this chapter, we explore this dilemma by first examining the fragmentation and inconsistency that lead us to propose this central question. We then look at fragmentation and inconsistency from a somewhat more positive perspective, describing the postmodern organization as inherently a hybrid made up of differing forms and dynamics.

Size and Complexity

While social philosophers, historians, and organizational consultants may not be able to agree on much, they all agree on two trends. First, organizations over the years have tended to become larger. Second, these same organizations have grown more complex. One of the obvious reasons for the growth of organizations is the massive increase in the size of the human population on this planet, which leads to increasingly dense human populations in any one area of the world. The noted sociologist and social theorist Emile Durkheim ([1893] 1933) was one of the first to observe that as the number of people inhabiting a particular area of land increases, there is a tendency for these people not to spread out evenly (which would provide each person with the maximum amount of space) but to cluster together (forming villages and, at a later date, cities).

Why did this clustering occur? Several good explanations have been offered. Teilhard de Chardin (1955) suggested that as people slowly populated the earth and began to bump up against others of the same species, they had to either continue a nomadic life-style and face ongoing conflict with other nomadic groups or establish cooperative relationships with other small groups and settle down in one spot.

> First of all come the incessant advances of multiplication. With the rapidly growing number of individuals the available land diminished. The groups pressed against one another. As a result migrations were on a smaller scale. The problem now was how to get the most out of ever more diminishing land, and we can well imagine that under pressure of this necessity the idea was born of conserving and reproducing on the spot what had hitherto been sought for and pursued far and wide. Agriculture and stock-breeding, the husbandman and the herdsman, replaced mere gathering and hunting [p. 205].

Riane Eisler (1987) has suggested that this decision between invasion, efforts at domination, and continuous conflict, on the one hand, and respect for boundaries, attempts at cooperation, and ongoing stability, on the other hand, has been central in defining the character of all societies. This critical choice—between domination and partnership—is still being made every day in our corporations and governments.

A second perspective on the clustering of people and the formation of organizations comes from the emerging field of chaos theory. In many different systems, there are forces, entities, and events that "attract" other forces, entities, or events (much as the corner of our living room or a space under our bed seems to attract dust or lost objects). The tendency for people to cluster as they increase in number exemplifies this "attractor" principle and is apparently not unique to the human species or even to sentient beings. One of the founders of chaos theory, Ilya Prigogine (Prigogine and Stengers, 1984), has observed that larvae in a specific insect population will tend to distribute widely when there is low density (small number of larvae in a specifically defined space) but will tend to cluster as the density increases and to form multiclusters with very high density. The formation of organizations is not a distinctive characteristic of homo sapiens. It may instead represent a much broader dynamic in many systems (especially those chaotic in form).

Emile Durkheim led the way among social theorists and observers in suggesting why organizations have tended to become more complex over the years. According to Durkheim, there is a tendency for societies to become more complex as they become larger primarily because there is an increasing possibility of struggle and violence in a densely populated world. Durkheim believed that increasing struggle and conflict create the need for specialization of functions: if people can do different jobs, they will be less likely to compete with one another. Rather than defeating and banishing people who are different from us and who compete with us for space and resources on a densely populated planet, we honor the differences. We provide specialized jobs and become dependent on one another. An effort to reduce social tension, according to Durkheim, is the primary reason for division of labor and the development of complex organizations. He doesn't believe that organizations need to become more complex simply because they have grown larger.

A second reason for the increasing complexity in organizations is the substantial increase in the proportion of human beings who now work in conjunction with other people, rather than working alone. Thus, while complexity leads to greater specialization of roles—and to greater individuality and even autonomy—it also leads to greater interdependence among members of a society, for they no longer can (or are unwilling to) provide all of the functions needed to maintain their society.

The central premise of this first of five chapters on the postmodern condition is that as modern organizations have grown larger and older, they have required an increasing proportion of resources to be devoted to integrative services, services needed to keep the organization from falling apart. A smaller proportion of resources is available for the direct services provided by modern organizations, thereby reducing their efficiency and ultimately their effectiveness.

As we enter the postmodern era, it appears that the integrative services offered—even if very extensive—often are insufficient to hold the organization together. Greater attention must be given to organizational culture and to creating a strong feeling of solidarity; otherwise, organizations will increasingly be experienced as fragmented and inconsistent. In one of the few detailed analyses (other than this book) of the postmodern organization, Stewart Clegg (1990, p. 11) emphasizes this very point and builds on postmodern perspectives on the arts to find inspiration for his analysis: "Postmodernity may well be premised on de-differentiation. Modernity, as the outcome of modernization, was premised on an increasing functional differentiation of phenomena. Postmodernization and postmodernity, on this account, would be distinguished by a reverse process. . . . De-differentiation is present in the postmodernist refusal to separate the author from his or her work or the audience from the performance; in the postmodernist transgression of the boundary (with no doubt greater or less success) between literature and theory, between high and popular culture, between what is properly cultural and what is properly social."

Clegg rightfully emphasizes the integration that comes with the direct connection between the person who provides the service (or performs the art) and the person receiving the service (appreciating the art). While, on the one hand, postmodernism emphasizes the disintegration of forms and functions, it also points the way to new forms of integration: through the reconnection of producer and consumer, and through an emphasis on relationships between people within organizations regardless of status or position.

Fragmentation and Inconsistency

Even with this postmodern emphasis on dedifferentiation and integration, key questions for many contemporary organizations remain: can the center hold? Will there be sufficient clarity of purpose in this organization for it to sustain its integrity? Will there be an adequate sense of differentiation of this organization from its surrounding turbulent environment for the organization to survive? We find that a sense of fragmentation and inconsistency—and an associated sense of edginess—exist at the macro- and microlevels of most contemporary public and private organizations. At a very mundane level, the fragmentation is evident in the type of bolts used in contemporary American automobiles. The engine blocks of many American cars, Peter Senge (1990) notes, require three different types of bolts, which in turn require three different types of wrenches and three different inventories of bolts. These three different types of bolts (which increase costs and decrease speed of assembly) are required because the design organizations in many large American automobile companies have three or more groups of engineers, each group responsible for one specific component of the engine block. Complexity and specialization have led to excessive isolation and inefficiency in these companies, as well as in many other large American corporations.

We find similar fragmentation in fast-growing computer companies that—according to Fred McAmis, an engineer/manager in a California high-tech firm—have stretch marks associated with their fast growth. These stretch marks are often manifest in frequent and counterproductive reorganizations, in a "hodgepodge of differing structures that always seem to have some fringe hanging out," in the failure of many divisions in these companies to coordinate their efforts with other divisions, in the lack of clearly established organizationwide priorities, and in a general sense of foreboding or panic (postmodern edginess).

Small organizations and small towns are not immune to these concerns if they have experienced rapid and unmanageable growth. The leader of a small-town hospital notes that her organization has grown dramatically during the last ten years and can no longer expand at its present location to meet growing, local health needs. This hospital has had to offer services through fourteen off-site centers. These widely distributed centers are difficult to administer, and coordination has become a nightmare. Similar stories are heard in many other organizations that have experienced rapid growth or are of large size.

Many utility companies, such as Pacific Bell, have recently decentralized as a way of coping with massive size and complexity. Vice presidents at Pacific Bell—like the general managers at Hewlett-Packard, IBM, and many other corporations—are asked to manage semiautonomous organizations not easily coordinated from the top, which requires that they acquire new skills and new attitudes regarding accountability and freedom of choice. Terrance Jakes, a mid-level manager at Pacific Bell, observes:

> Each of the [Pacific Bell] business units will have a vice president as its leader. The vice president will be responsible for all assets of that business unit, from the financial statement to the staffing of personnel. They will be running their own company. The success will depend on them and their teams. There will be a central or corporate staff, but this staff [will only provide] direction, guidelines and strategies.
>
> An example could be the switching machines that are used for dial tone and other services. The corporate staff will recommend various vendors that business units could use, [as well as providing] legal paperwork and other regulatory information. The business units can pick who they want and when they want the switching machines installed. They also will provide the features that their customers will need. [In this way], they can meet their different market needs.

They also will be responsible for the cost. . . . They
will need to be "jack of many trades."

We can move to the international level and find similar
issues of size, complexity, fragmentation, inconsistency, and edginess. In recent months, considerable attention has been directed
toward the dissolution of the Soviet Union and the emerging autonomy of the Soviet republics. We also find new authority and
responsibility being invested, potentially, in the United Nations, an
organization that has always had to balance issues of integration
and interdependency with concerns for national autonomy and differentiation of cultures and governmental forms.

Clearly, the new republics and the United Nations are not
alone in facing the extraordinary challenge of keeping large, diversified organizations together. "The center will not hold" in many
contemporary organizations. The myth of the superiority of bigness
has been destroyed, and growth is no longer considered the only—
or even the primary—path to efficiency and organizational prosperity. "In the seventies," according to Drucker (1989, p. 260), "the tide
turned. No longer is it the mark of good government to be bigger.
. . . We have moved away from the worship of size that characterized
the first three quarters of the century and especially the immediate
post–World War II period." Big businesses are divesting and restructuring to become smaller and more efficient. Government
agencies are shifting certain tasks to private vendors. Increasingly,
as Drucker notes, "The question of the right size for a task will
become a central one. Is this task best done by a bee, a humming-
bird, a mouse, a deer, or an elephant? All of them are needed, but
each for a different task and in a different ecology. The right size
will increasingly be whatever handles most effectively the information needed for task and function" (1989, pp. 260–261).

Integration and Differentiation

Largely in response to their growing size and complexity, with the
accompanying tendency toward fragmentation and inconsistency,
modern organizations have tended to emphasize structures and
procedures drawn up and reinforced in a systematic manner and

uniformly applied throughout the organization (Weber, 1947). Organizations were designed based on mechanistic models of efficiency rather than on agricultural or biological models of continuity, as in the premodern era. A critical issue arose, however, that created the seeds of destruction for this mechanistic model of organizational structure and growth and that led the way to a new, postmodern assumption about structure and growth. This issue concerns the need for integrative functions that compensate for the increasing differentiation in a growing organization.

Durkheim originally identified this theme in his analysis of the division of labor in modern organizations. He was certainly not the first social analyst to notice that jobs tend to become more specialized as organizations (and societies) become larger and older, but he was among the first to note the paradoxical relationship between differentiation and individual autonomy, on the one hand, and integration and interpersonal dependency, on the other hand, inherent in this division of labor.

Durkheim ([1893] 1933) observed, first, that there is an increasing differentiation of functions in all organisms as these organisms mature and become larger. Second, a division of labor is to be found in all sectors of society (economic, political, administrative, and judicial; aesthetic and scientific). He went on to note that a society in which each person provides a specialized service—thereby providing each individual with a distinct identity and autonomy—is also a society that requires each of its members to rely heavily on the competence and trustworthiness of other members of society who are also offering distinctive and indispensable services.

During the premodern era, when organizations were relatively undifferentiated, every person knew how to do virtually every job and was frequently involved in every aspect of the organization, whether an agricultural or a trade setting. As a result, no one had to rely on anyone else for the provision of specific, specialized services. By contrast, during the modern era, any one person can perform only a small percentage of the total number of jobs that need to be done to meet the needs of individuals in society and to maintain the stability of the society itself.

This interdependence of the modern era, according to Durkheim, creates a feeling of solidarity among members of a community. Yet, the specialization of functions also creates a feeling of isolation among these same members, for they cannot readily communicate about their work with one another. Specialized language is developed. Guilds and associations are created that bring workers together with those who do similar work. Durkheim uses the metaphor of the husband and wife to explain this paradoxical aspect of the division of labor. During the modern era, husbands and wives began to do quite different jobs. Men went off to work, and wives stayed home to perform domestic chores. While this differentiation of function helped to solidify marriages and made husbands and wives more dependent on one another (the husband depending on the wife for a clean home and the wife depending on the husband for a paycheck), it also created a gap between husband and wife as they increasingly began to live quite different lives.

A more contemporary parallel to Durkheim's intriguing analysis is offered by Lawrence and Lorsch (1967), who proposed that any organization must simultaneously become more finely differentiated (as it grows larger and older) and establish means for integrating these differentiated functions. According to Lawrence and Lorsch, the total proportion of resources in an organization devoted to integrative functions (administration, communication, monitoring, and so forth) increases substantially as the organization gets larger. Thus, as organizations become larger and more complex, increasing attention is given to those activities that enhance coordination and cooperation among the differentiated functions of the organization. In this way, the feeling of solidarity of which Durkheim wrote almost a century ago is amplified.

Much of our contemporary attention to the topic of organizational culture (for example, Deal and Kennedy, 1982; Schneider, 1990) exemplifies this notion of solidarity. The culture of an organization provides the glue that holds the organization's diverse elements together and creates a sense of continuity among those working in and leading the organization. Organizational culture, according to Schein (1985), is built on the learned responses of members of an organization not only to basic issues of organizational survival but also to the organization's need for integration and cohesion.

What then about the late days of the modern era in which we

now find ourselves? What might Durkheim have to say about the growing size and complexity of modern organizations and about job specialization in this era? He probably would have recognized, as have Lawrence and Lorsch (1967), that as an increasingly large proportion of the resources of an organization are devoted to the integrative functions of the organization—as the organization grows larger and older—this organization will be inclined to be less efficient and less competitive with other organizations in the same field that are smaller or younger. Figure 3.1 illustrates the relationship between size and maturation, on the one hand, and the proportion of resources devoted to direct (differentiated) and indirect (supportive and integrative) services, on the other hand. On the vertical axis of this graph I have placed the percentage of resources expended by an organization. These resources can be staff, money, time, facilities, or machinery. On the horizontal axis, I show increasing organizational age and size.

In general, as an organization gets older it tends to devote an increasingly large proportion of its resources to supportive and integrative services, even if the organization does not grow. The more powerful—and influential—variable, however, is size. The larger the organization, the greater the proportion of resources of all kinds devoted to integrative and supportive services (the upper right section of Figure 3.1). Very young and very small organizations would appear on the left side of the figure, with a small percentage of resources devoted to supportive and integrative services; very large and very old organizations would be located on the right side of the figure with a large percentage of resources dedicated to supportive and integrative services. IBM would be at the far right side (in terms of size), as would the federal government (in terms of both size and age).

While there certainly are exceptions to this model, it holds up in most organizational settings. Furthermore, once an organization gets bigger and integrative services begin to expand, it is very hard to downsize the organization. Even if the organization is reduced in size, the proportion of integrative services is likely to remain high. Mao tried to reduce integrative services when he moved middle managers and bureaucrats from the cities of China to the countryside, in order to provide more direct services (farming). According to most observers, he was not very successful in this endeavor.

Figure 3.1. The Growth/Age Dilemma.

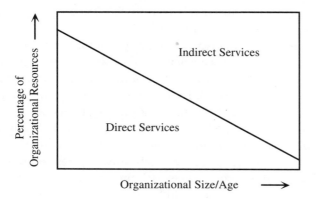

In American corporations, as Tom Peters notes, we may be reaching a point where there is little if any room for more integration. IBM is a prime example, especially in recent months with its Mao-like efforts at reducing its proportion of integrative services. A substantial proportion of the total resources (capital, labor, facilities) at IBM are devoted to indirect (integrative) rather than direct (differentiated) services. There are not sufficient resources in most postmodern organizations (especially those in a competitive market) to support a high ratio of indirect to direct services. IBM can't compete with much smaller hardware and software companies if only 5 to 10 percent of its work force is devoted to the direct production of hardware and software. Smaller computer companies hypothetically can produce products that are equal in quality to and lower in cost than those manufactured by IBM, provided that everyone is given equal access to the market. Integrative services have simply become too extensive and costly.

For IBM, this has meant a period of dismal performance during the late 1980s. *Fortune* magazine reported in July of 1991 (Woods, 1991, p. 41) that "revenue growth [in late 1986] was miserable, earnings growth was nonexistent, and IBM's stock, then $125 a share, had lost nearly $24 billion in market values from a peak of $99 billion just seven months earlier. . . . It is now 4½ years later. The stock was recently just below $100, which means another

$18 billion in market capitalization has been shredded into mega-bits. IBM's total revenues have dragged, rising over the past five years at an average annual rate of only 6.6%, against 13.4% for the data-processing industry as a whole."

While many other reasons can be given for the decline of IBM (such as too great an investment in hardware, flawed marketing strategies, and the general turbulence of the computer industry), one of the major reasons is IBM's size and percentage of integrative services. The recognition by IBM executives of this fact is evident in the November 26, 1991, announcement by IBM that it would move from its current monolithic structure to much smaller, semi-autonomous companies, perhaps including the creation of entirely new and independent companies with their own stock and board of directors: "The new IBM would resemble a holding company. Headquarters executives will be there to offer guidance—if needed. But heads of the new units, in theory, will act as CEOs. They'll present annual business plans and promise IBM a certain return on funds invested. If they succeed, they'll earn a share of the profits. Some may even be allowed to float a portion of their shares in public markets" (Verity, Peterson, Depke, and Schwartz, 1991, p. 113).

Decentralization certainly is not unique to IBM (or to Mao's China). Yet, in being undertaken by such a large company, this new initiative offers a substantial challenge—not unlike the comparable challenge being faced by the newly autonomous Soviet republics. Just as Gorbachev eventually had to relinquish his centralized authority to the republics, the CEO of IBM, John Akers, reports that "there are essentially no operational decisions made [at the central office level] anymore" (Verity, 1991, p. 28). IBM's attempt to form smaller work units will hopefully not only reduce the total number of employees needed to run the company (by an estimated twenty thousand workers) but also introduce a revitalizing spirit of innovation into the company: "Nothing will be sacred; every operation will have to justify its own existence" (Verity, 1991, p. 28).

There was initial skepticism about the ability of IBM to downsize and decentralize: "The news of radical surgery at IBM, a restructuring of the company into independent business-units, has been welcomed on Wall Street with about as much warmth as a flu outbreak. After an immediate but momentary upswing from 95 to 98, IBM's stock skidded as details of the wrenching plans became clear. Investors worry, analysts say, that the turmoil of the wide-ranging reorganization will hurt IBM's sales, before it helps" (Verity, 1991, p. 28). Yet, there is also growing recognition that IBM can thrive only if it does "trim down, be more competitive and serve its customers better. . . . Its streamlining should make the U.S. industry stronger and better able to battle its main opponent, Japan" (Verity, 1991, p. 28).

The ongoing saga of IBM (which may be quite different by the time this book is published) points to the importance of organizations making careful decisions at frequent intervals about size and complexity. IBM executives found out that it is not easy to remain large and monolithic in a postmodern world and that it is also not easy to downsize or decentralize, once the monolith has been created. Integrative services and the employees who provide these services simply do not go away. Services that once kept the organization together soon become cancerous and hazardous to the continuing survival of the organization.

If we look elsewhere in American corporate life, we find many examples of organizations that either remained small and preserved a distinctive market niche or that aggressively avoided the tendency toward increased integrative services. Certainly, one of the best-known examples of the latter strategy is Wal-Mart, which recently became the largest retail organization in the United States— while preserving a relatively small central administration. Wal-Mart has eliminated several steps in its distribution system, which yields lower costs and increases access to the producers of merchandise that Wal-Mart sells. Wal-Mart also encourages direct communication between the highest and lowest levels of the organization (thereby reducing the typical distortions of communication that come with the movement of information through multiple levels of midlevel management): "A satellite communications system allows . . . [Wal-Mart] employees to transmit their suggestions to their store manager, who, in turn, might send the suggestion on to headquarters. Glass [Wal-Mart president] claims that Wal-Mart gets most of its ideas at the grass roots level" (Sawaya, 1992, p. 169). Yet, Wal-Mart is a very large corporation and confronts many of the same problems as other large corporations, such as IBM. Sam Walton (the founder of Wal-Mart) tried to do much of the integration himself, by visiting each of his stores at least once a year. However, as noted in a recent *Fortune* article, "the creation has simply outgrown the creator; nobody could visit 1,650 stores plus 200 Sam's Clubs and still get around to the 150 or so store openings Wal-Mart holds every year" (Huey, 1991a, p. 47). Shortly before his death, Sam Walton expressed his concern about the growing "bureaucracy" (integrative services) at Wal-Mart:

> "We're gettin' just like Sears Roebuck in some ways," he says. "We got so many back office people workin' off the floor, not doin' a thing to help our customers." . . . "It's hard to believe we have one buyer just to buy Big Chief tablets and another just to buy tennis balls. We used to have one buyer for five departments." At store after store he pounds away on this theme. "I'd like to see the buyers come into the stores and sell one day a week," he says to one store group. "That'd put their noses in it. They get these big egos and start acting like the cock o' the walk when these conmen salesmen tell them how great they are."
>
> "I'm proud of what we've accomplished, but I do not like hearing we're the biggest retailer in the world. I don't want Wal-Mart going soft" [Huey, 1991a, pp. 54, 58].

Another problem now facing Wal-Mart is its devastating impact on other businesses in the small communities it serves. In many instances—at least as documented in a recent *Time* magazine article (Sidey, 1992)—small (premodern) businesses, which form the backbone of small-town America, have been driven out of business by minimalls created around new Wal-Mart stores built on the outskirts of town. Over the long run, in destroying small-town businesses, Wal-Mart may be eliminating its own base of support.

Wal-Mart's CEO, David Glass—like IBM's CEO, John Akers—must make some difficult decisions regarding the size of the organization he leads and the appropriate role to be played by his organization in the small communities it serves. During the modern era, growth was the primary criterion of success. For men like Glass and Akers, growth must be tempered with the recognition of the important, but eventually debilitating, role often played by integrative services in large organizations.

We don't have to look just at corporations to find examples of inefficiency in large and older organizations. The same principle applies to large, old universities, which have a high proportion of indirect services, as compared to younger and smaller colleges and universities, which have a much larger proportion of their resources devoted to the direct services of the institution (teaching, research, and community service). Whereas a major university, such as Stanford or the University of Michigan, must charge a large administrative overhead (often more than 80 percent) for grants they receive, a small independent graduate school (such as the one I head) need charge a very small administrative overhead or none at all.

Similarly, many of the large American charities are now floundering because of high overhead expenses. *Forbes* magazine (Cook, 1991a, p. 180) reports that only 5 percent of the nearly $4 million that the American Heart Disease Prevention Foundation raised in 1990 went to the programs for which the group was organized. The American Cancer Society similarly commits only 42 percent of its spending to program services, while the Leukemia Society of America is able to allocate only 43 percent of its revenues to direct services. As these organizations experience success in raising money, they become larger organizations and, as a result, are less efficient in expending the money they raise. Consequently, they must continue to raise even more funds to provide the same amount of service. This, in turn, leads to the substantial allocation of agency funds to fundraising activities (for example, 90 percent of the revenues of the American Heart Disease Prevention Foundation goes to fundraising), leading to even greater expansion in the indirect services of the agency.

Similar analyses of integration and differentiation in large organizations can be done on the cost of providing public services in urban areas. The optimal size for most cities appears to be about 200,000 to 400,000 people. Public services (such as police, fire, utilities, transportation, and communication) can be provided at a lower cost per citizen in a moderate-size community than in a small community. However, once a city grows larger than about 400,000, the costs per citizen begin to increase exponentially. The cost of providing services to each new resident in New York City, for example, is much greater than the cost of providing services to new residents in Eugene, Oregon. Thus, Eugene residents either receive better services or pay lower city taxes than residents of New York City.

Why is this the case? Primarily, the cost for services in large cities is a result of an increasingly large proportion of the city's budget being devoted to indirect services and a decreasing proportion of the city's budget being allocated to direct services. Some of the indirect services support the direct services provided (such as the role of dispatchers in a fire department, transportation system, or emergency road service). However, a considerable amount of the indirect services are integrative functions that do nothing more (or less) than hold the organization together (such as accounting, management, interagency communication). A diminishing percentage of the total services relate directly to the mission of the department (for example, policing the streets, fighting fires, or driving buses).

Similar problems regarding integration on a massive, public scale can be found in the (former) Soviet Union. In an effort to integrate the disparate cultures and nationalities in the Soviet Union and to provide proof for the Marxist emphasis on statewide planning and the formation of uniform and equitable policies and procedures, a single governmental system was constructed. In essence, the Soviet Union operated as a single, huge organization, with a very large proportion of its once considerable resources devoted to indirect services (primarily integration). Men and women in Russia and the other republics report having devoted virtually their entire work life to filling out forms and reporting on (fictitious) progress toward accomplishing a statewide five-year plan, one completely inappropriate to their own distinctive culture and local resources.

The failure of Mao to bring about a countrywide transition and the failure of the Soviet Union to establish an efficient centralized government have been frequently replicated in American institutions. Many attempts have been made to eliminate one or more levels of midlevel management—the recent efforts by IBM being a prime example. Governmental leaders have tried to substantially reduce, without a major revolution, the massive bureaucracy of federal and state agencies. Put simply, once an organization gets large, it is hard to keep down its integrative services (as Sam Walton discovered) or to reduce its size (as John Akers and others at IBM are about to discover). Usually, some form of transformation in structures, values, and attitudes is needed—as is now occurring in the former Soviet republics. The problem of size can best be solved by keeping an organization relatively small in the first place, a principle that flies directly in the face of modern traditions.

Leaving the Age of Giants

In seeking the sources of and potential solutions to the problems of size frequently found in postmodern organizations, one must look backward in time. First, I suggest that we look back to the modern era—the age of giants—to find the sources of many of our contemporary problems of size and complexity, specifically examining the interplay between the need for both differentiation and integration of functions within large and complex organizations. Second, I suggest that we look back to the premodern era—a simpler place and time—for potential solutions to our current problems. While it was appropriate for the early proponents of modern-day social institutions to denigrate the premodern era in order to justify the establishment of uniform bureaucracies and efficient, large-scale organizations, we should now reexamine these abandoned premodern forms and dynamics.

What are the sources of contemporary, postmodern conditions of fragmentation and complexity? How did we get to the point where we can't even determine whether or not we have solved our problems or met our goals? In large part, these conditions arise from the modern emphasis on size. We have been, as Tom Peters notes (1987, pp. 15-16), in an often destructive and short-sighted age of giants.

> Big, not best, has always been the American calling card. In fact, I bet you can't drive more than seventy-

five miles in any direction, from anywhere in the
United States, without running into a "biggest in the
world" of some sort. Wide-open spaces and an apparently limitless frontier set it all in motion. U.S.
farmers, starting with the Pilgrims, would cultivate
land, wear it out, and blithely move west five miles.
Today almost every farm you see is a history lesson
told by hunks of rusted cars and agricultural equipment, and homes and yards filled with broken Christmas toys and power lawn mowers.

The primary objective of modern organizations has been to
become and stay large. Corporate leaders still consider their companies (and themselves as managers) successful if they are one of the
Fortune 500. Human service agencies define themselves first and
foremost in terms of the number of clients they serve, the size of their
library, the number of professional staff they have hired, and the size
of the building they occupy. By contrast, the premodern individual
concentrated on the *process* of growth itself as the vital element of
the organization. Emphasis in modern organizations has been
placed on the *outcome* (rather than the process) of growth, this
outcome being large size. This emphasis on size is no more graphi-
cally illustrated than by the modern American romance with the
automobile. The number of cubic inches in the motor was the primary criterion for determining the quality of an automobile, just
as the size of the company making the automobile was considered
key for judging the quality and success of the company. With the
oil embargo of the 1970s and the emerging emphasis on efficiency
rather than power, this era came to an end (Peters, 1987).

As a result of the modern-day emphasis on bigness, rapid
growth has often destroyed organizations (especially if it occurs in
the startup phase). Modern liberals, for instance, placed great emphasis on large-scale housing projects for the urban poor prior to
and during the era of Lyndon Johnson's "Great Society." These
housing projects were noted for their large size, the uniformity of
their architecture, and the efficiency of their carefully planned operations. Unfortunately, as well intended as these massive public
housing projects were, they led to "the destruction of the fabric of

the traditional city and its older neighborhood culture (by way of the radical disjunction of the new Utopian high-modernist building from its surrounding context)" (Jameson, 1991, p. 2). Planners and city "fathers" sat in high-rise corporate buildings designing the future lives and reweaving the social fabric for masses of anonymous men, women, and children who wished to have an improved life—but not at the cost of their families, neighborhoods, or customs. A quest for uniformity led to homogenization and alienation, two of the most important and troublesome legacies left by modern leaders for the postmodern world to address.

As we examine the characteristics of the modern organization, we find that problems associated with bigness emerge in many different forms: inability to manage large numbers of people, slowness of response to rapidly changing conditions, and so forth. One of the most far-reaching problems associated with size, however, has rarely been fully acknowledged and has only recently come to broader awareness through discoveries in the physical sciences. This is the problem of scale and measurement. In essence, we now find it hard to measure anything of importance to discover either the extent and scope of the problems we face or whether or not the problem has ever been solved. Teilhard de Chardin, the extraordinary scientist and theologian, identified this fundamental difficulty more than half a century ago ([1937] 1955). He wrote of a world that looks quite different depending on the scale being used to measure it. "If there is one thing that has been clearly brought out by the latest advances of physics, it is that in our experience there are 'spheres' or 'levels' of different kinds in the unity of nature, each of them distinguished by the dominance of certain factors which are imperceptible or negligible in a neighboring sphere or on an adjacent level" (1955, p. 54).

Thus, even as early as the 1930s, there was a sense that the stability of scientific measurement was in doubt, that the level of analysis greatly influences the results obtained. We find this even more dramatically stated and illustrated in some of the recent findings from chaos theorists. In his informative and accessible account of chaos theory, James Gleick (1987) offers a wonderful story about the difficulty of measuring the length of the English coastline. The protagonist in this story, Benoit Mandelbrot (one of the leading figures in the field of chaos theory research), had come across a fascinating observation regarding the length of the English coastline in an obscure article by an English scientist, Lewis F. Richardson. In checking through several encyclopedias, Richardson discovered discrepancies of at least 20 percent in the published lengths of the coastlines of Spain, Portugal, Belgium, and the Netherlands. Why would there be such great differences in the measurement of things that seem so tangible?

Mandelbrot proposed that the differences had to do with the way the coastline was measured. The size of a cove, for instance, might be measured in a very rough manner by computing the distance (using a straight line) between one side of the cove and the other side of the cove. We could also measure the size of the cove by drawing a curve that roughly follows the boundary of the cliff surrounding the cove. This second measure would yield a greater length than would the initial straight-line measure.

At an even more detailed level, we could measure the size of the cove by using a yardstick and taking into account all of the larger jagged edges of the rocks on the cliff, or we could even move down to the bottom of the cliff and measure the jagged boundary of the cove at this level. Once again, this more finely differentiated measurement would yield a larger number with regard to length than would the previous two measures (done using a straight line and a curve). We could move even further to a macroscopic or even microscopic level of measurement that would yield even greater numbers. Gleick (1987, p. 96) notes that "an observer trying to estimate the length of England's coastline from a satellite will make a smaller guess than an observer trying to walk its coves and beaches, who will make a smaller guess in turn than a snail negotiating every pebble."

As Mandelbrot discovered, the length of any coastline is ultimately—in a sense—infinitely long. "Common sense suggests that, although these estimates [of the length of the English coastline] continue to get larger, they will approach some particular final value, the true length of the coastline. The measurements should converge, in other words. . . . But Mandelbrot found that as the scale of measurement becomes smaller, the measured length of a coastline rises without limit, bays and peninsulas revealing ever-smaller subbays and subpeninsulas—at least down to atomic scale, where the process does finally come to an end. Perhaps" (Gleick, 1987, p. 96).

The issue of measurement and scale certainly comes into play in all large-scale organizations. The larger the organization, the more difficult this question becomes. At one level of analysis, for instance, a corporation looks very successful. Its short-term profits and investments look impressive; morale is great among the executive staff; competitors look weak and disorganized. At another level, however, the corporation looks like a disaster waiting to happen: longer-term financial projections forecast major losses, personnel reports suggest slowly brewing labor problems, marketing analyses predict drops in consumer demand, the entry of new competitors into the marketplace—along with technological breakthroughs—will change all of the current rules of the game. Which level of analysis should we believe? They are both correct. However, one report is likely to be sent to the corporate board of directors and stockholders and another report to the executive officers of the corporation. Which report, if any, will the union leaders receive?

Even in a small organization, the scale and measurement problem can be profound. The owner of a small consulting firm suggests that "this idea that different realities exist dependent upon the vantage point from which one observes the organization can be difficult to conceptualize, if not impossible to believe." He notes that his organization is a small S-Corporation from the perspective of the Internal Revenue Service of the United States government. It is a minimally capitalized company with gross revenues of less than $500,000 in 1990. There are three full-time employees, five to ten part-time employees, a president, vice president, secretary, and treasurer. At one level, it is essential that the organization be clearly and consistently organized and that it look as traditional as possible. By contrast, from the perspective of the owners, the organization is primarily intended to fulfill their own interests in autonomy and in one of their shared hobbies (which is at the heart of the business). From the perspective of its customers, the organization is usually considered part of a totally separate organization that markets its services, or it isn't even considered an organization at all since it is run out of the home of one of the owners.

If the IRS took either of these latter two (owner or customer) perspectives, then it would probably see chaos rather than the order conveyed in the organization's tax returns, corporate papers, and other legal documents. The IRS might try to rectify this chaotic situation by asking the owners of this organization to clarify its boundaries with regard to its affiliation with the second organization and the location of the business in their home. Similarly, if customers saw that this was a small independent business rather than part of the larger marketing firm, they might take their business elsewhere, for this organization would seem to be "unbusinesslike" and chaotic. Finally, if the owners were truly restricted by the guidelines of the IRS or compiled with the expectations of their customers for a "real" business, then they would probably fold up their tent and move into some other line of work.

The problem of scale and measurement may go even deeper in our postmodern world. A member of the staff in a major governmental accounting office recently spoke with me about problems in his office. The U.S. government simply can't measure anything of importance with any accuracy, given the enormous size of the organization. Costs can only be estimated, for the assignment of expenses throughout the government to particular line items is often arbitrary. Only a very small percentage of the bills paid by the federal government can be reviewed by an auditor, for the time and complexity associated with reviewing all bills would be prohibitive. Thus, we approximate the costs of governmental programs, much as we approximate the population in the United States based on our latest census report.

Thus, whether attempting to measure a coastline, accurately portray a small consulting firm, or keep track of the federal dollar, we are constantly readjusting our construction of truth and reality. Just as we should be able to tell a school child the length of the English coastline, so should we be able to tell an American taxpayer what the population or the federal deficit of the United States is at any point in time. Apparently, neither can be done. We must learn to live with this ambiguity in measurement; this is part of the postmodern condition.

The implications of this shifting awareness of the relationship between size and accuracy of measurement are profound for any leader who seeks to monitor and hopefully control the operations of his or her organization. If we can't even measure what is happening in the organization, how can we recognize its current problems or know for sure that we have solved these problems, let alone plan for its future?

Yet, the problems of measurement also open up new options in the formulation of second-order strategies for change. We have the option of working toward shifts in perspectives and frames of reference, rather than focusing on shifts in the underlying "reality." We can, for example, solve a problem (that is, a discrepancy between the current state and a desired state) by shifting the desired state rather than by trying to change our current state. In Los Angeles, for instance, the problem of air pollution could be solved not by reducing pollution but by changing the standards for acceptable levels of pollution. It is usually much easier to change the standards than to alter reality.

Back to a Simpler Place and Time?

Part of the postmodern response to the problems associated with size and complexity—and the attendant problems of scale and measurement—should be the reexamination of those values and structures prevalent in premodern times, with a partial return to smallness and, in particular, to manageable size. As we look back to the premodern era for suggestions on how to live in our postmodern age, we find that the primary organizational dynamic of that period was one of people coming together to work together. As people came together under conditions of increasing population density, they initially formed relatively simple organizations. Durkheim described the premodern era as one in which everyone did essentially the same work as his or her neighbor. Until the twentieth century, most people in the Western world were involved in the business of farming. A much smaller number were involved in crafts and production. Men and women working in the service industry were small in number until the second half of the twentieth century. Robert Heilbruner (1973, p. 51) reports that "roughly speaking, 70 to 80 percent of the people who lived in America in 1800 were essentially farmers. The other 20 or 30 percent were split between two other broad categories of occupations. Some of them—black-smiths, tanners, printers—handled goods of various sorts. Some of them—legislators, merchants, clerks—provided services of various sorts. I don't think any figures show how the 20 or 30 percent that weren't essentially farmers were divided between service and goods, but however the division fell, in any event, the proportions in either category were clearly small."

All members of the family assisted with household chores and with the farm or craft shop that the family ran. Durkheim ([1893] 1933) spoke of this as a form of "mechanical solidarity." Premodern people felt close to each other because they shared the same values, the same perspectives on work and society, and a collective unconsciousness (to use Carl Jung's term) regarding the essential nature of reality.

In the premodern world, an emphasis was also placed on planning for and leading organizations toward increasing size. The focus was the *process* of growth, rather than on size, per se. Much as premodern people celebrated the growth of crops or livestock, they also celebrated the gradual and organically based growth of family and family-based products. Kenneth Boulding (1953, pp. 64–65) makes an important distinction between what he calls "simple growth," which has to do with the "growth or decline of a single variable or quantity by accretion or depletion," and what he terms "structural growth," which involves not just a greater or lesser amount of a single variable or quantity but also the addition of new elements or operations to the existing organization.

Premodern growth is of the first type. Organizations grew by adding more of the same thing: more acres of farmland, more tools, more members of the family to do work. In the musical *Carousel,* Mr. Snow, a premodern New England fisherman, sings about adding more and more boats to his fleet, much as he dreams of adding more and more children to his family. While Carrie (Mr. Snow's wife-to-be) was not especially enamored of the growth in her figure that would accompany the growth in her family, she no doubt would have accepted the premodern notion that a large family is needed to sustain a growing family business. The modern organization, by contrast, typically defines growth in terms not only of greater size (simple growth) but also greater complexity (structural growth). As the modern organization grows larger, it also changes form, thereby making growth that much more stressful and difficult.

Throughout the premodern era, the analogy between agriculture and business was strong, as it should be today, in the postmodern era. Organic models of organizational life prevailed during the premodern era; an organization was a living being, just as a plant or animal is living. Both organizations and plant life, furthermore, embodied the spirit of some deity and were therefore considered spiritual in nature and guided by divine direction. Non-Western cultures are often permeated with a sense of the spiritual in all natural things (what anthropologists call *animism*). Totems and other societal symbols of importance incorporated the images of both people and animals to convey the essential values and dreams of the organization (family, tribe, culture).

Today we often ignore these premodern elements in our organizations. We have remnants of these elements in the names we assign to our sports teams (the Chicago "Bears") and in our use of mascots. Advertisers are also aware of the power of animistic images in conveying something about the spirit of an organization (the Federal Express eagle or Dean Witter's bull). Even Wall Street reaches for animal images when speaking of the rise ("bull") and fall ("bear") of the value of stocks. The question remains whether these premodern remnants hold anything other than marginal value in our society. Are the premodern strategies of gradual, simple, and organic growth still viable in an emerging postmodern world of structural fragmentation and unanticipated change? Is it just wishful thinking, or is there some reality in the notion of a return to smaller and simpler organizational forms?

The premodern era does have at least partial answers for our emerging postmodern era. While the premodern era primarily helps us set the agenda, with regard to reemerging values, it can also provide us with some important insights about the human enterprise. We certainly cannot simply recreate the simpler premodern structures and processes, as many "small is beautiful" and "back to basics" neo-conservatives and neo-liberals would have us do. We can, however, learn from the accumulated wisdom of this long era in the development of world civilizations. Typically, one of the first steps taken in the formulation of any modernist perspective is the bashing of premodern modes: "we are no longer going to use the old 'horse and buggy' . . . let me show you the new, 'modern' way in which we build houses [or grow peas or produce widgets]." Virtually all major societal transformations begin with denigrating the previous dominant era (much as I am doing a bit of a hatchet job on the modern era in this book). This is quite understandable. However, once an era is replaced by another perspective or set of values, then the old era can be revalued and reexamined. New lessons can be learned from very old sages and forgotten or repressed societies, much as Riane Eisler suggests we do in returning to the lessons about partnership and cooperation from the pre-Christian cultures of Europe (Eisler, 1987). We turn repeatedly to valuable lessons from the discounted premodern era throughout this book.

We are living on the edge of both order and chaos and must learn how to survive in this new world. Order and stability will come, in part, from acknowledging continuity with the past and stripping away the modern blinders that have prevented us from clearly seeing our premodern needs and perspectives. Many people assume that the fragmented and inconsistent complexity of contemporary organizations is symptomatic of a transitional phase. Postmodernism is nothing more than a world shifting gears to some new form or model. The alternative, however, is also possible: fragmented and inconsistent postmodern organizations may themselves be the new models and may be around for a rather long period of time. If this is our new reality, then we need to stop waiting for things to get clear and consistent and look instead toward a mixture of old and new forms—premodern, modern, and postmodern.

Chapter 4

Mission and Boundaries: Who Are We?

In some ways, the future is the cause of our current behavior.
We have a vision or an image of where we wish to head and
the kind of organization we wish to create, and we act in
ways that we believe are in pursuit of creating that future.

The alternative, which is the dependent choice, is to
act on a future of someone else's creation. We ask the organization to tell us its vision, its values, and how it wants us
to operate, and then that becomes our guidepost.

The payoff for autonomy is that we live our own life
and have control over our own destiny. The payoff for dependency is that if we act on someone else's choice and it
does not work out well, it is not our fault.

Peter Block, *The Empowered Manager*

Contemporary organizational con-
sultants and theorists generally agree that it is useful to conceive of
organizations as systems. All systems are defined by two traits. First,
they have one or more reasons for existence—a mission or purpose.
A random assembly of people (such as those walking down a street)
is not considered a system—nor is it considered by anyone to be an
organization. At the point, however, when these people stop at a
street corner and wait for the light to change, they are briefly considered a system and an organization. They have a common purpose: waiting for the light to change. They also are considered a
temporary system or organization because they are governed by a

specific set of rules or norms (as represented by the stop light). This group of people can be distinguished from other groups of people because the actions of all of its members are governed by a common set of constraints (the laws about crossing a street on a green light). These constraints are what systems theorists call boundaries, a second trait common to all systems.

I propose, with regard to these two central traits of all organizations, that the premodern organization typically had unclear boundaries (particularly between work and family life) and an unclear mission. There was little need for a clear definition of organizational purposes since the work of the premodern organization was primarily providing sufficient food and shelter for the family. Furthermore, even among those working in the trades, a mission statement was unnecessary since the product spoke for itself. A system of bartering (for example, the farmer's market) eliminated the need for any substantial monetary system.

During the modern era, by contrast, boundaries were quite clear, while mission statements tended to remain unclear or inconsistent. In modern organizations, clear distinctions were made between the places where employees worked and where they lived, relaxed, and worshipped. We knew when we were entering and leaving a modern organization and often defined this organization solely by its existence rather than by its specific mission or purpose. Thus, during the modern era, large organizations could buy up other organizations with relatively little regard for compatibility of mission and purpose and could diversify their enterprises primarily for monetary or market gain, disregarding founding purpose or cause. In many cases, mergers and acquisitions resulted in impressive short-term financial gain and even in the rebirth of organizations that had been poorly managed or had become stagnant. Longer-term consequences, however, often were much less positive and sometimes were even destructive to both organizations.

Frequently, the absence of a clear mission in modern organizations was hidden behind the facade of fiscal accountability; the organization existed to produce a profit for the owner or the shareholders. Such a statement of mission in the modern world heightened confusion and inconsistency in the identification and maintenance of long-term goals and sustaining values. While profits were often essential ("the mother's milk") to the existence of modern organizations, they failed to be adequate reasons for organizations' existence by the end of the twentieth century. Profits rarely provided sufficient guidance to steer the leaders of modern organizations through the increasingly turbulent waters of the later years of the modern era.

Postmodern conditions have precipitated a crisis with regard to both mission and boundaries. In order to survive, most postmodern organizations have formulated clearer mission statements, in part because they usually no longer have clear boundaries. As "specialty shops" in postmodern corporate and human service "malls," these organizations must find their own distinctive niches and become more adaptive in producing, marketing, and delivering products and services. Leaders of organizations in the postmodern world must repeatedly reexamine organizational purposes and values, for the world is constantly changing and demanding new and different products and services. Without a clear sense of purpose and values, organizations soon splinter or become aimless vagabonds or scavengers that feed destructively on other organizations and segments of society.

In this chapter, I focus on the organizational dimensions of mission and boundary and address one of the central questions of any organization: "who are we?" I begin this discussion with the presentation of my basic premise: postmodern organizations don't need (and may not even want) clear boundaries if they are to respond effectively to the turbulent postmodern environment. However, precisely because of boundary ambiguity, postmodern organizations need clarity and commitment regarding their mission and values. I then turn to postmodern models of the visionary organization with clear mission and the flexible organization with unclear boundaries. From this discussion, I move to a direct consideration of our basic question—"who are we?"—which requires examining the interplay between mission and boundaries and the troubling ambiguity of identity in a postmodern world.

The Nature of Mission and Boundaries

Contrary to what the word seems to imply, a system boundary is typically not a physical entity; rather, it is an event or series of events (such as stopping at a street corner for a light to change) that tells one that something specific is required if one is to belong with these other people. All organizations and all systems have boundaries. When they lose their boundaries (by invasion or acquisition, for instance), organizations and systems cease to exist. Though all organizations and systems have a purpose (or mission) and boundaries, the mission and boundaries can be relatively clear or obscure. Heavily boundaried systems are called closed systems. Living biological systems can never be totally closed; if they were, they would die. According to traditional systems theory, a thriving system is likely to be quite open, with highly permeable boundaries—especially if this system is located in a highly turbulent environment.

In the postmodern world, organizations tend to become less bounded and more open. However, postmodern organizations that survive have some core purpose or mission that provides continuity—an anchor—during turbulent periods. A postmodern perspective suggests that there are essential ingredients in the founding structure and dynamics of any system or organization that remain intact throughout the life of the system. A successful organization is relatively closed with respect to certain styles or patterns—the culture—of the organization. These styles or patterns remain the prevalent means by which an organization brings in new resources and information from the outside world, works on these resources and information, and produces something of value that is subsequently exported to the world. However, established cultures may not be adequate to the task of preserving the integrity of postmodern organizations. Contemporary organizations must continually address the issue of mission and values—the question of "who are we?"—if they are to remain viable.

Postmodern organizations are usually the inverse of modern organizations with regard to mission and boundaries: modern organizations typically have clear boundaries but unclear missions, whereas postmodern organizations usually have unclear or changing boundaries but have clear and consistent missions. The shopping malls of the 1990s exemplify the postmodern interplay between unclear boundaries and clear mission. Boundaries are often unclear in malls. Shops often blend into one another. Tables are set up in open areas to serve shoppers who have bought lunch in one of several adjacent restaurants. Events that affect the entire mall (for example, Christmas decorations or arts and crafts fairs) know no boundaries, nor do the more enduring general themes that many malls embrace (Old West, New England, Mexican, European). Yet, each of the stores located in the mall has a very clear mission. It specializes in a unique product or service and would get in trouble with other stores in the mall if it began to diversify. A variant on the shopping mall, the theme park (Disneyworld, Sea World) offers specialized lands with clear missions, while diffusing the boundaries with activities and themes that overarch the specializations. In a similar manner we can look to the new gourmet supermarkets that provide small specialty areas (often independently owned) within a single building.

An excellent example of the modern organizational tendency toward clear boundaries and unclear mission is the modern college campus. A typical college campus established during the modern era (between the 1600s and the early 1900s) is clearly different from "off-campus"; you know when you've entered the campus of a modern university (such as Harvard). Even more important, you know when you have been admitted to Harvard as a student. After undergoing a highly demanding and selective admissions process, you may be fortunate enough to be admitted to this distinguished institution. In many ways, admission to Harvard will have a greater impact on the rest of your life than will anything that you learn while enrolled as a student at Harvard.

While a modern organization (such as Harvard) is defined by its boundaries rather than by its mission, a postmodern organization (almost any community college in the United States) is defined not by its boundaries, but rather by its mission. Community colleges are much less selective in the admission of students than is Harvard University. Architectural boundaries are much less imposing than at Harvard. While Harvard has gates and walls surrounding most of the campus and many other highly selective modern colleges and universities have guards at the front gate to check visitors and students in and out, most community colleges have no restrictions on movement on and off campus. Many of these colleges even hold some of their courses in other locations or in storefront operations. Other collegiate organizations that primarily serve adult students (for example, business schools) often rent space for classes and run the school out of multipurpose office buildings. Yet each of these unbounded colleges and schools has a very clear mission. Any one of these schools would go out of business if it didn't have a clear sense of the students that it serves and the product that it offers.

Vision and Purpose

Harvard University and many other established modern organizations have survived into the postmodern era because of their substantial resources and reputation. Most contemporary organizations, however, do not have these advantages, and they must be clear about their mission if they are to survive. Drucker (1989) writes about a new pluralism in our postmodern society in which single-purpose institutions dominate. These institutions must have carefully articulated statements of mission. Tom Peters (1987, p. 166) similarly concludes that "being unique—standing out from the growing crowd of competitors, products and services—is an essential for survival. Such uniqueness, to be implemented, must be understood and lived by everyone in the organization. While niche-market-oriented, higher-value-added strategies are increasingly the winning hand, low-cost producers can be successful. On the other hand, an 'in between' or 'stuck in the middle'—i.e. not unique—strategy is unfailingly disastrous." An organization that defines a specific product or service as needed by at least a small segment of society is more likely to be successful in our chaotic, postmodern world than is an organization that tries to appeal to a much broader audience with a variety of unrelated products or services.

Mission, vision, and purpose are sacred rather than secular concerns, whether we are speaking of the international level, the organizational level, or the level of personal identity. A clear organizational vision comes in many forms. Some organizations identify a set of guiding principles; others issue a statement of vision and values. One division of a large corporation located on the Gulf Coast has articulated a set of five outcomes on which it bases its operations. One of the outcomes envisions "a people-oriented plant." Employees are intimately involved in the operation of their plant, "to produce quality products in a safe and efficient manner." A second outcome concerns a "customer-oriented plant," while a third is about a "cost-effective plant." The fourth outcome labels this company "a concerned corporate citizen," and the fifth identifies "a multiskill plant." This company's outcome statements are concrete and explicit. They speak about the specific ways this organization must function if it is to be considered successful.

Senge (1990) suggests that the vision of an organization is not valuable relative to other visions but is inherently valuable. According to Senge, one does not choose from among the best of several possible visions. An organization—or person—is instead drawn to a specific vision that remains the driving force behind the organization throughout its history. Noted theologian Paul Tillich (1957) stated that the identification of one's ultimate concern is essential to living in our contemporary world. A similar statement could undoubtedly be made about the central role of visions in our current organizations. Senge's emphasis on the intrinsic value of a shared vision might readily be derived from Tillich's notion of an ultimate concern, the shared vision being based on the gradual and thoughtful integration and synthesis of concerns that are of ultimate importance for individuals in the organization: "Visions that are truly shared take time to emerge. They grow as a by-product of interactions of individual visions. Experience suggests that visions that are genuinely shared require ongoing conversation where individuals not only feel free to express their dreams, but learn how to listen to each others' dreams. Out of this listening, new insights into what is possible gradually emerge" (Senge, 1990, p. 217–218).

In such a setting, communication takes on a particularly important form and purpose. Storytelling becomes prevalent. Stories of success and victory, of sacrifice and devotion, of service and commitment become the fertile soil for the emergence of Senge's shared vision and the formulation of a clear statement of mission. These are critical for any postmodern organization that wishes to thrive rather than just survive.

For shared visions and clear mission statements to emerge in postmodern organizations, there must be clarity of personal vision and personal mission. Identity is a particularly important and problematic aspect of personal vision and mission, especially in the

turbulent and edgy world in which we now live. We need greater
clarity regarding our personal identity (who am I really?) because
our personal boundaries are less clear; we are constantly changing
roles. In a recent discussion I had with a group of busy corporate
and human service managers, attention turned to their common
experience of living through very complex workdays. They noted
that they are required to play many different roles: subordinate,
colleague, supervisor, salesperson, patient listener, storyteller, in-
spector, and negotiator. They also talked about using a wide variety
of different approaches to solve the diverse problems that seem to
impinge on their job from every possible angle. By the end of the
workday, they often had forgotten what they had done eight hours
earlier (or was it actually eight years ago) at the beginning of the
day. Each day seems like an entire career. Working like this is ex-
hilarating, but also a bit tiresome and disorienting. We're not sure
who we are—or have been—at the end of such a day, and these kinds
of days are all too typical for many people in contemporary
organizations.

We often allow complex workdays and the many external
forces associated with each of these days to dictate something as
important as our personal feelings and emotions. Arlie Hochschild
(1983) writes about the ways in which contemporary men and
women can become quite confused about their own feelings because
they must control them so carefully on the job. For example, Delta
Airline flight attendants and bill collectors both learn how to manage their emotions so they can more effectively do their jobs. Flight
attendants learn how to be enthusiastic about their passengers so
they can be friendly and hospitable, even when a passenger is rude.
Conversely, bill collectors learn how to develop a feeling of disgust
for their clients so they can be immune to the hard-luck stories
clients are likely to tell. Hochschild compares the training received
by Delta Airline employees to the "deep acting" taught to would-
be actors and actresses. The flight attendant and the bill collector,
like the method actor or actress, learns how to manage emotions to
more effectively control his or her own behavior.

Unfortunately, when these employees become skillful at such
management, they can no longer rely on their emotions to provide
them with an accurate sense of their real attitudes, values, and feel-

ings about other people or events. They have learned how to con themselves, and no longer know who they really are. Experts in human relations argue that we should learn how to better control our emotions, yet they do not address the impact of this control on our tenuous sense of self in this turbulent and complex postmodern world.

To what extent do managers in contemporary organizations learn how to control their own emotions as they move through complex and often contradictory workdays? At the end of the day, how do they recognize their "real" feelings, having effectively controlled and modified their feelings all day? Similarly, to what extent does the postmodern therapist, physician, minister, nurse, or social worker learn to manage her heart when working with a variety of needy clients or patients, and to what extent is this human service professional likely to be confused about her emotions at the end of a long, hard day of work? These are important questions to ponder as we prepare ourselves and our children for the postmodern world.

Flexibility and Responsiveness

While most successful postmodern organizations have clear missions, many do not have clear boundaries. In fact, it is precisely because of ambiguous boundaries that many of these organizations (such as American community colleges) need clear mission statements. Conversely, with a clear mission statement, there is often less of a need for clear and substantial boundaries. As we look at many American corporations we find abundant examples of unclear boundaries. The most obvious examples are institutions with such weak boundaries that they have been successfully "invaded" (acquired) by or merged with other organizations.

> Everywhere you look these days, archrivals are falling
> into each other's embrace. So far this year [1991], 5 of
> the nations' top 10 banks—including Chemical Bank,
> Manufacturers Hanover, Bank of America, and Secur-
> ity Pacific—have announced megamergers. Mean-
> while, airlines such as United, Delta, and American
> are evolving into supercarriers as they subsume the

routes of flailing competitors such as Pan Am and
TWA. And then there's the proposed research collaboration between Apple Computer Inc., once the arche-
typal innovative startup, and its corpocratic nemesis
IBM. That alliance of the industry's No. 1 and No. 2
would radically alter the dynamics of the $93 billion
personal-computer   industry   [Bremuer,   Rebello,
Schiller, and Weber, 1991, p. 86].

These mergers are quite understandable, given the need for
American corporations to compete against foreign companies that
work in close coordination with one another (often under government auspices). Many of the major manufacturers of tools and heavy
equipment in the United States (for example, Giddings and Lewis,
Ingersoll-Rand, Caterpillar) are initiating mergers with sister institutions in large part to compete effectively with foreign companies.
Mergers also are being precipitated by the large startup costs associated with the development of many new products and services, by
the increasing capacity (through computers, facsimile machines, and
so forth) of organizations to manage the flow of information in large
and complex systems, and by the continuing assumption that there
is economy in scale (which does apply in some industrial and service
sectors, such as construction and sewage). We can expect more
mergers in the future and a continuing erosion, as a result, of the
boundaries surrounding many organizations.
      In each of the above instances, organizations merge with
another organization that has a different culture and often a different mission. In many instances, these mergers and acquisitions do
not work because they destroy the mission of one or both of the
organizations. Boundaries that are let down prior to the identification of a commonly shared mission are not easily reestablished. One
or both of these merging organizations are likely to be set adrift
without an appropriate and anchoring sense of purpose, vision, or
value (the Continental–Eastern Airline merger comes immediately
to mind).
      Other large corporations have not focused on the acquisition
of other companies in the same field but on the diversification of
products or services, within the context of a specific mission or

purpose. The Clorox Corporation, for instance, now produces not only bleach but also Kingsford Charcoal, Hidden Valley Ranch Dressing, Liquid Plumber, B and B Mushrooms, and a host of other consumer products. Wells Fargo Bank offers not only traditional banking services but also has nonbanking worldwide subsidiaries in such areas as agricultural credit, business credit, capital market investments, insurance services, investment advising, leasing, realty advisement, securities clearance, and realty finance. Anheuser-Busch offers beer for every possible taste. I recently encountered a sign at an Anheuser-Busch distribution center in Texas that never seemed to come to an end: Budweiser, Bud Light, Bud Dry, Michelob, Michelob Dark, Michelob Light, Michelob Dry, Busch, Busch Light, Natural Light, Carlsberg, Carlsberg Light, and beverages called Cobra and Elephant. This didn't even include the nonalcoholic Anheuser-Busch products. Clearly, this company has decided to define itself as a beer- (or more broadly, beverage-) producing organization that builds on the reputation and broad distribution of a single product (Budweiser). In this way, Anheuser-Busch exemplifies the postmodern combination of a modern emphasis on size and mass production of goods that are of general appeal (Budweiser) with a premodern emphasis on small, specialized markets and distinctive products. Perhaps, the resurgence of premodern microbreweries has helped to propel Anheuser-Busch into this postmodern stance.

How diversified should a corporation become, even if it has a clear mission? This is a central question, perhaps as important as the issue of appropriate organizational size and complexity. Should Anheuser-Busch move into a product line other than beer? What about Clorox's abandonment of bleach as its basic product? At least Anheuser-Busch kept Budweiser Beer. Should McDonald's sell lasagna or corn on the cob? (Michael Quinlan, CEO of this corporation, is encouraging more freedom for the company's franchises [Therrien, 1991a].) Is McDonald's in the business of selling relatively low-cost, highly convenient hamburgers in a clean setting or is it more broadly in the business of fast-food marketing? The company certainly moved beyond hamburgers and milk shakes when it opened playlands for young customers and when it began offering salad bars and main courses other than hamburgers. How far should the company go in redefining its basic mission?

A similar question can be asked of the Sara Lee Corporation, which is known for baked goods but has expanded during the past decade into panty hose and purses (Therrian, 1991b, p. 50). This Chicago-based conglomerate produces Hanes underwear, L'eggs nylons, Bali bras, and many other products. It appears that Sara Lee's chairman, John Bryan, looks for products that are not particularly glamorous (such as undergarments) and whose primary manufacturers are small and complacent. In essence, Sara Lee is in the business of producing mundane goods and does so with a strong base of experience and investor credibility.

Many smaller companies have also diversified. The Keystone Company was founded in Houston, Texas, as a producer of oil well valves. The founder of this relatively small company, C. K. Stillwagon, has kept the company in the valve business (mission) yet has loosened company boundaries by shifting to the production of valves for electric power plants, aquariums, paper product companies—and Anheuser-Busch's breweries (Autry, 1991, p. 100). Keystone also serves customers in twenty-six other countries. The lesson to be learned from Keystone and other postmodern companies is to carefully and periodically identify what you do well (clear mission) and then do this in many different settings (loose boundaries).

In other cases, the key to developing an effective marketing strategy in a small organization is not to expand into many different settings (as Keystone has done) but rather to find a very specific niche and fill it with specialized, high-quality products or services. Quarterdeck Office Systems has made a living over the past decade filling gaps in the Microsoft software product line. While Quarterdeck can't keep up with Microsoft's extensive research and development efforts, it can offer unique programs that complement those developed by Microsoft. Quarterdeck sells primarily to users of older Microsoft programs who wish to beef up their existing "user friendly" computer systems rather than buying one of the new Microsoft Windows programs, which some users find to be less friendly (Pitta, 1991, p. 193). While Quarterdeck will probably never be a large organization and must remain flexible to respond to

Microsoft programming, it may survive in our turbulent postmodern world.

We are likely in the future to find more of these "gap-filling" organizations that can run circles around their larger, more cumbersome sister institutions. In essence, it seems that the leaders of successful postmodern organizations must know their organization and what business they are in. As a result, postmodern organizations will be much more flexible regarding boundaries. They will establish their own market niches and shift with the changing market, while preserving a specific identity and purpose. They are likely to be much more open than modern organizations to changes in clientele and may even move across previously restrictive boundaries (such as product line or national boundaries).

In dropping boundaries, postmodern organizations are likely to be more fully responsive to changing technologies, shifting customer needs, and new sources of revenue. They are more likely than modern organizations to include their customers and clients in the design of new products or services and to borrow freely (sometimes almost illegally) from the research and development efforts of other organizations. According to *Fortune* magazine (Pare, 1991), the Fortune 500 companies of the 1990s will not only have a sharp focus (clear mission), deep pockets, and intelligent employees but also the capacity to be sensitive and highly responsive to the shifting needs of their customers and the changing character of technology in their field.

> The race is often won by those who get a new idea to market fastest and best rather than by those who create it. Amid the cornfields south of Crawford, Indiana, sits a $270 million case in point. Here Nucor Corp. is operating a revolutionary new minimill that can roll scrap metal into steel slabs in a single, continuous process. Conventional mills require three to four steps to do that and take three to four times longer. Never mind that the technology was developed by Germany's SMS Schloemann-Siemag. For now, Nucor has the only plant in the world that employs it. Says CEO Kenneth Iverson, "American corporations have

done a pretty good job inventing stuff, but a lousy job commercializing it. That's going to change" [p. 59].

If they are to survive, high-tech firms must break down the traditional boundary between producer and consumer. According to Fred Wydler, an engineer in such a firm, these firms must "form a closer than usual alliance between the people who visit customers and the people who design products." If they can form this alliance, they will not only be more responsive to customer needs but may reduce costs by bypassing various "middlemen" (a common product of the modern era).

Charles Schwab made quite a mark when he eliminated the middleman—and accompanying commission—in the trading of stock. Other companies have further reduced the costs associated with stock trading through the formation of electronic trading systems. Bernard L. Madoof Investment Securities, for instance, "pays brokers a penny a share to get their market orders. This saves that $26.50 fee per one thousand shares to the NYSE, and puts a little extra money in the broker's pockets" (Slutsker, 1992, p. 48). In order to compete with these low-cost trading services, other firms are now investing in software programs and in other ways to reduce the middleman in stock transactions that do not require the expertise of a stock broker.

In many instances, product designers will themselves become the salespeople who meet with potential clients. Some corporations now encourage their customers to design products themselves through computer programs developed by the corporation. Specifications for the new product are then conveyed by modem to the corporation's assembly line. The newly designed product comes off the line and is sent to the customer within two hours. A 1991 *Fortune* article (Huey, 1991b, p. 140) provides three examples. Customers in Japan can order a Toyota with any features they want on Monday and pick it up on Friday. Motorola pagers can be modified when ordered, and shipped out within two hours. Some banks now advertise that they can prepare and process a mortgage application within twenty-four hours.

Clearly the boundaries between customer and corporation in these instances are minimal and highly flexible. This is the central ingredient in any successful postmodern organization that seeks to establish a clear mission while allowing its boundaries to become more diffuse. "As such applications of technology develop, they are certain to spell profound change in the way customers order and receive goods, the way manufacturers plan and finance inventories, and the way people in the sales chain earn their living. It may be possible that a niche will always exist out there for companies that don't want to change, for executives who are willing to hang their hat on the tried and true. But if so, it's a damned small niche" (Huey, 1991b, p. 140).

Social service agencies, hospitals, and banks must also be able to respond in a flexible manner to changing client needs, as well as to shifting local, state, and federal regulations and funding priorities. Many nonprofit organizations in the United States have recently established for-profit subsidiaries whose income can be placed in reserve for the financial "hard times" that the nonprofit will inevitably face in the future. Alternatively, such funds can be used to support an underfunded valued human service activity. A college in New York State ran its own roller rink for many years. Revenues from this enterprise helped to fund a variety of the college's innovative programs. A comprehensive human service agency in Illinois offers corporate training and substance abuse counseling that are not only of value to their corporate clients but also provide revenues for other programs such as halfway houses and adolescent alcoholism programs. Deemed important by the agency's board and staff, we are likely to find abundant examples in the near future of mixed private and public institutions, especially if our society continues to reduce its financial support for human service agencies.

Troubling Ambiguities

In his penetrating and controversial analysis of postmodernism, Frederick Jameson (1991, p. 115) speaks of the "troubling ambiguities" of boundaries that exist in this new era, for example, boundaries between the "inside" and "outside" of many buildings and between the "high culture" and "mass culture" of our society. Jameson uses the Westin Bonaventure Hotel in Los Angeles to illustrate his conclusion that postmodern architecture produces buildings inconsistent with regard to boundaries. Entrances to the Bonaventure Hotel are rather unimpressive, whereas the lobby area (as in many contemporary buildings) is remarkable and spacious. When inside the hotel, one seems to be in a world unto itself (not unlike Disneyland or other popular theme parks). Yet, once within the space of the hotel, other boundaries are diffuse. One feels uneasy riding up and down in glass-enclosed elevators, not knowing whether one is floating in the air or solidly encased. The revolving cocktail lounge at the top of the building leaves one with an uneasy, unclear sense about whether one is inside the building or on top of the building. A further sense of confusion and edginess is created by the absence of any clear markers showing which of four towers one is in at any point in time.

We find the same confusion and complexity regarding boundaries inside postmodern organizations as we find inside Jameson's postmodern buildings. In many instances, we don't know if we are "inside" or "outside" an organization, or even if we are "at home," "on the road," or "at work," given the proliferation of car phones, home computers, and home-based facsimile machines. *Fortune* magazine (Huey, 1992) describes the "mobile office": an automobile equipped with cellular phone, pager, dictation machine, laptop computer (for the traffic jam), car fax machine, and cassette player (books on tape). Given this gadget-filled vehicle, when do I begin work each day? Is my commute a time when I can collect my thoughts, make the transition from home to work, and perhaps even daydream a bit, or is this the start of my busy workday? (The automobile has also become a part of our home. We find "quality time" with our children as we transport them to school or build close friendships with the men and women with whom we commute. The automobile even becomes a setting for microwave ovens and all of those remarkable domestic chores that we observe people doing while driving, from changing diapers to flossing teeth.)

Even when we are out of town, our motel or hotel room becomes our office, to an extent that the traveling salesman of the modern era could not even imagine. *Fortune* magazine (Bylinsky, 1991b, p. 98) proclaims:

Welcome to the world of bits, bauds, modems, lap-
tops, faxes, E-mail, on-line data services, log-on
names, voice mail, pagers, cellular phones, and an
electronic cornucopia of new hardware. An adven-
turous breed of top managers and professionals—call
them the wired executives—stay on top of business
wherever they are, anywhere in the world, with highly
portable computers and telecommunication devices
that liberate them from the constraints of the office.
Universally, these peripatetic executives praise their
newfound freedom. More than that, their use of electronic devices has made them enormously more productive and has saved them huge amounts of time in
the office, on the road, and at home.

Yet, we might wonder about the long-term consequences of
this newfound freedom and productivity. When does the executive
relax, at the end of a hard day on the road? Not many years ago,
we could relax when we finally settled into our seat on an airplane,
knowing there was little we could do other than read, sleep, or jot
down a few notes. Now we can bring along our portable computer
and make use of the sky phones to keep in close contact with our
office. Is this a good thing? Is the edginess of the postmodern era
in part a continuing confusion about what is work, what is home,
and what is leisure? Is the time we save with our wonderful new
devices time that we take away from our own lives and the lives of
people with whom we don't work (our friends and family)? Are we
more likely to keep appointments that we have made with other
people in our lives than to keep the appointments that we have
made with ourselves?

Boundaries at home are equally as ambiguous and troubling
for many of us. Even with phone answering systems to screen our
calls, we are inundated with unsolicited sales pitches or late-night
calls for assistance from the nightshift manager in the computer
division of our company. It's hard for many of us to have a "quiet
night at home."

Home has also become the setting for purchasing goods—
courtesy of the prospering television marketing services: "While the

recession and heavy debt have laid waste to many old-line retailers, QVC ('Quality, Value, Convenience'), a 24-hour cable channel that reaches over 40 million homes, is posting record sales—estimated by analysts to come in at a little under $1 billion for the fiscal year ending next January 31 [1992]. . . . Emboldened, QVC has started a new channel that specializes in clothing. 'At the same time retailers were wondering where their customers were, our phones were jammed,' says Joseph Segel, QVC's founder and chairman" (Lubove, 1991, p. 164).

The not-yet-successful computerized checking systems and highly successful information retrieval services (compact disks that hold extensive reference services and modems that link with large-scale data base systems) have also changed many of our homes. We are moving toward the electronic village Marshall McLuhan prophesied and in doing so have muddled the boundaries between home and commerce, as well as between home and work.

At a macrolevel, we find the same "troubling ambiguity" in current world affairs. The world we now live in has witnessed the simultaneous destruction of large multinational states and the resurrection of smaller nation-states that had been engulfed by their larger and more powerful neighboring states during most of the twentieth century. We have seen the demise of large conglomerate states—the British Empire and the Soviet Union—within the past fifty years. We have also seen a growing push toward division and dissolution in many other nation-states, such as Canada, Yugoslavia, Czechoslovakia, the United Kingdom, and India. Even within the United States, we find this tendency toward "balkanized" communities (Phillips, 1978). Ben Wattenburg (1990) identifies the United States as the source—and a prime example—of diffuse boundaries, while Robert Bellah and his colleagues (1985) describes a world of American "enclaves," each with a distinctive identity and mission but characterized by very loose or inconsistent boundaries.

In essence, the boundaries of most nation-states have been forever altered by the pervasive influence of international currency and investment, oil, and rapid communication. Peter Drucker (1989) observes that the independent nation-state is now only one of four decision-making units in the world's economy. Economic regions represent a second unit, the world economy of money, credit, and investment is a third unit, and transnational enterprise is the fourth. Each of these units influences the world economy and is interdependent with the other three.

A masterful, though disturbing, scene in Paddy Chayefsky's postmodern film classic, *Network,* illustrates the interplay between these four interdependent units. Ned Beatty, in the role of a powerful international businessman, speaks to Peter Finch, who plays the role of a renegade newscaster. Beatty reminds Finch that national boundaries no longer exist. The governments that used to control these boundaries have been replaced by corporate boards and stockholders. National currency has been replaced by the currency of oil. The new world order will be run like a business, not like a government. This new world order has no purpose other than the provision of profits to its anonymous stockholders and the establishment of a peaceful, business-as-usual environment. People are tranquilized by their own personal consumption of commodities skillfully marketed by those who control the international business conglomerates.

Reality tends to replicate Chayefsky's troubling vision of the postmodern world. Robert Reich (1991, p. 77) writes about the creation of a "purer form of capitalism, practiced globally by managers who are more distant, more economically driven—in essence more coldly rational in their decisions, having shed the old affiliations with people and place." According to Reich (1991, p. 77), "Today, corporate decisions about production and location are driven by the dictates of global competition, not by national allegiances. Witness IBM's recent decision to transfer 120 executives and the headquarters of its $10 billion per year communications business to Europe, a move that is partly symbolic—a recognition that globalization must take companies beyond their older borders—and partly practical—an opportunity for IBM to capitalize on the expected growth in the European market."

The Salman Rushdie controversy is a real-life drama that highlights the trend toward globalization. His book *The Satanic Verses* was threatening because it cut across national, religious, and cultural boundaries. Rushdie, in turn, has been hounded across national boundaries; he cannot find safety simply by moving to another part of the world.

While the postmodern world is noted for its diffuse boundaries, this new world order is also composed of discrete, competing
entities that will never allow global tranquility to exist. We have
seen the reemergence of small nation-states (such as in the Baltic
region of the former Soviet Union) and of nationalities within
countries (such as in Central Europe, Yugoslavia, and the Middle
East). While efforts are being made to bring people together and to
minimize differences—as in the creation of a unified European
Community—there is a simultaneous movement toward articulat-
ing and even exaggerating differences in religion, politics, culture,
and language. At the heart of this emphasis on differences and
national character is the new postmodern emphasis on mission and
purpose.

When Boundaries Were Clear

Any thorough examination of mission and boundaries in our
emerging postmodern era requires a look backward to the modern
and premodern eras. What are the remnants of the modern era that
we must still contend with, and what are sources of guidance from
both the modern and premodern eras to help us prepare for a postmodern world of clear mission and unclear boundaries?

I have proposed that the postmodern organization is likely
to be one in which mission is clear and boundaries are unclear.
What kinds of resistance are we likely to encounter as we move to
this type of organization? The resistance is likely to center around
the modern-day emphasis on both size and control. As modern organizations became larger, they needed clear boundaries and barriers to keep these organizations under control and integrated. The
emergence of boundaries in modern life occurred in both private
and public spheres. According to Jameson (1991) the modern era
was typified by the emergence of private rooms in homes. Whereas
in premodern times, men, women, and children often slept together
in the same room, the modern home was built with private bed-
rooms, studies, parlors, and living rooms. Corridors were built to
connect these isolated living units. These changes in architecture,
in turn, reflected the modern emergence of a sense of self—a personal identity.

Modern individuals placed great emphasis on distinctive individual identity. Personal boundaries were clearly drawn. Furthermore, those few personal boundaries that did exist in the premodern world shifted in the modern world. In his exceptional analysis of private and public man, Richard Sennett (1976) proposed that people in Western society tended to be quite candid in public life prior to the eighteenth century, while they had definite boundaries (cosmetics, formal dress, manners) in their private lives. Norbert Elias (quoted in Anderson, 1990) has observed that the sight of totally naked people was quite unremarkable in Germany and elsewhere until the sixteenth century. This changed in the eighteenth century with the emergence of modernism. Modern man retreated into his private life and created a public mask to protect him from other people in his public life. Thus personal boundaries became particularly important in public life.

Personal boundaries were further expanded and reinforced with regard to the differentiation between the world of work, on the one hand, and the worlds of family and leisure, on the other hand. Peter Drucker (1989) notes that divisions between work and family in the modern era were established even in areas of human welfare (for example, health and education) that had been connected with the family in the premodern world: "A hundred and fifty years ago social tasks were either not done at all or done primarily in the family, whether bringing up and educating children or taking care of the sick and old. Now social tasks are increasingly done in and through organized institutions—the business enterprise, the labor union, the hospital and the health-care system, the child-care center, the school, the university, and so on" (p. 77).

While personal boundaries were critical in the modern world, there was much less clarity and consistency when it came to mission and purpose in the modern world. The modern-day supermarket exemplifies an emphasis on clear boundaries and the absence of a clear sense of mission. We know when we have entered a supermarket; the electric-eye doors and signs tell us quite clearly. Signs that tell us where to drop off our shopping carts let us know at what point we are moving outside the supermarket's boundaries. Yet, the supermarket doesn't have a very clear mission. It contains many different products and seems to specialize in not specializing.

We can find anything from soup to nuts (and bolts and drugs, and lawn furniture, and small televisions).

Modern corporations are noted for their imposing high-rise structures. One steps into a new world when entering the lobby of one of these large, monolithic buildings. High levels of security and thick walls separate this corporation from the rest of the world. The sense of privilege, status, and boundaries is particularly evident when one attempts to access the executive offices of the corporation. These heavily reinforced boundaries are marked and protected by guards, receptionists, secretaries, carpeted waiting rooms, and closed doors. Similarly extensive and imposing boundaries are found in the modern professional offices of physicians, lawyers, and psychiatrists.

In contrast with their visible and clear boundaries, the mission statements of most modern organizations do not provide much clarity or guidance for those who work in or evaluate these institutions. No one cares much about the mission of Harvard University. "Veritas" (truth) is not exactly a grounded, definitive statement about the mission and purpose of this school. Similarly, who knows what the real mission statement is for IBM or General Electric. We hear a variety of marketing slogans associated with these companies ("Progress Is Our Most Important Product!") but know little about their founding mission, about revisions in their mission statements, or about how these vague slogans translate into real priorities and actions.

Apparently, in most modern organizations, the mere presence of the organization (and the highly bounded edifice that it has created) is itself justification for its existence. As a result, many public and private organizations were left alone during the modern era to manage their own affairs. The leaders of these organizations were accountable to no one outside the organization. Corporations polluted streams located on or adjacent to their property. Research laboratory scientists determined the projects on which they were going to work. Human service agencies determined who they would assist and how they would provide this assistance. Government agencies operated with minimal oversight by outside, civilian groups.

An investigator in the United States Armed Forces, for instance, speaks about the mission of his unit as being "very broad": you did everything and anything that would get the job done. No one questioned whether or not a specific type of investigation was appropriate to his division. Because of the thick boundaries that protected this agency from outside civilian intrusion, no one external to the agency had sufficient knowledge of the unit's operations to even engage in a discussion about its mission and purpose. At the federal level, we find many instances of unclear mission and very clear, impenetrable boundaries: the Federal Bureau of Investigation, the Central Intelligence Agency. In our newly emerging postmodern era, we have seen changes in these agencies as they have become more accountable to legislative bodies and as they have had to clarify—and then act more consistently with regard to—their own mission statements.

When We Could Do Our Own Thing

In the premodern world, organizations typically had both unclear missions and unclear boundaries. People simply did what they had to do, often in order to survive. One would never ask a farmer in the old days—or today for that matter—what his or her "mission" was. A farmer was simply in the business of raising food for his or her family to eat and for bartering for things the family needed. A craftsman or artisan would be just as confused (or bemused) as the premodern farmer if asked the same question. She would simply show the inquirer what she was working on at the time. Forty years ago, C. Wright Mills (quoted in Best, 1973, p. 11) observed:

> The craftsman has an image of the completed product, and even [if] he does not make it all, he sees the place of his part in the whole, and thus understands the meaning of his exertion in terms of that whole. The satisfaction he has in the result infuses the means of achieving it, and in this way his work is not only meaningful to him but also partakes of the consummatory satisfaction he has in the product. If work, in some of its phases, has the taint of travail and vexation and mechanical drudgery, still the craftsman is carried

over these junctures by keen anticipation. He may
even gain positive satisfaction from encountering a
resistance and conquering it, feeling his work and will
as powerfully victorious over the recalcitrance of
materials and the malice of things. Indeed, without
this resistance he would gain less satisfaction in being
finally victorious over that which at first obstinately
resists his will.

Obviously, many people involved in contemporary agriculture are no longer "farmers"; they are in "agribusiness." Similarly,
men and women who participate in crafts often are involved in
large-scale production (especially if they are living and working in
a third-world country) and share very little of Mills's sense of crafts-
manship. For them (or at least for their bosses), clarity of mission
is very important. Are we going to raise soybeans or corn? How
many of these small carved statues or "starving artist" pictures do
we need to produce today? As crafts and the arts have become businesses, the issue of mission and purpose have become quite serious
and appropriate. In his musical *Sunday in the Park with George*,
Steven Sondheim's second-act protagonist sings about the problem
of having to market his art. His modern concerns contrast sharply
with those of his premodern grandfather, George Seurat, whose
indifference to business and other mundane aspects of life is featured in the first act of the play.

We do, however, have elements of the premodern as well as
the modern era in our contemporary world. Alongside modern,
heavily bounded corporations, we find other organizations that
look very premodern with regard to mission and boundaries. The
farmers' markets that have once again become popular in our society offer a contemporary example. Typically found in an open
area at the center or periphery of a city, this "organization" does not
have clear boundaries. One can never declare with any assurance
that the farmers' market starts here and stops there. The mission of
the market isn't very clear either. Roughly, the market is set up for
the exchange of commodities and services; however, this includes
everything from fruits and vegetables to entertainment provided by
street musicians and mimes. The farmers' market is often unclear

with regard to a second set of boundaries: time. Farmers' markets tend to open roughly at a certain time of day and to close roughly at another time. Yet, because the market is composed of independent vendors, these time boundaries are rarely honored. Furthermore, many farmers' markets do not open every day. They may not be consistent with regard to the days they are open. Many contemporary farmers' markets (and their sister institutions, flea markets, antique auctions, and street fairs) open on an infrequent, spontaneous, or seasonal basis. Such markets contrast sharply with the modern supermarket and the postmodern mall.

As in the premodern era, for many of us, in our personal and work lives, neither mission nor boundaries are very clear. We are left, in essence, to do our own thing, to exist and even survive by picking up odd jobs, freelancing, piecing together a set of part-time appointments, living off contracts or royalties. Boundaries were unclear in premodern times because things tended to be very small and personal. A premodern family didn't need to stake out its territory, as a modern nation-state must do. Men and women were farmers or craftspeople. They knew the land they owned or the object they produced because they planted and harvested it or crafted it with their own hands, like their parents and grandparents had done for many years before them.

Richard Harris plays the role of a premodern man living in our contemporary world in Jim Sheridan's screen adaptation of John Keane's play called *The Field*. As an Irish farmer, Harris is unable to comprehend how a lush, green field that he personally brought to life (at the sacrifice of his relationships with other members of his family) could be sold by its legal owner to an "outsider" (an American) who had nothing to do with its restoration. For the character played by Harris, one establishes rights to a piece of property by working the land and nourishing it.

Some men and women in the premodern era owned small businesses inherited from their parents or grandparents. No one in the community doubted that they owned their shops, and there was no need for deeds of ownership for either the property or the business. Frequently, shopkeepers lived near their business or even on the premises (above the store, in the rear of the shop, alongside the inn). Their entire life was devoted to business, much as their postmodern equivalents, such as owners of bed-and-breakfast inns, often speak of the all-consuming nature of their business.

Today, we find that both mission and boundaries are important. Still, the premodern organization continues to exist in our contemporary world. Many businesses are still concerned more with ongoing processes (building something or repairing something) than with outcomes. We still find skilled craftspeople, gardeners who derive great satisfaction from landscaping a new home, and family physicians who care deeply about their patients.

There are other premodern remnants in our contemporary society: artisans, bed-and-breakfast inn owners, farmers' markets. Given that many of these remnants quite successfully fill a niche in our society, perhaps we should look to other remnants for solutions to our pressing, present-day problems. Is it just a yearning for a simpler place and time that leads us to reexamine the premodern era, or are there important lessons from this era that have been forgotten? My analyses throughout this book point to the enduring value of these premodern lessons.

Who Are We? The Interplay Between Mission and Boundaries

The emphasis on clarity of mission in postmodern organizations may reflect the need to survive the diffusion of boundaries commonplace in our postmodern world. Mission statements are often appropriately described as anchors: the holding point that prevents the organization from going adrift or being pulled away by a compelling tide or current. Contemporary organizations may need to be securely anchored if they are to effectively confront a confusing and constantly changing environment or if they are to avoid being swept away by a powerful, yet short-term, market trend or customer demand.

Unfortunately, the metaphor of an organizational anchor may be appropriate only in a large organization with substantial resources. Can most organizations be as indifferent to changing tides and currents as the metaphor of the ground anchor implies? The secure anchor may be appropriate if current postmodern conditions are temporary. However, what if this turbulent and unpredictable period is the long-term state of things in our society? Will an emphasis on clear and unchanging mission statements be appropriate over the long term?

An alternative metaphor may be more appropriate in the postmodern world. This is the metaphor of the sea anchor. While the traditional ground anchor requires relatively shallow water and a stable bottom to hold the boat securely in place, a sea anchor can be used in deep water (a state known to most postmodern leaders) or when the sea bottom is unstable (once again, a common postmodern condition). A sea anchor is not used to prevent a ship from moving when there is a prevailing tide or current; it slows down this movement. The sea anchor is used primarily to help stabilize a ship when it encounters rough seas or high wind. The sea anchor enables a ship to survive under highly turbulent and critical conditions, as well as to resist the pull of the ship toward another location (as a result of tides, currents, waves, and so forth).

Flexible mission statements may similarly serve as sea anchors for our organizations as they encounter highly turbulent and even life-threatening conditions, and as they attempt to move with, yet resist, shifting tides of market demands, environmental conditions, and unpredicted opportunities. Edgar Schein (1978; 1980) writes about "career anchors" that provide both stability and flexibility as we move into new jobs and new work environments. A similar model may be appropriate in establishing mission statements as sea anchors in postmodern organizations.

What will be the bases for these flexible, yet steadying, sea anchors? With regard to mission, the central purpose of an organization must be deeply rooted in the organization. The mission of an organization may be one of those initial elements that can't be added at a later time. Furthermore, the mission cannot readily be changed. It can, however, be expanded as conditions change. The railroad industry in the United States, for instance, might have expanded its mission in the early part of this century to include not only the running of trains but also, more broadly, the management of transportation systems. If the industry had expanded its mission, the railroads might have devoted less energy to competing against and attempting to block the expansion of the newly emerging air travel industry. We might have found a Santa Fe airline company today or a Great Northern conglomerate of airline, railroad, and trucking enterprises.

Clearly, as we look forward to a new era in which change is unpredictable and variable, in which customer needs and demands change frequently, and in which boundaries between organizations become ambiguous and often troubling, there will be many defining moments for most institutions. The leaders of these organizations must decide whether or not they are in the business of running railroads or transportation systems, providing low-cost medical services or generating revenues for hospital stockholders, offering liberal arts education or career advancement training programs. There will be no more important—or difficult—task for leaders of postmodern organizations to accomplish than defining the guiding mission and purposes for their institutions.

Chapter 5

Leadership: Who Moves Us and How?

I can find little spirit in terms such as *role model, participative leader, facilitator,* or *CEO.* My spirit recoils at doing anything to, for, or about the people around me in one minute. I can't follow a cookbook's five easy steps or someone's can't-miss method if what I am about has my spirit and that of others at stake—has "spiritual validity," so to speak. What metaphors and images are real for me as I move into my spiritual leadership? Am I a voyager, a knight, a quarterback, a chaplain, a father or mother, a servant?

Peter Vaill, *Managing as a Performing Art*

$\mathbf{A}$s I have observed in this book, many contemporary organizations are now moving into a postmodern phase typified by small-to-moderate size, fragmentation and inconsistency, and clear mission but unclear boundaries. The leaders of these organizations must find new ways to provide both direction and support for those with whom they work. In creating and moving into these new roles, postmodern leaders must overcome the ghosts of premodern and modern assumptions about leadership, while also retaining many of the valuable lessons learned and taught by premodern and modern leaders.

As we look back to these earlier eras, we find that leaders in the premodern era tended to be "great men," who were selected for their character and education. Great men not only led organizations, they also influenced history and established societal values. Leaders were either born to greatness or provided with an elitist program of liberal arts and mentorship. They tended to exert authority through a paternalistic concern for the welfare and proper education of those who depended on them. By contrast, the more democratic modern era tends to emphasize structures, processes, and procedures that ensure the appropriate expression of leadership and influence. Events—not great men—determine the course of modern history, and values are identified as products of the system and bureaucracy rather than as products of any specific individual(s). Those who head modern organizations typically define themselves as managers rather than leaders. Modern authority is expressed through rules, regulations, roles, and organizational structures.

The postmodern world has called both the premodern and modern notions of leadership into question. The postmodern leader is neither inherently great nor merely a product of a system or bureaucracy. Individual leadership can be effective and influential if applied at the right time, in the right place, in the right manner, and with regard to the right problem or goal. This contingent or situational model of leadership requires careful consideration of both individual and organizational character and style. It also requires a tolerance for ambiguity, a recognition of the need for one to learn from his or her mistakes, and a clear sense of personal mission and purpose. It is ultimately spiritual rather than secular in nature.

Postmodern organizations tend to be flatter than their modern-day counterparts and therefore encourage more collaboration and less direct exertion of authority than did either their premodern or modern counterparts. Peter Drucker (1989) suggests that new postmodern organizations are likely to resemble organizations rarely studied by either practicing managers or students of management and administration: the hospital, the university, and the symphony orchestra. The identification of these nontraditional modes of organizational life is somewhat paradoxical, given that hospitals, universities, and even symphony orchestras are now becoming more businesslike. Drucker (1989, p. 214) provides wonderful food for thought (or song for the ear) when describing a form of leadership in symphony orchestras that is very postmodern in character and form.

> There are probably few orchestra conductors who could coax even one note out of a French horn, let alone show the horn player how to do it. But the conductor knows how to focus the horn player's skill and knowledge on the orchestra's joint performance. This focus is the model for the leader of an information-based [postmodern] organization. . . . Another requirement of the information-based organization is that everyone take information responsibility. The bassoonist in the orchestra does so every time she plays a note. . . . The key to such a system is that everyone asks: Who in this organization depends on me for what information? And on whom, in turn, do I depend? The list will always include superiors and subordinates. The most important names, however, will be those of *colleagues,* people with whom one's primary relationship is coordination.

In this chapter, we explore these new forms of postmodern leadership by asking, "who moves us and how?"

The Butterfly Effect and Self-Organized Criticality

The postmodern leader is not only an orchestra conductor; he or she also exemplifies the "butterfly" in contemporary chaos theory. The so-called "butterfly effect" is a small event that occurs in a specific place and at a specific time. It has a profound impact on the world around it and on worlds that may be far removed from the "fluttering of the butterfly's wings." The concept of the butterfly effect was first introduced in the field of weather prediction. For many years, weather forecasters had hoped to significantly improve their predictive abilities through the development of increasingly complex computer models of weather patterning. They discovered that they could not move beyond a certain point in terms of improved predictability because specific conditions that exist in one small region of the world may influence the weather pattern of an entire continent for a period of time. Soon the influential region changes and weather conditions are strongly influenced by yet another small event—another fluttering of butterfly wings—at one particular place and at one particular point in time.

We are keenly aware of the butterfly effect in the United States. On several occasions, the warming of a small body of water (El Niño) off the western coast of Central America helped to determine the weather conditions (including drought) throughout the West Coast and the Rocky Mountain regions of the United States. In a more tangible manner, we can observe the butterfly effect in operation when we add sand to a sandpile on a beach or in a sandbox (Bak and Chen, 1991). The pile of sand will accept many grains of sand without changing its shape. The new grains slide down the slope of the pile (making it slightly larger) or they remain near the top of the pile (making it slightly taller). However, at a particular point in time and at a particular place on the top or side of the sandpile, one additional grain of sand (the precipitating event or critical incident) will start an avalanche and the sandpile will be dramatically altered in shape and even size (some of the sand falling away from the pile may become part of a new pile). We cannot specify ahead of time which grain of sand will start the avalanche or what the sandpile will look like after the change has occurred.

Bak and Chen (1991, p. 46) consider the butterfly effect and sandpile avalanches to be examples of a phenomenon they call "self-organized criticality": "Many composite systems naturally evolve to a critical state in which a minor event starts a chain reaction that can affect any number of elements in the system. Although composite systems produce more minor events than catastrophes, chain reactions of all sizes are an integral part of the dynamics. According to the theory, the mechanism that leads to minor events is the same one that leads to major events. Furthermore, composite systems never reach equilibrium but instead evolve from one metastable state to the next."

According to chaos theorists and researchers like Bak and Chen, initial events will have the greatest impact on a system if it is in a chaotic state, and the least impact if the system is in an ordered state. In an adaptive state—as found in a sandpile or a snowpack—the impact is likely to be short term. In the case of the sandpile, for instance, there is short-term adjustment to the addition of a single grain of sand. Similarly, a snowpile can readily accommodate an additional snowflake. Adaptive systems usually have the capacity to adjust and rework themselves into an orderly, solid state. At certain points, however, adaptive systems reach a supercritical state and can no longer adjust to the addition of new elements. The sandpile can no longer accommodate an extra grain of sand. The one additional snowflake makes the snowpile unwieldy. At this point the system becomes unstable and an avalanche occurs. Portions of the sandpile take on a very different form—in essence, forming a new stabilized state—and the system can once again adjust easily to the addition of a few new elements.

Organizations are mechanisms that can learn and adjust, much as the sandpile or snowpile accommodate additions. Organizational theorists speak of this short-term adaptation to change as first-order or single-loop learning (Argyris and Schön, 1974). Yet, at a supercritical stage, organizations can no longer adjust; they can no longer accept one additional crisis. An avalanche begins within the organization, and this institution changes in a profound manner. Organizational theorists speak of this irreversible transformation as second-order or double-loop change. The theory of self-organized criticality suggests that small events, such as a change in leadership, will usually produce only minor alterations in the structure and dynamics of the organization (the sandpile will get a bit bigger or a bit taller). However, sometimes the change in leadership will create a major alteration (an avalanche or, in systems terms, a "catastrophe"). Bak and Chen propose that the same processes are involved in the initiation of both the minor and major changes and that the onset of the major event cannot be predicted, in part because the same process brings about both outcomes.

It appears that the precipitating event in any instance of self-organized criticality serves two functions. First, it provides a structure for the dramatic rearrangement of the existing elements of the system. This is what occurs when an avalanche begins in the Swiss Alps or in a laboratory sandbox. The snow or sand begins to move in a specific direction and at a specific speed, rather than being random in either direction or movement. During the 1989 San Francisco/Oakland earthquake, homes and bridges began to vibrate in a specific patterned manner. Second, the precipitating event brings about the importation of resources from elsewhere in the system. The self-organized criticality of a system, in this instance, becomes an attractor of additional resources. It pulls them in from the surrounding area, initially, and then from more distance locations to bring about the dramatic rearrangement of the existing system and the existing resources within this system. Thus, the precipitating grain of sand leads not only to coordination of the direction and speed of neighboring pieces of sand but also to importation of grains of sand quite a distance from the one that was just dropped on the sandpile.

These two functions of self-organized criticality are mentioned because they may provide a key to the effective functioning of postmodern leaders. We may come to recognize a new kind of leadership. In the postmodern era, change introduced by a leader may begin to spread and import resources from elsewhere in the system, leading to an avalanche that even the leader could not have predicted, and certainly cannot control. This is not new; Martin Luther introduced a change he could not control and that eventually led in directions he directly opposed. The same could be said about Brutus (one of Caesar's assassins), Henry VIII, and even Gandhi. Our growing recognition and understanding of this function of self-organization, however, may be new and profound. While women and men in leadership positions do not always know if they will be able to precipitate a major change (avalanche), they must be prepared to provide direction once the movement begins, as well as to help attract—or at least prepare for—the external resources likely to fuel and expand the change once it starts.

Similar to the performance of weather and to the sandpile avalanche, we find major changes in the lives of organizations and countries spinning off from seemingly small events precipitated by individuals or small groups of people. The actions of a single jurist initiated the divestiture of AT&T—an avalanche in the field of communications. Decisions by a small group of Mid-East leaders precipitated an oil crisis in the early 1970s that altered the world economy. Avalanches of slightly smaller magnitude occur with the revelation of a sexual liaison between a presidential candidate and a fashion model, of a possible case of sexual harassment by a Supreme Court nominee, with the unanticipated death of a choreographer, or with the disclosure of impropriety in a major Wall Street investment firm.

Who Moves Us and How?

What will be the nature of this new postmodern leader, who must live with avalanches and butterfly wings? I propose that during the postmodern era, great leadership takes place in a specific place and context, at a specific time in history. The low-key and little-known CEO at Wal-Mart, David Glass, suggests that he is "nothing more than a representative of the collective efforts of our company's 350,000 associates [Wal-Mart's term for employees]" (Sellers, 1991a, p. 80). In the past, he probably left the more charismatic leadership role to Wal-Mart's founder, Sam Walton. What will happen now that Walton is no longer living? Frank Shrontz, Boeing CEO, indicates that "instant change by a CEO is impossible in a capital-intensive company with long lead times for product development. . . . The most you hope for is a shift in direction over five or even ten years" (Sellers, 1991a, p. 80). Yet, CEOs play an important role in postmodern organizations. According to a recent *Fortune* magazine article (Sellers, 1991a, p. 80), they serve three critical functions: "setting the strategic direction, aligning the employees behind the strategy so they can carry it out, and developing a successor." Yet each of these functions will be successful only at certain times and in certain places.

As David Glass notes, you need the support of the employees before you set the strategy, rather than soliciting it afterward. Several old jokes describe the leader as someone who discovers the direction in which his or her organization is already moving and then runs around in front of the organization in order to provide it "with leadership and direction," while being primarily concerned, in reality, with not being trampled by the herd. There is some truth in this, as David Glass has wisely revealed. Frank Shrontz has pointed to yet another factor regarding the effectiveness of CEOs. Their success may not be evident for five to ten years, when the gradual and often subtle impact they may have had on the vision and culture of the organization begins to bear fruit. El Niño has been influencing the weather patterns on the North American continent for many years, yet we have only recently discovered its impact. Similarly, the impact the beating of a leader's wings has on the tangible operations of an organization may not be discovered for many years.

As a prime example of these factors of leadership, we need only look at the rise (and recent fall) of Michel Gorbachev in the Soviet Union. He was in the right place, at the right time, to bring about an avalanche. Would he have been successful at another point in history? Probably not. As David Glass noted, the effectiveness of a postmodern leader is heavily dependent on his or her many "associates" (in this case, Soviet citizens). Will Gorbachev regain his power, or, like El Niño, will his influence fade, as yet another grain of sand (a new leader, such as Boris Yeltsin) is added to the sandpile of Soviet, Russian, and world history? Will Gorbachev's presidency be positively evaluated five or ten years from now or will he go down in history as a relatively minor figure? Will the new leader(s) in this part of the world have a minor impact or could their actions precipitate another major revolution in Russia, in the other new republics, or even throughout the world? We must await the outcome but should try to learn from this dramatic example of fluttering butterflies and self-organized societal avalanches.

Situational Leadership and the "Jerk"

From the perspective of self-organized criticality, postmodern theories of leadership tend to be highly situational in nature. Modern leadership and management theory, exemplified by the work of Blake and Mouton (1984), emphasizes the acquisition of the specific skills and attitudes appropriate to one, correct mode of leadership (the so-called "consensus-building" model). The postmodern theory of leadership, exemplified by the work of Hershey and Blanchard (1977) (and even more insightfully but less popularly by the work of Fiedler, 1967, Vroom and Yetton, 1973, and Woodward, 1958), emphasizes the relativity of leadership. Effective leadership depends on the use of specific styles of leadership in particular settings and in addressing specific tasks. No one style is always effective. Rather, we must learn when and how to use a specific style.

Even the situational leadership theorists, however, provide an inadequate model for the transitional, liquid, self-organized systems described in this book. We can't even find consistency on when a specific leadership style works or doesn't work. At certain times, a particular kind of butterfly will make a difference, provided it is in the right place and time. At other times, this same butterfly will be ineffective, even if the situation very closely resembles a previously successful situation. Sometimes El Niño is influential; at other times it is not.

Flexibility in style, therefore, must be supplemented by a commitment to learning if postmodern leadership is to be effective. As Argyris and Schön (1978)—and more recently Senge (1990)— have observed, we are effective leaders not because we avoid making mistakes but because we learn from our mistakes.

The postmodern model of leadership is based on the assumption that history is the unfolding of simultaneous or sequential elements of both reason and irrationality. At one level, there is reason in the emergence of appropriate leadership. Situational leadership theorists, such as Hershey and Blanchard, define specific criteria for determining the appropriate leadership style. At another level, there is nothing but chaos. Appropriate styles of leadership and, more important, the effectiveness of a specific leader can neither be predicted nor even fully understood after the fact.

The characterization of any phenomenon in an organization (for example, worker morale) is often influenced more by the measuring procedure than by the phenomenon itself. Similarly, in the assessment of leadership effectiveness, the relative success of a leader is often determined less by the leader being studied than by the level at which the analysis is being conducted and by the nature of the criteria of effectiveness being used. Certain criteria and levels of analysis produce clear conclusions about the nature of effective postmodern leadership; other criteria and levels of analysis tend to produce either contradictory conclusions or a muddle of images and impressions about effective leadership.

At one level, the behavior of virtually any leader is understandable and even predictable. At another level, however, the behavior of this same leader is inexplicable and unpredictable. At the global level, for example, we can examine the behavior of one of our current archenemies, Saddam Hussein. Saddam is understandably described as a mad man, one willing to sacrifice his people and his country for a vision of regional domination that is neither appropriate nor achievable. His behavior exemplifies a theory of chaotic—or at least nonrational—leadership. Yet, as one examines the life of Saddam and the history of his country and region, many of his dreams begin to make more sense—and the strategies and actions of the American government begin to seem more chaotic and inappropriate. It is not unusual for one part or level of a system to begin to look increasingly chaotic or arbitrary precisely at the point when another part or level of the system becomes clearer and more purposeful.

At a much closer level, we can look at the behavior of almost any corporate executive to uncover both the chaos and order of postmodern leadership. The leaders of one high-tech firm are accused by one of its managers of allowing the corporation to slide rather than walk into a new organizational structure that may be much too complex and incompatible with the founding vision of the organization. A common complaint in other organizations concerns the unwillingness or inability of company leaders to encourage open and honest communication. The managers in another organization suggest that their president is a "dangerous" visionary, who always seems to shift his concerns to a higher level when crisis appears. On occasion, most corporate executives (and other leaders of our society) seem, in the words of Robert Hochheiser (1987, p. 1), to behave like "jerks."

> Do you think of your boss as a grade A unadulterated jerk whose brains are on vacation? Does he act like a world-class bozo who would get the Nobel Prize in bungling if there were such an award? . . . You're not alone—at one time or another, most of us have felt that we reported to bosses who wouldn't know a sound management concept if it bit them on the nose.

They raise hell with us if we screw up, but then they
display an almost total lack of ability to do anything
right, and we suffer for their mistakes.

Hochheiser offers several intriguing reasons why bosses become jerks (self-interest, limited vision, working at a level beyond
one's competence, and so forth); however, most important, he
speaks of the ways in which the system colludes to turn bosses into
jerks and suggests strategies for working within this system (making
your boss look competent) rather than fighting it and losing the
battle (and job).

Hochheiser's jerks—like the corporate leaders described
above—seem to be making decisions and operating in a manner that
contradicts their own best interests and the best interests of the
organization. None of us are immune when we assume leadership
roles. We sometimes (or oftentimes) behave like jerks with the people who report to us. Colman and Bexton (1975) (from the Tavistock Institute in Great Britain) suggest that we as members of
groups produce and collude in sustaining the competencies and
incompetencies ("jerkness") of those who serve as leaders of our
groups. I noted earlier that we tend to have a premodern attraction
to leaders who are wise, great warriors, or visionaries. We also,
however, wish our leaders to be incompetent, because in this postmodern world we are ambivalent about our dependency on the wise
leader.

Alternatively, we (and the warrior leader) need a strong
enemy in order to justify our actions; therefore, we can never totally
defeat our enemy. Or we are ambivalent because we need to keep our
dreams intact, and if these dreams are ever successfully enacted, they
will be modified by reality. At times and in certain ways we want
the wise leader to appear foolish, so that we don't always have to
feel so foolish. We want the brave leader to lose to the powerful
enemy, for the enemy defines the identity of our noble and just
group. We want the vision or dream to remain unrealized and the
leader in charge of the dream to fail, because we want the dream to
remain a pure, unrealized, always present wish.

The theories of Chris Argyris and Donald Schön (Argyris and
Schon, 1974; Argyris, 1982; Schön, 1983) suggest yet another reason

why we act like jerks in our postmodern world: the theories of leadership and management we espouse and believe that we follow are, in fact, incompatible with our actual behavior and the assumptions ("theories-in-use") that underlie our behavior. We exist in organizations that never or rarely encourage the disclosure and discussion of discrepancies between espoused theories and theories-in-use. Hence, leaders continue to act without personal insight and in a manner both counterproductive and incompatible with their own values and goals.

Both of these explanations are credible. Neither, however, does full justice to the complex and demanding conditions that leaders now face in a postmodern world. We exist in a world that is changing so rapidly and in such unpredictable ways that a group's collusions in the creation of incompetencies among its leaders must constantly shift, for leaders must continually be incompetent or untrustworthy in whole new ways. Sometimes the group helps the leader become an ineffective communicator; at other times, the group helps the leader become a great communicator who is highly manipulative and can no longer be trusted, as in the case of our city manager.

In a postmodern world, the espoused theory and the theories-in-use must not only be compatible (and hopefully identical) but frequently changed because of shifting internal and external environmental conditions. A president may initially believe that his visionary concerns at times of crisis help employee morale. He can be confronted with the contradictory evidence if, in fact, his behavior lowers morale. However, a few days later, the president may introduce "vision" because the crisis is itself caused by a lack of vision or long-term perspectives. In this latter case, the president may be correct in using this strategy. Under shifting conditions, how is the president (and organization) going to learn?

Leaving the Age of Management

As we leave the modern world, what can we learn about leadership from this short-lived era and from the much longer one that preceded it? First, it should be noted that premodern notions of leadership were generally sacred in nature. A great leader was somehow an emissary of God. He succeeded his father by God's will or possessed great skill or wisdom, given to him by God. Just as God was paternal in character, so were the leaders of secular institutions. Our very notions of leadership and organizational structure came from sacred sources (the church) or from the military (which has always been a quasi-religious institution). The modern world attempted to divorce itself from the sacred, especially in the ongoing operations of its organizations. As Max Weber noted, bureaucracy not only eliminated nepotism, it also drove the sacred out of organizations. In the modern era, men and women turned to secular priests—called professionals—rather than to sacred sources (clergy) for their inspiration and guidance. They turned to lawyers, physicians, and computer programmers. Professionals who wore the secular vestments of psychiatry or psychology became the modern-day recipients of confession and sources of absolution (Bellah and others, 1985).

But this did not last very long. Mankind insists on living in a world that is sacred in nature. Postmodern organizations—and the postmodern world in general—are once again a blend of secular and sacred.

> To outward appearance, the modern world was born of an anti-religious movement: man becoming self-sufficient and reason supplanting belief. Our generation and the two that preceded it have heard little but talk of the conflict between science and faith; indeed it seemed at one moment a foregone conclusion that the former was destined to take the place of the latter. But as the tension is prolonged, the conflict visibly seems to need to be resolved in terms of an entirely different form of equilibrium—not in elimination, nor duality, but in synthesis. After close on two centuries of passionate struggles, neither science nor faith has succeeded in discrediting its adversary. On the contrary, it becomes obvious that neither can develop normally without the other. And the reason is simple: the same life animates both. Neither in its impetus nor its achievements can science go to its limits without

becoming tinged with mysticism and charged with
faith [Teilhard de Chardin, 1955, p. 293].

When we look for the emergence of a new type of leader in
a complex postmodern world, it is essential that we understand and
appreciate the nature of modern notions about leadership, for this
is the standard against which the postmodern model of leadership
is judged (and often found wanting or at least very threatening).
Max Weber (1947) proclaimed near the beginning of the modern era
that formal, equitable bureaucratic structures had replaced the ar-
bitrariness of premodern organizations. Leaders, according to
Weber, were now influencing organizations through their formal
bureaucratic positions, rather than because of any charismatic presence, possession of valuable expertise, or impressive list of accomplishments. Furthermore, leaders provided systematic guidance to
organizations as they confronted accelerating change both within
and without. Leaders with considerable training and managerial
skills provided the continuity and planning needed not only to
survive but to thrive in the "future shock" of the modern era.

In the modern era, we looked not to the great man of the
premodern era nor did we anticipate the situational leader of
the postmodern world. Rather, we relied on the great system and the
great plan as implemented by the competent manager. Individual
leaders became anonymous or even invisible in a modern world of
"organization men" and "men in gray flannel suits." Schools of
management flourished during the modern era in part because leadership was assumed to be something that could be nurtured (and
controlled) in a systematic manner and also because of a growing
recognition that organizations needed to be carefully managed if
they were to survive repeated change. According to Drucker (1989,
p. 221), "Rarely in human history has any institution emerged as
quickly as management or had as great an impact as fast. In less
than one hundred fifty years, management has transformed the social and economic fabric of the world's developed countries. . . .
The truly important problems managers face do not come from
technology or politics; they do not originate outside of management
and enterprise. They are problems caused by the very success of
management itself. . . . The performance of management has con-

verted the workforce from one composed largely of unskilled labor-ers to one of highly educated knowledge workers." Perhaps, as Drucker suggests, there has been no more important development in our society during the modern era than the emergence of man-agement as the dominant (though salient) form of social control.

Given this emphasis on management, primary attention was given to the development of policies and procedures to enable men and women to exert authority in a leadership role. The paternalism of the premodern era was no longer appropriate, for as Sennett (1981) suggests, it is no longer acceptable in the modern world to make a pretense of care when a leader is exerting authority. Autonomous, bureaucratic authority is Sennett's replacement for paternalism.

Modern theories of leadership are distinguished from the pre-modern in that modern theories tend to emphasize events and sys-tems and de-emphasize characteristics of the individual who assumes a leadership position, which was the primary orientation in the premodern world. The old debate of whether man makes history or history makes man is resolved in favor of history as the active agent in modern leadership theory. One of the first modern philosophers and social analysts, Hegel, described history as the unfolding of reason, as a universal order or process. Marx agreed with this model. Along with Hegel, Marx has been crucial in de-veloping our modern notion about leaders as products of their times and social orders. Thus, while premodern models of leadership were founded on myth, the modern model of leadership is built on a solid base of history and reason (thereby, supposedly being objective and value free).

A second aspect of modern theories of leadership is the equa-tion often drawn between leadership and management. The terms *manager* and *leader* are interchangeable in most modern manage-ment and leadership theories. Emphasis is placed on the develop-ment of policies and procedures that enable men and women to exert appropriate and effective authority. According to Richard Sen-nett (1981), modern notions of leadership and management evolved from the assumption that authority should be based on the posses-sion of appropriate skills and attitudes, not on ownership of a busi-ness or on formal position in an organization. The autonomous authority that Sennett describes relies heavily on rational judgment and clarity of policy and procedure, which, in turn, often leads to a sense that those in authority are indifferent to our personal welfare.

A Chinese businessman with whom I work recently provided the analogy of the silkworm to describe modern notions about leadership. While the premodern leader lived in a world of potential (the cocoon) and the postmodern leader flutters as a butterfly in a turbulent world, the modern leader lives in a world of daily work. He or she simply goes about the business of fulfilling the functions of his or her job. There is nothing terribly special about the silkworm, though it (and many highly successful modern-day leaders) have created products of great beauty and complexity. The silkworm is industrious and knowledgeable, and these are the critical ingredients of successful modern leadership. We are left with an impression of the diligent, systematic spinner of silkened managerial threads by organizational men and women who may never be seen but who are essential to the very fabric of the modern corporation.

The unsung heros of modern organizations such as IBM and AT&T are the many executive and line managers who go about the rather mundane practice of daily leadership. Yet, in the modern world, we often long for the charismatic leader who will save our organization or even our country. In spite of this wish, we still tend to select men and women who are quietly competent. In the 1988 presidential election we were attracted to men who were good bureaucrats rather than challenging leaders. Jesse Jackson (and perhaps Pat Robertson) were exceptions. They may have been throwbacks to the premodern era, where character and charisma seemed to make a real difference. Yet, we chose two potential leaders (Bush and Dukakis) who claimed to be good managers of people and the economy, of world affairs and of our governmental institutions. The issue becomes: do we need something more than good management in our emerging postmodern world?

Is There Still a Time for Kings and Queens?

Max Weber wrote extensively about the transition in leadership and organizational functioning from the premodern to the modern era.

He noted the movement from a "charismatic" and "traditional" mode of leadership to a "legal-rational" form. As Peter Dews (1987, p. 151) notes in summarizing the argument made by Weber, "In modern societies power does not depend upon the prowess and prestige of individuals but is exercised through an impersonal administrative machinery operating in accordance with abstract rules." While this shift corrected the widespread abuse of power, there have also been profound costs, as noted not only by Max Weber but also by the Marxist-based Frankfurt School in Germany and the postmodern social historian, Michel Foucault, in France.

In his studies of confinement, surveillance, and social control, Foucault emphasizes the shift from an external form of coercion and control (the visible chains) to a more pernicious internal control (the invisible chains). Similarly, for Weber as well as the Frankfurt School, "it is the social forms engendered by purposive or instrumental rationality, with their indifference to personal ties, and their crushing of idiosyncrasy and spontaneity, which represent a profounder threat to human freedom than the class oppression specific to capitalist society" (Dews, 1987, p. 151). Similar sentiments are expressed by postmodern American social historians and analysts such as Richard Sennett and Arlie Hochschild, who write about the rationalization ("autonomous love") and internalization ("the managed heart") of control in American life. While at one level our social institutions seem to be more benevolent and responsive to individual needs, at another level they have become more subtly repressive and controlling. Control is now more efficient and, because it is less visible, more effective.

The dominant leadership myth from the premodern era is the "great man." If we just wait long enough, the great man will come along to rescue us. Some organizational theorists (for example, Bion, 1961; Colman and Bexton, 1975) describe groups that hold a "dependency assumption": group members are inadequate and need a wise leader on whom all members of the group can rely for guidance and nurturance. Other groups make a "flight/fight assumption" regarding a hostile external world and need a forceful and brave warrior-leader. According to the Tavistock theorists, another group assumption centers on the visionary leader who points the way to a world that does not yet (and never can) exist.

This third image of leadership, called the "pairing assumption," requires the group to wait or search for the missing element (the leader's "lover") who is needed to fulfill the leader's dream. This "lover" might be a pot of money, societal recognition, or another person. All three of these models of leadership were dominant in the premodern world and, according to the Tavistock theorists, continue to determine the unconscious or at least regressive aspects of group life in contemporary organizations.

Even if groups in the premodern world somehow avoided the creation of "great man" myths, they still embraced the notion of leader as parental in form and character. All three of these assumptions tended to be quite paternalistic—especially the dependency assumption—for they enact interpersonal dynamics founded in the relationships between children and their parents. One of the most provocative and insightful analyses of this premodern emphasis on paternalistic leadership is offered by Richard Sennett (1981, p. 84): "Paternalism stands at one extreme of the images of authority. . . . It is power exercised for the good of others. No hereditary obligation binds a person to do so, nor do religious injunctions. The care for others is the authority's gift, and he will bestow it only so long as it serves his interests."

Sennett proposes that patrimonial authority gained ascendancy in the nineteenth century as the dominant mode of control exerted by "real" fathers in family-run businesses. This patrimonial system gave way during the latter stages of the premodern era to the quasi-paternal authority exerted by male leaders who continued to appeal to familial models of obedience and commitment: "In a paternalistic society, males . . . dominate. The domination is based on their roles as fathers: protectors, stern judges, the strong. But this basis is symbolic rather than material as in a patrimonial order [where 'real' fathers exerted their authority over other members of the family who helped run the business]" (Sennett, 1981, pp. 53–54).

In the premodern world, leadership was exerted primarily through this paternalistic mode of authority. Leaders felt that they had the right (as surrogate fathers) to control the behavior of their followers both inside and outside the organization. An excellent example of this is found in the Broadway musical *Carousel*. The owner of the mill in which Julie Jordon (the heroine of the play) works instructs Julie to return to her home (owned by the mill) when he discovers she is spending time with the notorious womanizer, Billy Bigelow. The mill owner felt he had the right (and responsibility) to protect Julie's virtue, even though her behavior had nothing to do with her work as a mill employee.

This paternalism was also exhibited in the *in loco parentis* policies of many American colleges and universities. As with Julie's boss, collegiate leaders believed they had the right and responsibility to determine the hours their students (particularly female students) were to return to the dormitory and even to monitor the table manners and dress of their students. Both the mill owner and the college president in premodern America felt that their purpose as a leader was not just to produce textiles or provide education but also to mold character and shape the values of the new generation of "uncivilized" (often foreign-born) men and women.

The boundaryless purview of premodern leadership is still evident in many organizations. However, because laws have been enacted that prevent employers from dictating the conduct of their employees or from firing an employee for behavior (for example, intoxication) that occurs off the job, paternalistic influence on life away from work now takes on much subtler forms. We find the life-styles (rather than just the corporate policies and record of success) of corporate leaders featured in magazines, television programs, and books. Rather than focusing on the character or values of the successful corporate leader, the media tend to focus on acquisition and consumption of wealth. Emphasis is placed on form rather than substance. This new attention to the leader's behavior away from the job may ultimately have much greater influence on the employee's behavior off the job than did the older, more coercive forms of paternalism. Young men and women may emulate the life-styles of "the rich and famous" without necessarily knowing much about how these successful men and women arrived at their current position and wealth. Even if the "rich and famous" are the same age as their youthful admirers, they play a role that once was assumed by parental figures. They provide a model of how life is to be lived.

In the premodern era, leaders were either born with specific skills and talents ("leaders are born, not made") or were provided with excellent education. In the United States, this premodern concept of leadership is exemplified in the colonial liberal arts colleges, such as Harvard and Yale. These colleges were established (like their British counterparts, Oxford and Cambridge) to mold the character and increase the wisdom of the young men who were about to assume positions of leadership in their communities (as ministers, lawyers, or physicians). These wealthy young men did not go to college in order to find a job. Rather, they were already assured of a comfortable life and were now receiving the most expensive and extensive training available for their inevitable leadership positions. We still find remnants of this era in elitist collegiate institutions (such as Yale, Harvard, Stanford, or St. Johns) and in informal (or formal, but secretive) corporate training and career track programs for the young men and (in some cases) young women who show "high potential."

The premodern image of leadership is based on myth rather than on history (the latter is the dominant mode of analysis in the modern era's model of leadership). Myth is centered in the telling of stories about the great man's exploits and wisdom. As we look to new, postmodern models of leadership, we must recognize these premodern myths, for they are still very influential in our society; they have only been covered over (not superseded) by modern, rational models of leadership and management. In terms used by the Tavistock Institute theorists (Colman and Bexton, 1975), these myths and stories of the premodern era help to create and recreate the collective group culture. The members collude regarding the veracity and meaning of these stories of leadership, ensuring that the stories are never changed and that the "truth" behind these stories is never told.

In our own past, as Americans, we had many "great men" myths, ranging from the stories about George Washington and Abraham Lincoln to those about Franklin Roosevelt and Douglas MacArthur. We wait for the great leader who is born and educated to leadership. Perhaps the enduring myth of John Kennedy and his Camelot and of Martin Luther King and his dream are the closest we have come in our own times to this dream of leadership, though both myths are now tarnished (as perhaps all such myths will be in a media-dominated postmodern world).

Our Chinese businessman spoke of the premodern world as

illustrating a cocoon model of leadership. We assume that leadership is waiting there for us, full of potential. We see the cocoon and spend our time dreaming of what will happen when it opens up and how beautiful the butterfly inside must be, rather than noting the beauty of the cocoon itself. We spend our time speaking of what John Kennedy or Martin Luther King might have done and how our society might have been transformed, if only they had lived. We, of course, don't know what would have happened if they had lived. Modern and postmodern leadership theory suggests that they probably would have been regular human beings, like the rest of us, with some successes and some failures.

Our discussion of postmodern leadership, as it relates to premodern and modern models of leadership, leads us to a central question. Not only must we ask "who moves us and how?" We must also ask: "can we live with our leaders being 'regular' human beings, or is it essential that we give birth to exemplary men and women who hold great potential, whom we subsequently dishonor or destroy?" Another central question emerges: "how can a man or woman live under such conditions as a leader, whether butterfly, silkworm, or cocoon?" Clearly, the normal modern preparation of managers for leadership roles is inadequate. A new form of leadership is needed if our organizations are to survive the transition to a new era.

New Leadership and the Rogue Event

What will be the nature of the newly emerging postmodern leader? He or she will be one who can master the unexpected, and often unwanted. He or she (and more often, it will be she) must be able to tolerate ambiguity. Most important, the postmodern leader will acknowledge and even generally anticipate the occurrence and impact of rogue events, which profoundly affect and determine the ultimate success of a leader or group. Rogue events cannot be predicted. We can only predict that they will occur and that when they do, they often have a substantial impact on the life and dynamics of a group.

Bateson (1979) describes a rogue event when he writes about the problem of predicting where bubbles will first arise in a pot of water being heated to the boiling point. The bubbles will first appear and the boiling will begin at a place in the body of water where there is a flaw or foreign element (thus, the value of shaking a little salt in a pot of water to get it to boil sooner). We usually cannot predict where the first bubble will be located. We can only predict that as we raise the temperature of the water to 212 degrees, boiling will begin somewhere in the pot of water. Similarly, we usually cannot predict where honesty, service to others, or sacrifice will first be manifest by individuals or where visionary and courageous leadership will emerge in a group. We can only hope that a David will emerge to slay Goliath. We can, however, create conditions (though education, group development, encouraging policies and procedures) to maximize the possibility that someone will take on this role. We can also encourage the group to help the newly emerging leader become successful and nourished in this role, rather than colluding with him or her to fulfill fears (and hopes) about the emerging leader's "jerkness."

Senge (1990) identifies several conditions that underlie the rogue event. First, he notes that cause and effect are not closely related in time and space in many complex human systems: "When we play as children, problems are never far away from their solutions—as long, at least, as we confine our play to one group of toys. Years later, as managers, we tend to believe that the world works the same way. If there is a problem on the manufacturing line, we look for a cause in manufacturing. If salespeople can't meet targets, we think we need new sales incentives or promotions" (p. 63).

Thus, in some instances, a highly influential action or situation is defined by us as a rogue event or a leader seems to be acting like a jerk, because we have been unable or unwilling to look beyond immediate cause-and-effect relationships to identify the real causes of the rogue event or jerky behavior. A change in accounting practices resolves our manufacturing problem and we are surprised. It is a rogue event because we had failed to connect accounting to manufacturing. We are surprised by the impact a slight change in a product line has on the effectiveness of a sales campaign because we had previously ignored the intimate relationship between product design and sales. A leader becomes unexpectedly ineffective in motivating her employees because the relationship between lower employee morale and the company's new compensation package is not recognized.

Second, Senge (1990, p. 64) notes that small changes can produce big results; "small, well-focused actions can sometimes produce significant, enduring improvements, if they're in the right place." This principle, which systems thinkers call *leveraging*, parallels the chaos theory concept of self-organizing criticality and is illustrated by Buckminster Fuller in the use of trim tabs on the rudder of a ship.

> A trim tab is a small "rudder on the rudder." . . . It is only a fraction the size of the rudder. Its function is to make it easier to turn the rudder, which, then, makes it easier to turn the ship. The larger the ship, the more important is the trim tab because a large volume of water flowing around the rudder can make it difficult to turn.
>
> Ships turn because their rear end is "sucked around." The rudder, by being turned into the oncoming water, compresses the water flow and creates a pressure differential. The pressure differential pulls the stern in the opposite direction as the rudder is turned. . . . The trim tab . . . does the same for the rudder. When it is turned to one side or the other, it compresses the water flowing around the rudder and creates a small pressure differential that "sucks the rudder" in the desired direction. . . .
>
> The entire system—the ship, the rudder, and the trim tab—is marvelously engineered through the principle of leverage. . . . So, too, are the high-leverage changes in human systems [Senge, 1990, pp. 64–65].

Rogue events and the precipitation of organizational avalanches are often like the trim tab, small forces that affect larger ones, which in turn bring about massive change in an organization. Postmodern leadership may be effective when it operates like a trim tab. A leader may not be able to turn the ship or organization himself or herself, for the organization is simply too big, too complex, and too unwieldly for any one person to make a major impact. Rather, the effective postmodern leader will pick a specific rogue event that has already occurred or will help to create a small, roguish event that will, in turn, affect other moderately large events, which in turn may bring about significant organizationwide changes.

Often, as in the case of Fuller's trim tab, one will actually produce, use, or encourage a rogue event that moves an organization in a direction opposite to that which is intended. The reaction against this event will, in turn, create new momentum that moves the organization in the desired direction. One is reminded of the biblical tale in which the wise King Solomon offers to cut a child in half in order to resolve a conflict over custody of the child by two contending women. The horrible prospect of such an act drives one of the women (the true mother) in the opposite direction. She is willing to give up the child in order to spare its life. In this way, the true mother was discovered, and the possibility of an inhumane act leds to humanity and resolution of the conflict.

An excellent, real-life example of leverage and rogue events in corporate life concerns the emergence of courage and honesty among a group of corporate executives in a major American financial institution. I was consulting with a senior vice president of this institution, who had a reputation among his vice presidential subordinates of being very demanding and intimidating. The senior vice president knew that he was discouraging risk-taking behavior through his abrupt manner and wanted to change his style of leadership in order to encourage more creative problem solving on the part of his staff during a particularly turbulent transition in the life of his institution. A consulting team collected extensive information from his vice presidents on his leadership behavior, much of which was quite critical. After reporting this information back to the senior vice president (which he received quite openly), the team met with him and all of his subordinates at a retreat site and presented an oral summation of the interview data. The immediate and highly emotional reaction of his vice presidential reports to this presentation was an absolute and unqualified rejection of everything the consulting team had said: "You are a wonderful leader! How could the consultants have so grossly distorted the facts!"

Members of the consulting team began to wonder if they were at the right meeting or if they had been set up. After about twenty minutes of "killing the messenger," one of the vice presidents, who had been quiet, spoke up. He took a deep breath and then stated that "the information being presented by these people is accurate. I've talked with many of you in my office or in the hall about these very issues. I'm tired of beating around the bush. Let's bring this stuff out in the open!" After a short pause, during which everyone looked at the senior vice president for his reaction (which was somewhere between neutral and appreciative of the vice president's candor), the other vice presidents began cautiously to state their own concerns and to verify that the information contained in the oral report was accurate. The meeting was productive, and tangible steps were taken to alleviate some of the personal and structural problems this group of financial leaders faced.

The vice president who first spoke up exhibited courage, as did the senior vice president who contracted with the consulting team in the first place to present their critical report (without editing) to all of the vice presidents. Perhaps both men were simply tired of the old way of operating and were willing to take risks in order to change things. Perhaps both men had sufficient job security to take a chance. Maybe I was witness to a very special kind of organizational courage.

Typically, when courage does occur in an organization, it operates like a self-organized system (the butterfly or sandpile effect) or like a rogue event. It is unpredictable, momentary, surprising, and often transformative. We usually cannot determine beforehand when courage will be exhibited or who will be the courageous person, though we are often terrific Monday morning quarterbacks. As in the case of Bateson's pot of heated water, we cannot accurately predict when or where the first bubble of courage will form or when it will come to the surface. We can continue to heat the pot (in the case just presented, by offering information never before presented in a public setting) and perhaps sprinkle a few grains of salt (words of encouragement or the use of supportive retreat settings) to encourage the water to begin boiling. In some cases, unfortunately, one can continue to heat the water and sprinkle salt on the surface, and still find that nothing changes. The prognosis for a similar organization is not very positive in this turbulent postmodern era.

A second example of a rogue event, as it relates to leadership, comes from a quite different source: John Lennon of the Beatles. Lennon often told a story about the police who were protecting the Beatles at a concert in Los Angeles. The crowd became very excited during the concert and began to storm the stage, located in the middle of a baseball field. The police began clubbing members of the crowd and serious injury was imminent, as members of the crowd became more agitated and the police grew more anxious about their own safety, as well as the safety of the Beatles. In a remarkable rogue event, John Lennon suddenly stopped the concert and calmly told the police that "these people will not harm us, so please don't harm them." The crowd and the police immediately stopped the confrontation, everyone quieted down, and the Beatles completed their concert with no further incidents.

Using my Chinese colleague's analogy, the postmodern leader is a butterfly. This type of leader knows that he or she has a limited time to live (or to be credible) and must constantly change directions with the wind. The butterfly is not protected in the cocoon (the premodern leader) nor does this leader do the mundane and safe managerial work of the silkworm (the modern leader). The butterfly is not always valued for its practicality, as is the silkworm, nor does it have the potential of the cocoon. The butterfly leader is a real person, rather than a mythic possibility. The butterfly leader must find purpose and value in subtle ways, for the moments of glory are at best brief and often not even acknowledged. Tomas, the protagonist in Kundera's *The Unbearable Lightness of Being* (1984), deeply loves Tereza. Yet, he knows that Tereza loves him by chance and could just as easily have fallen in love with someone else. Like Tomas, we must find meaning and purpose in the seemingly random and chance events that propel us into positions of leadership or that place the people for whom we work in positions of leadership.

Postmodern leaders and followers must be clear about personal and institutional mission and purpose, while fluttering in a turbulent environment. We must find value in the work that others do (with our support and guidance) and in the success that our organization has achieved—even when we had intended something else to occur. In some instances, we may even confront situations in which, acting like a trim tab, we help our organization achieve the exact opposite of what we had hoped or intended. We can be successful as leaders in the postmodern world—and find satisfaction in this highly demanding role—only if we acknowledge and anticipate this new, more turbulent reality.

Chapter 6

Communication:
How Do We
Tell Our Story?

The stories people tell have a way of taking care of them.

Gary Holstun Lopez, *Crow and Weasel*

In setting the stage for postmodernism, Gregory Bateson (1979) had much to say about communication and conversation, and about the critical role played by both relationships and conversations within organizations. According to Bateson, any organizational transition is best understood not as a shift in the rate of production or in the flow of energy in the organization but rather as a change in the relationships among members of the system or organization. This emphasis on relationships is decidedly postmodern and flies in the face of the modern emphasis on production and energy transformation. Ilya Prigogine (Prigogine and Stengers, 1984) suggests that the modern emphasis on energy builds on a Newtonian worldview, which reduces all physical phenomena to the action of forces, such as gravitational attraction, heat, electricity, and magnetism—the pendulum model from Chapter One. Both Prigogine and Bateson believe that some nonorganic systems are appropriately described in terms of forces or the flow of energy or materials between two or more objects. Organic (and even some nonorganic) systems, however, are more accurately described by changes in relationships—the model of fire I described in Chapter One.

One individual cannot have a relationship. Relationships exist between two or more people and are defined jointly by the involved participants. A relationship, in other words, is something more than the sum of its parts (participants in the relationship). It has a life of its own and exists as a separate entity. Harry Stack Sullivan (1953) speaks of relationship as a central ingredient, even with reference to our definition of self. Traits (such as aggression) are to be found in relationships or in the organization or in culture, not in the individual (Bateson, 1979). My identity as a person is defined by my relationship with other people, not in terms of any enduring personality characteristics. No man is an island. He lives with—and defines himself in terms of—other people.

Organizational processes require energy (production, flow of resources, capital) but are themselves manipulations of information or relationships. I kick a dog and the dog is pushed forward. This represents a flow of energy from my foot to the dog. Such a flow is important in a nonorganic world (which exists only on paper). Both the dog and I are objects in this world of linear cause and effect. However, in the real world, when I kick a dog, the dog either turns around and bites me or runs off to sulk in the corner. The dog's reaction depends not so much on the flow of energy (velocity of the foot and weight of the foot and boot) as on the nature of my relationship with the dog (flow of information or relationship). Both the dog and I are living beings who exist in relationships.

Causality in organic and complex inorganic systems (hence in all human organizations) is always cyclical: I kick the dog; the dog bites me back. I get even madder at the dog and kick him again (or shout at the dog and get out of his way). My behavior influences the behavior of other living beings, which, in turn, influences my subsequent behavior. Causality never moves backward, however, and many forms of change (for example, fire) are irreversible.

In the area of communication, as in all dynamic systems, time serves as a mediator between cause and effect. We call something a "cause" because it precedes that which we called the "effect." Organizational problems are often difficult to diagnose and solve because of differences in the ways a cycle of causes and effects is punctuated (Watzlawick, Beavin, and Jackson, 1967). From a postmodern perspective, there are no causes of organizational problems nor is there a beginning to any conversation. It is more appropriate to conceive of an organization or conversation as an ongoing process (a living entity or fire) rather than as a structure or machine (a mechanical entity such as a pendulum).

Premodern cultures often used particular animals (totemism) to describe the nature of their society. Only during the brief modern era of Western civilization do we find organizations described as machines. An animal is a relationship, a process (Bateson, 1979). The postmodern era must return to a conception of organizations as processes and relationships rather than structures. Specifically, I propose that the postmodern world is based primarily on verbal communication and storytelling. While the visual form of communication that was dominant during the modern era may allow us to ignore the contextual and interactive nature of relationships and communication, the premodern and postmodern emphasis on verbal communication and conversation requires us to examine these dimensions of relationship and communication in much greater depth.

The Verbal Mode: What Do People Say?

The postmodern world has returned to a seemingly premodern emphasis on the spoken word. Rapid communication devices (in particular, the telephone and in the near future, teleconferencing) make the written word passé. Marshall McLuhan (1964) heralded our entrance into the postmodern era with his description of the global electronic village. A recent *Business Week* article (Coy, 1991a) demonstrates that McLuhan was probably right. Coy comments on the increasing use of the telephone and on the new technologies that are emerging to support an oral mode of communication. Organizations are beginning to reduce the number of secretaries and clerks they employ, as they move back to oral communication. Even the newest writing-based mode of communication—electronic mail—more closely resembles oral speech than it does formal written communication. In place of the formal typed written memorandum (which typically is carefully edited and reviewed by multiple sources), the new E-mail message tends to be handwritten or informally typed. It is usually spontaneous and considered off-the-record, to be followed up, if necessary, by a more formally written proposal (which is meant for public consumption). Even formal written communication has changed with the introduction of facsimile machines. There can literally be a conversation back and forth between two people in distant locations through a facsimile machine. Our postmodern world has become quasi-oral and instantaneous.

Even without the electronic media, our contemporary world is one in which oral, face-to-face communication is once again dominant.

> Without a script or any rehearsal, Mike Walsh, CEO of Union Pacific Railroad, holds the stage for 5½ hours as employees from 24 sites across the country fire questions at him via satellite. With disarming candor, Walsh, 48, answers queries on everything from job security to workplace safety.
>
> Mattel's CEO, John Amerman, whose belief that employees should have fun has helped turn around the toymaker, wants to announce quarterly results with a splash. The 59-year-old executive puts the message into a rap routine, which he delivers to his assembled workers, backed up by a group of secretaries called the Rappettes.
>
> At UNUM Corp., CEO James F. Orr, III, invites all 5,500 employees to sound off to him through the insurance company's ubiquitous electronic mail system. Every night he sits down with that day's messages. Sometimes he answers with a personal phone call the next day (Rice, 1991a, p. 111).

While these examples may smack of show business and sexism, they also speak to the growing appreciation of verbal communication. *Fortune* magazine (Rice, 1991a, p. 111) similarly observed that "talk back and forth within the organization, up and down the hierarchy [is increasing]. . . . It's the free flow of information inside the company that enables you to identify and attack problems fast, say, when customer service representatives first get an earful about some quality glitch, or salesmen in the field encounter a new competitor."

At a societal level, we find a renewed emphasis on verbal communication and conversation in a recent successful television series about the Civil War. This program emphasized the stories told by men and women who were alive during this tumultuous period of American history. The women's movement in America emphasizes the discovery or rediscovery of voice by women. The men's movement similarly builds on the stories being told by men about their fathers, themselves, and their sons. Organizational stories become grist for the mill in the formulation of institutional visions, identification of dominant cultural themes, and generation of appropriate solutions to long-standing institutional problems.

Truth and Lies

A central question has emerged regarding analyses of postmodern communication: how do we know what is true? During the modern era, the medium used to convey information or ideas was often invisible. Very little attention was paid to how a message was delivered; instead, we focused on the content of the message. As we enter the postmodern era, however, we look carefully at the way communication occurs, for the medium does make a significant difference in the message conveyed.

Jameson (1991) reminds us that words are readily recognized, whereas visual images are more slowly assimilated. We immediately recognize a song or childhood jingle, while struggling to recognize an old picture from our youth or a postcard from some place we know we have been. Visual messages can be ignored, whereas auditory messages cannot. The growing predominance of auditory messages in postmodern organizations may lead to a condition whereby information can less readily be ignored today than it could a decade ago. We are more likely to answer the phone than to answer a letter.

Though we may be less likely to ignore oral postmodern messages, this does not automatically mean that we are more likely (or even just as likely) to believe the message received. In this postmodern world of oral messages, "disinformation" and public image management are just as important and influential as information and reality (Anderson, 1990). It is indeed ironic that one of the most successful advertising campaigns of our time features a man ("Joe Isuzu") who is lying. We appreciate the candor, on the one hand, of a car company that acknowledges the fragility of truth in advertisement; yet we also know that this candor is itself a lie or at least part of a cleverly constructed message to sell us cars. Similarly, we think we are watching a legitimate commercial for one product, then a pink rabbit marches across the screen telling us that we are really watching a commercial for a battery that keeps going and going. Thus we are both knowledgeable and naive. We are lied to, and are lied to about being lied to. We are fooled, told we have been fooled, and seem to enjoy being fooled.

The mixture of truth and lies is found in abundance throughout our culture. New, postmodern novels—such as those written by E. L. Doctorow (1975) or Gabriel Garcia Marquez (1990)—intermingle historical figures (Harry Houdini, Sigmund Freud, Simon Bolivar) and events (the shooting of Stanford White, Bolivar's conquest of South America) with fictitious characters and events. A recent, controversial film about the assassination of President Kennedy (*JFK*) contains elements that are true, others that are clearly fictitious, and yet others that may or may not be true. No clear distinctions are drawn between these three; they are intermingled in a movie that is meant to both entertain and persuade moviegoers to reach a particular conclusion concerning an assassination plot.

The contemporary sculptures of Duane Hanson present figures that are so realistic and placed at such appropriate places in the galleries and museums in which they are displayed that one is uncertain about whether or not they are statues or real people (Jameson, 1991). I recently walked through the French quarter in New Orleans and discovered people around me who were from another era. They were statues—but not of famous war heroes or presidents; rather they were statues of butchers, customers, and young children who may have frequented those very buildings many years ago. I was faced with the almost ghostly presence of other people from another time who were occupying the same space and doing pretty much the same thing (buying and selling) as other people around me.

Jameson employs Plato's concept of the *simulacrum* to convey an important point about this new postmodern interplay between truth and lies. The simulacrum is an "identical copy for which no original has ever existed" (Jameson, 1991, p. 18). Thus, we look at a French quarter or Hanson sculpture or read a Doctorow novel and believe, at one level, that we are seeing or reading a faithful rendering of a real person or event. Everything seems real, including the details, the discontinuities, the mixture of beauty and ugliness. Yet, none of it is true; we have been presented with a very "accurate" portrait of a person or event that never existed. While novels, sculptures, and other works of art of the premodern and modern eras often attempted to portray something about the world in realistic fashion, the new modes of art have moved this realism one step further; there may actually be confusion about what is or is not real or about what once was real. We no longer know what is fact and what is a mixture of fact and fiction; we no longer know if this is a real person or a real door in the art gallery we attend.

We see this strange mixture of truth and lies operating in many organizations, both large and small. An organizational fiction is created that everyone is supposed to accept as true, yet which no one believes to be true. Yet, if the fiction is repeated often enough and long enough, then perhaps someone will begin to believe it. If nothing else, at least the teller of the tale may begin to believe his or her own lies, if for no other reason than to reduce the cognitive dissonance (Festinger, 1957) usually associated with the consistent telling of lies. If we tell stories about unicorns in many settings and from many different perspectives, then eventually at least one person is likely to suggest (or at least begin to believe) that unicorns must in fact exist, since there are so many stories told about them. We have many organizational unicorns to contend with in our society; some of us might nominate "worker democracies," while others might point to the "balanced federal budget" or "peace through a strong defense."

At a moderately large public relations firm that I will call Co-Action Associates, quarterly companywide meetings are held, at which the "amazing success of the past quarter" is announced and documented with a large volume of statistics. Ambitious plans for the next quarter's growth and success build on these upbeat reports. Impressive organizational unicorns are clearly evident—and are at some level acknowledged as true—among members of Co-Action Associates. During the three months between these meetings, however, voicemail messages spell out a different story: inadequate funds, discontented employees, cancelled events. No explanation is offered for the discrepancy between the formal announcements and the informal communications. Hence, the informal messages at Co-Action gain increasing credibility. Members of the organization begin to believe that this public relations firm is trying to "P.R." its own employees. Whispering and gossip are rampant.

A similar dynamic seems to be prevalent in many large contemporary organizations, whether public or private, low-tech or high-tech. In his journalistic account of the rise and fall of the Bank of America, Gary Hester (1988) describes a yearly ritual at the bank involving the senior financial officer on New Year's Eve. This senior officer would gather together the financial reports from all of the bank's divisions and at the stroke of midnight would come out of his office and announce to the assembled senior executives that the bank had once again exceeded its financial projections for the year. At this time all of the executives would celebrate the start of a new year. Unfortunately, these pronouncements of financial success were never based on reality.

This financial wizard was able to manipulate the figures in such a way that success was always achieved for the past year. While the other executives knew at some level that these figures did not make sense and that the reality of the bank's financial status was actually one of gradual deterioration, no one was willing to confront the lie, possibly out of fear for their jobs or, perhaps, out of fear of the implications of the negative financial reality for their own personal sense of effectiveness. A dose of reality would force change (as it ultimately did) in this highly stable and respected financial institution. So the ritual continued for many years, and lies were spun out in abundance. Bank executives, like congressmen, congresswomen, and the rest of us, often do not want to hear the bad news about finances, whether personal, organizational, or national in scope.

The same thing has occurred at a rapidly growing high-tech firm in California that I will call Tell-Vic. Many of the formal written reports at Tell-Vic seem to be for external consumption and for internal auditors who need to prepare legally credible reports on the organization's functioning. As in the case of the Bank of America, the executives at Tell-Vic are able to manipulate the numbers to achieve their financial objectives. However, unlike the Bank of America, there are new forms of informal communication that make it harder to sustain the corporate lie. Much as in the case of Co-Action Associates—or, for that matter, in the Tiananmen Square massacre—new telecommunication devices (such as voice-mail and facsimile machines) tend to reduce the ability of leaders at Tell-Vic to control the flow of information in the organization. The "real" communication at Tell-Vic occurs through informal conversations, small group meetings, and "the indispensable voice-mail," which is widely available at Tell-Vic.

The training coordinator at an electronics firm I will call Rigtonics notes that E-mail systems (as well as the extensive use of cross-functional task forces) in her company have helped to create a new communication pipeline for nontraditional groups and dissidents in the organization. She suggests that the absence of honest communication from the top of the organization has created a vacuum that tends to be filled by rumor and gossip.

> Company meetings at [Rigtonics] are . . . a postmodern sheep in modern wolves' clothing. The meetings are lavish, multimedia extravaganzas, yet fraught with censorship. . . . A subtle form of censorship can be seen in how the "open" question-and-answer session is handled by the CEO; always the master of ceremonies for these meetings. The employees are invited to write their questions on 3 x 5 cards and submit them to be read [out loud] and answered by the CEO at the

end of the meeting. The cards are collected by representatives from the Internal Communications
Department, who sort them into appropriate categories, and finally some of them are read aloud and answered by the CEO.

As a result of this restriction on interaction with high-level executives, employees at Rigtonics tend to rely on informal sources of
information (whispering).

The training coordinator, however, recently had an opportunity to bypass the formal lines of authority in order to communicate directly with the CEO of Rigtonics.

As task force coordinator, I was required to present an
outline of the program to the CEO. My time with the
CEO would allow me to sort out the degree of truth
of three different rumors: (1) he is extremely critical
about the quality of presentations, (2) he did not trust
his executive team, and (3) he was an uninspiring
leader. For me, the truth turned out to be a CEO who
was comfortable with an informal discussion rather
than a presentation. He was not critical in any way,
and I found him genuinely inspiring in his enthusiasm about the company. However, he did voice a lack
of trust in the public-speaking ability of his entire
staff.

Thus, the CEO shared with his employees a preference for more
informal modes of communication. Yet the answer for Rigtonics's
communication problems is not simply making the CEO more accessible to his employees. The company is too large and complex
for this to occur in anything other than a symbolic manner (as is
now the case with the 3 x 5 cards).

Furthermore, as noted by the training manager, there is insufficient time in the workday for this type of informal communication. "I understand the role gossip and rumor play in postmodern
organizations, but I found the necessity to meet the CEO in person
a time-consuming way to filter truth from rumor. Much can be

learned about an organization by listening to its whispers. Unfortunately, much time and energy is wasted by those generating rumors and those trying to find the truth. My own postmodern organization design would include a culture built on a vision of truth; giving consideration to the difficulty that many people have telling it, yet constantly striving to underline its value."

Books about informal and nonverbal communication abounded in the 1960s and 1970s, in large part because we learned not to trust the formal written messages that people sent us. We are moving into an increasingly heterogeneous world in which more and more people we work with are in some sense strangers to us, either because we have had no previous contact with them or because they come from a different cultural background. Gossip and related informal networks of communication become central to postmodern organizations, though they obviously played a significant role in modern organizations (and probably in premodern organizations) as well. The primary conveyor of organizational precedent and culture in the postmodern organization may be the person who gossips. This person may be even more effective in the postmodern organization than in the modern organization, given the presence of new communication technologies that significantly increase the speed and expand the range of informal communication in the organization.

We need to find new and more effective ways to make use of informal communication in the postmodern organization. We must reconceive the role of gossip, given that gossip is usually viewed in a negative light. As the authors of *Women's Ways of Knowing* (Belenky and others, 1986) have shown us, gossip may be an important contextual way of gaining information. Organizations have devalued and misunderstood gossip for many years, in part because it has been used primarily by people without much power as an alternative mode of communication and influence to the male-dominated formal channels. Eisler (1987) writes of the role of gossip-related communication in the building of partnership societies as opposed to the more formal modes of communication (pronouncements, policies, memoranda, proposals), which tend to support societies based on domination. The discounting of gossip and related forms of informal, contextual communication may be a tactic of individuals who seek to control or dominate an organization from above, through the use of formal, abstracted modes of communication. The postmodern world increasingly demands a mixture of both formal and informal communication to establish credibility and trust in settings where truth and lies intermingle.

Organizations as Relationships and Conversations

According to Bateson (1979, p. 113), the reinforcement of specific behaviors in an organization is influential because it points to "rightness," that is, it defines the norms of the organization. Behaviorists, by contrast, would have us believe that rewards work because they tend to reinforce specific behaviors. When an employee does a good job preparing a report, according to many behaviorists, we reward him with a raise and then expect him to perform at this high level even more frequently as a result of the reward. In many ways, behaviorists are still trying to reify an inorganic world in which there is a transfer of energy by means of reinforcement. They are not much further along than the example of the man kicking the dog. They change the behavior of the pendulum by giving it an extra push.

We are now discovering that Gregory Bateson was correct. Reinforcement primarily concerns the transfer of information, not the transfer of energy. Thus, reinforcement becomes a vehicle for communication, rather than for the control of behavior. Reinforcement tells us about the nature of appropriate behavior and about the consequences of inappropriate behavior. It does not simply increase the probability of specific actions. The raise in salary serves not just as a motivator but also as an organizational sign that the employee is doing the right thing in the right way.

Bateson's notions about reinforcement work even in the behaviorist's own backyard: the "Skinner box" (an animal cage containing a lever that a pigeon learns to press with its beak and a slot where a food pellet is placed after the lever is pushed). We discover that a pigeon in this box may be pressing the lever not because of the pellet that will roll into the slot but because the lever defines (along with the pellet) the rules and sequence of behavior appropriate in this Skinner box game. We know that this is the case because we can reverse the sequence of events and the pigeon will perform correctly. Specifically, we can "condition" a pigeon to eat a pellet in order to be given the chance to press the lever. Thus, in this instance the lever-pressing behavior, not the pellet, becomes the reinforcing behavior.

This outcome may give us some ideas about overeating behavior. Rather than being a reinforcement or an end in itself, eating food becomes the behavior the overeater performs in order to obtain some other reinforcer (parental approval, reduced stress, and so forth). Food becomes a means to another end, just as salary increase may be interpreted in a variety of ways and may not necessarily increase the employee's future production of good reports. The reinforcement might be reversed in the case of the employee, just as in the case of the pigeon. A salary increase may signify that the employee is now moving up to a position in which he will be given responsibility for preparing a certain kind of report. He may find this increased responsibility and recognition more important than the salary increase, provided, of course, that his current salary meets the employee's basic needs for food, shelter, and other "hygiene" factors (Herzberg, 1966).

Reinforcement tells us about context or, more generally, about our culture. The learning of context by means of reinforcement is more important, according to Bateson (1979), than the learning of specific skills or specific behaviors through reinforcement. We can, in turn, only learn about a specific context (culture) of an organization by knowing other contexts, that is, other organizations. Given this conception, organizational consultants are of particular value as cultural anthropologists.

"Cosmopolitan-locals" (Grimes and Berger, 1970) play a central role in the diffusion of innovations. "Cosmopolitan-locals" are men and women who "have seen the world" but who are also knowledgeable about the unique dynamics and culture of their own organization, that is, the organization's patterns of reinforcement. They have worked in a variety of organizations and have rich and diverse experiences in addressing a number of problems in many different settings. They are less likely to be frightened by change and readily gain a sense of the culture or context of reinforcements in any organizational setting. They rapidly learn how to play the game in any institution and are of great value with specific regard to the promotion of change and the definition of organizational contexts.

If communication is an important ingredient in organizations, then reinforcement is a form of "punctuation" (an indication that a sequence of events has come to an end) of conversations that occur in the organization. Such punctuation becomes a critical variable in determining the life and nature of the organization by helping to define cause and effect relationships. Senge (1990, p. 21) offers a wonderful example of this desire for punctuation: "Two children get into a scrap on the playground and you come over to untangle them. Lucy says, 'I hit him because he took my ball.' Tommy says, 'I took her ball because she won't let me play with her airplane.' Lucy says, 'He can't play with my airplane because he broke the propeller.' Wise adults that we are, we say, 'Now, now, children—just get along with each other.' But are we really any different in the way we explain the entanglements we find ourselves caught in? We are conditioned to see life as a series of events, and for every event, we think there is one obvious cause.

The major area of debate for Lucy and Tommy is defining the "beginning" of the problem. Furthermore, the point when their argument (conversation) began ("who started it") defines the nature of each participant's role and defines our sense of cause and effect. If Lucy begins the argument, then Tommy is likely to play a defensive, reactive role, arguing that he "didn't start it!"—whereas the roles are likely to be reversed if they define the argument as being "started" by Tommy.

The "social construction of reality" (Berger and Luckmann, 1967) is strongly influenced by the ways ongoing processes and complex causal relationships are "punctuated" as "events."

> Conversations in organizations are dominated by concern with events: last month's sales, the new budget cuts, last quarter's earnings, who just got promoted or fired, the new product our competitors just announced, the delay that just was announced in our new product, and so on. The media reinforces an emphasis on short-term events—after all, if it's more than two days old it's no longer "news." Focusing on

events leads to "event" explanations: "The Dow Jones average dropped sixteen points today," announced the newspaper, "because low fourth-quarter profits were announced yesterday." Such explanations may be true as far as they go, but they distract us from seeing the longer-term patterns of change that lie behind the events and from understanding the causes of those patterns [Senge, 1990, p. 21].

The rate and type of delay of communication flow between various parties in the organization is also critical (Forrester, 1961, 1969, 1971; Senge, 1990). Virtually all organizations—and the feedback systems within them—experience some form of delay. At a global level, the delay in the transmission and receipt of diplomatic papers at Versailles may have played a major role in starting World War I; the possible delay in diplomatic papers (in this case, offers of surrender) from Japan through Scandinavia to the United States may have prevented the end of World War II prior to the dropping of the atomic bomb on Hiroshima. Messages are missed. The "phone tag" and "answering machine ping-pong" games so prevalent in contemporary organizational life may account for many of the important dynamics—and, in particular, the important failures—of postmodern organizations.

Delays in communication not only prevent information from being received in a timely manner, which can create instability and breakdown. Delays often are misinterpreted. They are frequently attributed to inefficiency ("why in the world does it take so long to get a response to my request!"), incompetence ("how could these people be so stupid as to move so slowly on this order!"), or malevolence ("this is just 'politics' as usual!"). Fred McAmis, a manager at a high-tech firm, observes: "From the employees' point of view it often looks like political games are being played to satisfy the egos of executive management, but that may be too simple of an explanation, reflecting more the frustration felt than any critical thought. What seems to be a more realistic assessment is that [this company] outgrows its strategy as soon as it becomes implemented."

According to this manager, the plans made by the executives of his company always seem a little out of date. There is delay in the flow of information to these executives. This is particularly critical given that they work in a highly volatile and competitive environment. The consequences of such delays also affect the employees, who interpret late decisions and resistance to new ideas as signs of outmoded perspectives.

It is not at all unusual for valuable information in an organization to flow upward rather than downward, which leads to the common—and valid—perception of employees that the boss doesn't know what is really going on. These types of delays can be avoided if, as Richard Beckhard (1969) has proposed, organizations are designed to ensure that decisions are made at the point where maximum, relevant information is available. Unfortunately, many organizations do not recognize the critical role played by communication delays and hence find other reasons for the problems caused by such delays.

Organizations as Conversations

A postmodern perspective—as I have extrapolated it from European deconstructionist theory—suggests an even more radical notion about both the form of communication within organizations and also the very nature and purpose of organizations. From a deconstructionist perspective, organizations can be characterized as a series of concurrent and sequential conversations between people. These conversations (oral and written) may lead to the purchase or distribution of goods or to the initiation of machine-based production processes. However, the goods and machines are *parts* of the organization, whereas conversations are the *essence* of the organization.

From a slightly different perspective, I propose that the product of all organizations is conversation or, more broadly, information. While organizations produce many other things (services, commodities, energy), they share one function: they all produce conversation. Some organizations produce nothing other than conversation (for example, government regulatory agencies), while other organizations, such as small farms, craftshops, and small factories, typically produce very little conversation relative to other services or goods they offer or create. As organizations become increasingly complex, a greater proportion of resources in the organization typically goes to this conversation function.

Conversation is needed to sustain integration among the diverse, differentiated parts of the organization. Conversations tend to bind people together; talk is the glue in most organizations. The role of conversation as glue is especially important in ostensibly secular organizations that lack history, continuity, or unifying myths. The notion of conversation as a form of integration has implications for a postmodern theory of leadership. A postmodern leader must be first and foremost a conversationalist. She must be sensitive to and able to influence the conversations that take place.

As in the case of many postmodern observations, children are often the sources of real insight about our society. I first heard of organizations as extended conversations from my son, Jason, and soon had it confirmed by my daughter, Katy, when they were both less than ten years of age. We were attending a month-long experimental college that brought together faculty and students (along with their families) from colleges throughout the United States to create a new form of education to fully integrate family care and learning. As the dean of this temporary college, I was curious about my children's reactions to the environment in which I usually work. After the first full day of the program (planning sessions, coordination, decision making, a bit of conflict management), I asked Jason what he saw going on. He said that he had seen and heard a lot of people sitting around talking, but not much else. A day later, I asked Katy about her impressions. She also commented that there seemed to be a lot of talking going on and not much else.

I began to look at our month-long experiment in a new light. Yes indeed, it was mostly talking. Furthermore, the more I thought about it, the more I was convinced that this is exactly what this temporary college should have been; talking should have been at the heart of the matter. Conversation in this setting, as in most settings, was legitimate, not a waste of time. Talking was not only the basis for education in this college, it also formed the basis for the creation of community in this highly productive and memorable temporary college. During the month the college existed, the participants in the experimental program visited several utopian farms in New England, as well as several local businesses. Sure enough, most of what seemed to be happening was talk. There was very little action (even on the farm). There was mostly talking about farming and telling stories about what had already happened in the organization. Years later, when I was reading the deconstructionist's radical perspective on society, I was reminded of my children's precocious and prophetic foray into the same realm of social observation and critique.

Conversation as Dialogue and Ordering Process

The description of organizations as a series of conversations is extended and further clarified by Senge (1990), who distinguishes between two kinds of conversation: dialogue and discussion. He notes that the term *discussion* comes from the same root as the words percussion and concussion. Whereas discussions tend to resemble ping-pong games and emphasize win-lose competition, *dialogue*, is intended "to go beyond any one individual's understanding. . . . In dialogue, individuals gain insights that simply could not be achieved individually. . . . [The] group explores complex difficult issues from many points of view. Individuals suspend their assumptions but they communicate their assumptions freely. The result is a free exploration that brings to the surface the full depth of people's experience and thought, and yet can move beyond their individual views" (p. 241).

Senge points to an observation made by Werner Heisenberg when describing dialogue: "science is rooted in conversations. The cooperation of different people may culminate in scientific results of the utmost importance" (p. 241). Heisenberg suggests that his conversations with fellow scientists such as Einstein and Bohr had a lasting impact on his thinking. We can readily point to other examples of intensive and extensive conversation and interaction (dialogue) that led to extraordinary productivity by a group of composers ("Les Six" in Russia), authors (Paris of the 1920s), or corporate engineers (the Eagle Project, described by Kidder, 1981). Argyris (1982) offers a similar "dialogical" model in his description of "advocacy with inquiry," suggesting that effective reasoning, learning, and action occur in interaction with other men and women who encourage us to test our assumptions, as they are testing their own. We test assumptions by engaging in brief action-oriented experiments that bring new information to bear on our perceptions of the world.

A second deconstructionist theory about conversations can be extrapolated to organizations. This theory concerns the role of conversation in preserving order and continuity. Narratives and conversations, in general, follow irreversible processes, and this irreversibility provides an organization with stability and ultimately order. Narratives involve a series of decisions about which direction to take in forming and telling a story. Numerous bifurcations (decision points) occur. The story moves in one direction and can never return to another narrative structure or theme without taking into account the previous choices that have been made. A story that begins with the theme of administrative incompetence, for instance, can never be a story of administrative dedication, even if the story line later turns to instances of commitment and service; it will then be a story of incompetence *and* dedication, not merely one of dedication. Like fire, a story can never be undone; it always changes reality in an irreversible manner.

Formal modern-day communication, by contrast, is reversible. It operates like a pendulum, seeking out balance and equity. One can "white-out," deny, or even contradict previous statements. We are all acquainted with self-canceling phrases and pronouncements in formal communiques and think nothing of passively reading statements that simply make no sense. Informal communications are different; they are irreversible. We pay attention to them and accept all their aspects (slips-of-the-tongue, tone of voice, posture, and so forth) as accurate representations of a complex and often contradictory world. Thus, the sequence of a verbally communicated story is critical. We can't start over again or white-out what we have already said. The informal conversations (not the formal, usually written, communication) provide the order in the organization, for they do not allow the organization to reverse itself or vacillate between different modes or styles. Shifts in the content or style of informal conversation are irreversible, which adds to the accumulating precedence of the organization and its ongoing progression.

Order is also introduced to an organization through the use of language as a legitimatizing process. A central problem in all organizations is legitimation: who is allowed to speak about what and at what time. These are the game rules. Every utterance or unit of conversation is a move in a language or conversation game. Conversations about conversations are in some sense metamoves that shift the rules or require a shift to another set of rules. These shifts alter the basic character of the organization and suggest the power of second-order change. Games have their own rules. There is no ultimate, legitimatizing authority that resides outside the game, hence legitimacy is always a central issue in the communication that takes place in organizations. Games are self-fulfilling and self-sealing, that is, they produce their own validation and justification and typically are not discussable (Argyris, 1982).

In a corporation with which I consult, complaints are rarely voiced publicly, and the assumption is widely shared that if complaints are made, they will be ignored or the complainer will be punished. The accompanying "indirect complaining" game requires that communication about organizational or interpersonal problems be informal and "secret." The assumption that complaints will be ignored and complainers punished is never tested, because complaints are never expressed; hence the assumption is never subjected to any verification. Furthermore, members of this organization can't even complain about the fact that complaints are unacceptable. Thus the assumption (and accompanying game) are self-sealing: they are not discussable (and their nondiscussability is itself nondiscussable). This dynamic is certainly not unique to this organization.

Communication games are local and temporary. A phrase commonly used by the postmodernists is that the world no longer has its "grand narrative." System theorists often tend to conceive of communication in a very general manner as the flow of information across boundaries. However, the actual character or form of information is distinctive to each organization. One organization with which I consult, for example, has established a pattern of "end running," with each member of the organization tending to bypass the people immediately above (supervisor) and below (subordinate) him or her. They primarily relate instead to those members of the organization two levels above or below them. Such a pattern encourages the destructive use of indirect confrontation and rumor. Another organization with which I work tends to undo all of its messages after they are first conveyed. The president and chair of the board are both very intuitive and visionary (as all of the previous chief executives of the organization have been). They make pronouncements and commit themselves to goals strongly opposed by those immediately below them (the vice presidents). The vice presidents in turn reframe and reinterpret each of the president's and chair's statements, changing the meaning and purpose of these statements. The third level of management then "unmakes" the vice presidents' pronouncements and so on down through the organization. In each instance, one must examine the individual case to obtain a clear sense of organizational communication and the rules of the game that help define this organization's dynamics and culture.

There certainly appears to be justification for the postmodern perspective on the role of conversation as a means of preserving order in organizations. One has only to look at the informal rules that determine the behavior of people in most organizations. These rules usually determine which people are allowed to talk together, what they can talk about when together, and the extent to which what they say can be told to other people. Other aspects of the informal rules and culture of an organization (dress codes and rituals) are established primarily to help determine the nature and extent of communication between various people in the organization. For example, in most organizations, those who wear work shirts can interact with those who wear coats and ties only in certain ways and at certain times. A man can kick the dog, but the dog can never bite back without serious consequences. The conversational rules within organizations have much to do with establishing and maintaining relationship rules.

The World of Visual Communication

The modern world was primarily visual, and we still see abundant evidence of this world in our contemporary society. In its later years, the modern era relied heavily on such visual media as film and television. We need very little documentation to make the case that we have been living in a television age—complete with MTV, televised wars, and an average of six hours of television per day in most households. We have witnessed increasing reliance on attention-grabbing graphics in corporate life, increasing use of videotaped presentations rather than brochures or other forms of printed advertising to sell a product or service, and greater use of videoconferencing and related video-mediated technologies in bringing together people from different locales.

Conversely, it should be noted that the predictions made ten to twenty years ago about the massive infusion of television into the daily operations of corporations have not come true. There are limits to the use of television; furthermore, television seems to be entering organizational life just when the visual medium is giving way to a return of oral media. A more lasting mode of visual communication in the modern world, especially in organizations, is the gaze, that is, visual surveillance. One of the major innovations in the design of office buildings during the latter phases of the modern era was the elimination of walls between offices. While this elimination of physical barriers allows for more informality and a sense of community, it also allows for greater surveillance and the watchful gaze of the boss.

A nineteenth-century version of a visually-based environment was proposed by the noted social reformer, Jeremy Bentham.

> In the famous panopticon of Jeremy Bentham . . . the building is a set of cages placed in a circle around a central observation tower, so that the inmates can be constantly observed by the doctors, workhouse managers, or prison guards. The inmates cannot talk to each other, nor can they see if the guards are observing them at any one time, since Bentham designed an ingenious set of louvers and blinds for the central guard tower. . . . There is control, but neither visual nor verbal interchange—or, rather, the initiation of all exchanges lies with the invisible guards, managers, and doctors [Sennett, 1981, p. 58].

Because the workers, prisoners, or patients could not determine if they were being observed, they internalized the control of their behavior. Bentham even suggested that the central tower need never be occupied, for those under observation would act as if they were being observed. Foucault noted in *Madness and Civilization* (1965) that chains can be removed from the madmen of society because they have internalized the chains (through a sense of shame or personal disgust). They have become "adjusted" citizens of society, having learned to control their own behavior. While the open architectural designs of modern organizations need not contribute to an internalization of control, it certainly is worth noting the role this design can play in the internalized management of both behavior and emotions. In the modern world, we see other people and know what they are doing. Privacy has been abandoned in a world of open, modularized office spaces. This, in turn, can lead to the internalization of control and new, more subtle modes of control, a central, continuing issue in many postmodern organizations.

The visual basis of modern organizations was also evident in their reliance on the printed word. In the modern world, scribes (in the form of secretaries) became indispensable, as were clerks. Whereas the premodern organization tended to rely on the storyteller to provide continuity, the scribe in modern organizations became the agent for preserving the precedents and culture of an organization, since these precedents and cultural characteristics were usually contained in the formal written policies and procedures of the organization. Secretarial and clerical roles began to flourish in the late nineteenth century. The white-collar worker was a growing presence in most organizations prior to World War II and became prevalent in America after the war. These men and women were typically in staff rather than line relationships, occupying positions such as secretary, clerk, administrative assistant, or staff associate to a specific manager or executive in the organization.

In their staff role, white-collar workers had no formal power. They were only as influential as their boss. They also typically were unable to change bosses and rarely moved from staff positions into higher line positions. A secretary, for instance, rarely became a manager. Instead, a secretary (usually a woman) would advance with her boss (usually a man) up the corporate ladder. If a secretary's boss didn't advance, then the secretary would not either. As Kanter (1977) noted, staff members in modern corporations were treated much as wives and servants were during the premodern era. While modern-day organizations were able to preserve uniformity up to a point, the huge increase in the number of staff assistants led to the increase in integrative services that typify the modern organization and ultimately to the organizational fragmentation that typifies the postmodern world.

When Stories Were Told

The primary mode of communication in the premodern world was oral. Men and women in organizations communicated with each other through face-to-face conversation. Because organizations tended to be small and simple, people didn't need much other than this face-to-face contact. As organizations grew larger, hierarchical structures were established (first in the military, then in civilian organizations). The hierarchical chain of command was established primarily to expedite the flow of face-to-face communication from person to person, not to ensure control. An order was given by the general to his lieutenants, who in turn conveyed the order to their sergeants, and so forth.

Oral communication was sufficient in the premodern world because men and women tended to know and trust the people with whom they had contact. Their contacts were usually with people from the same community or at least from the same society and culture. Everyone knew the values and life-style of everyone else, hence little needed to be written down; there was little chance of major misunderstandings.

Trust and understanding built not only on the words that were spoken but also on the visual, nonverbal gestures made to support and enhance the spoken words. Furthermore, the actions taken by members of the community in many ways spoke louder than did the words. Yet, oral communication was at the heart of premodern societies, particularly in organizational settings. The spoken words provided continuity and conveyed the heritage of the community, primarily through stories about past events and people.

What about our postmodern organization? In what way do the premodern elements of communication remain viable in our contemporary organizations? The key premodern element appears to be storytelling. Storytellers in both the premodern and postmodern eras (and perhaps the modern era as well) were the primary conveyers of organizational culture; they provided indispensable information about precedent and pattern, while ensuring continuity. The culture of the organization has always been conveyed through legendary stories of the "founder," the "great battle," or the "great recovery." Given the paternal and familial nature of most premodern organizations, the stories were often passed from father to son, or mother to daughter. They were stories about families as well as organizations. Time was set aside for the telling of stories, usually during a slack time in the business of the family (wintertime among farmers, weekends or summer holidays among shopowners). Special rooms called *parlors* (from the French word for speech) were set up in some societies for storytelling and its companion, gossip. Sunday afternoons were often spent visiting neighbors and talking about the events of the past week. In other cultures, saunas, sweat lodges, or local taverns or restaurants served as settings for these conversations. Inside organizations, the father, mother, or grandparent would speak at a special dinner about the history of the organization. Organizational anniversaries were celebrated with the same care as many contemporary marital anniversaries.

In many Asian countries, evening meals are still used for storytelling about the organizations in which those seated at the table work. Oftentimes, one or more members of the assembled group (usually an older member) is recognized for his or her contribution and a series of stories are told about this person's activities and achievements in the organization. In the United States, we still tell stories about early organizational history; however, we tend to use these occasions to bestow gold watches or tie clips in honor of an employee's anniversary with the company or the employee's retirement.

In some cases, however, we do much more in contemporary times about organizational storytelling. A group of faculty members from the United States and Canada, for instance, meet at a retreat location in Western Canada each summer in large part to tell stories about their individual organizations and about their shared history (over a twelve-year period). Christmas or retirement parties are also often occasions for the telling of organizational stories. The stories are old and have been told many times before. They often bear little resemblance to the truth; yet, they convey something important about the values and aspirations of the organization. Beneath the thin veneer of modern preoccupation with the written word, there is a hunger for the spoken word and, in particular, for the telling of stories.

In many fields that require communication (for example, marketing and law), the stories that are told in contemporary organizations become a central, if not the primary, ingredient in determining the nature of reality in that field.

> As we become aware of the social construction of reality—consciously, *publicly* aware—the boundary erodes between the kind of fiction we call art and the kind of fiction we call reality. History becomes another kind of storytelling, personal and social life becomes another kind of drama. . . . So, whether you get your literature from deconstructionist critics and university-press novelists, or from the latest item in the airport bookstore, or from the daily news, you are likely to get a similar subtext about the human condition: a message that life is a matter of telling ourselves stories about life, and of savoring stories about life told by others, and of living our lives according to such stories, and of creating ever-new and more complex stories about stories—and that this story making is not just about human life, but is human life [Anderson, 1990, pp. 99, 102].

If organizations are extended conversations, then the reality of an organization is conveyed primarily through the conversations (stories, memos, and so on) about the organization. An old joke conveyed by Anderson (1990, p. 75) tells it all: "Three umpires are sitting around over a beer and one says, 'There's balls and there's strikes, and I call 'em the way they are.' Another says, 'There's balls and there's strikes, and I call 'em the way I see 'em.' The third says, 'There's balls and there's strikes, and they ain't nothin' until I call 'em.' "

This story not only illustrates the primacy of conversation but also suggests that language is used to construct social realities, primarily by those people who have power. For Lyotard (1984), language and power are inextricably linked together. Lyotard also identifies a second factor—other than power—found in all social systems: desire. According to Lyotard (Dews, 1987), desire is expressed by those without power. Desire must be expressed therefore in a way that does not directly confront power. In its expression, however, desire tends to destroy or bypass formal language, much as in Freudian theory (Freud, [1900] 1965), where the dream destroys or bypasses the language spoken by the dreamer when awake.

What are the ways in which desire is expressed by those without power in organizations? First, informal language is used to bypass those in authority. Those without power use the language of gossip as the primary mode for expressing the inexpressible. Alternatively, desire may be expressed through nonexpression, that is, through the nonuse of language. Belenky and her colleagues (1986) discuss the role of silence in women's acquisition of knowledge. Perhaps silence becomes a way of expressing desire: we tell other people through nonspeaking that power in our organization (or family) has not connected with our own personal wishes, values, needs, or desires, thereby leading to alienation and silence.

While gossip, silence, and nonverbal communication may be important sources of information about desire in an organization, stories set the norms, values, and aspirations of an organization. The stories of an organization are critical conversations between the present and the past. Organizations exist at the present moment in time. The past life of an organization only exists in the present conversations, that is, in the stories, about the past and in the conversations that are now taking place (via archival records) about past conversations. Similarly, the organization's future is found in current conversations about the future.

Why have stories had such power in all three eras? Why is storytelling a central ingredient in the expression of desire and the reconstruction of reality—whether this reality be personal or organizational in nature? At the organizational level, stories are the primary ingredient of culture; organizations are often held together by stories and by their sister agent, the gossip network. Stories provide the glue because they offer us coherence and meaning (Anderson, 1990). Even though individual stories about life experiences and experiences within organizations may be distinctive, they inevitably contain and convey universal or at least organizationwide themes.

Stories also provide meaning for most of us. This is particularly the case in the secular (organizational) aspects of our life. "The struggle with meaning, the weaving of stories around our pains and joys, the conflict between different ways of making sense of the events of daily life—they are present in every form of therapy, and also present constantly in the existence of people who have never sat in a therapist's waiting room" (Anderson, 1990, pp. 139–140). Third, stories are (simply put) a great form of entertainment. We enjoy listening to stories and often find them the most comfortable and natural way in which to learn. Jesus was aware of this when he set many of his lessons and sermons in story form (parables). Successful religious leaders in our own times also make extensive use of stories, as do many of the "great communicators" in government and business. In the modern era we forgot (or tried to ignore the fact) that man is a storyteller and storylistener. We are beginning to reclaim and legitimize this versatile mode of communication.

What prevents storytelling and the use of words—such as covenant and sanctuary—whose popular usage predates modern times and which often are biblical in origin from becoming yet another mode of superficial change rather than of transformation? It seems there are several safeguards. First, neither stories nor old, sacred words are owned by any one person. They are repeated and modified by other members of the organization. Second, stories typically are repeated only if they seem to have some veracity, and old words only gain general public recognition if they are appropriate and illuminate our current situation. Otherwise, an alternative story is told about the lie the original storyteller conveyed or alternative words are used to convey the point. Third, a story is composed of nonverbal as well as verbal messages. Usually one or more elements of this complex message will convey the truth. At this point, in our complex and turbulent postmodern world, we can ask for little more than some clear sense of what another person or organization holds to be true. We gain this clear sense of another person's truth when we enter into dialogue with this person and allow our own sense of the truth to emerge. Whether or not organizations are nothing more (or less) than conversations, they certainly can be of value if they encourage this mutual search for the shared truth.

Chapter 7

Capital and Worker Values: What Matters in This Organization?

There is a quiet revolution taking place in many organizations. The source of the revolution is the growing realization that tighter controls, greater pressure, more clearly defined jobs, and tighter supervision have, in the last fifty years, run their course in their ability to give us the productivity gains we require to compete effectively in the world marketplace. Attention is shifting to the need for employees to personally take responsibility for the success of our businesses if we hope to survive and prosper.

Peter Block, *The Empowered Manager*

The fifth and final dimension of organizational life I discuss concerns the resources that fuel the organization: capital (provided by those who own the organization) and labor (provided by those who are employed by the organization). In essence, we look at the question, "what matters in this organization?" The values of an organization are ultimately defined by the relative weight given to the various forms of capital and labor available to an organization, and by the values held by those who own and are employed by the organization. My major premise is that the new capital of postmodern organizations is information and that the knowledge worker of the postmodern world looks for different kinds of rewards and forms of authority than was the case with either the modern or premodern worker. Specifically, the postmodern worker looks for meaningful work and for personal growth and maturation in the work setting. The knowledge worker is motivated by the opportunity to exert internalized control, which is manifest in a search for freedom and autonomy in the workplace, as well as by a seemingly contradictory search for psychological approval and the avoidance of shame.

Bell (1976) and Drucker (1989) suggest that the new postindustrial or postmodern form of capital is knowledge and that workers gain respect and even exert control in postmodern organizations because of their valued expertise and their command of information vital to the organization. As early as 1968, Drucker (quoted in Best, 1973, p. 59) offered the following description of changes in the contemporary work force.

> "Knowledge" rather than "science" [or technology] has become the foundation of [our] economy. . . . To be sure, science and scientists have suddenly moved into the center of the political, military and economic stage. But so have practically all the other knowledge people. It is not just the chemists, the physicists, and the engineers who get fat on consulting assignments. . . . Geographers, geologists, and mathematicians, economists and linguists, psychologists, anthropologists, and marketing men are all busy consulting with governments, with industry, with the foreign aid program and so on. Few areas of learning are not in demand by the organizations of our pluralist society.

Ample evidence of this new form of capital is found in many contemporary organizations. One-third of the employees in a Japanese firm have recently been "liberated" from routine and mundane jobs and have been reassigned to rebuild the company every ten years and to stay five years ahead of their competitors. These employees represent the future for this company. Financial reserves are no longer the answer for this company, nor the goal. Similar changes are occurring in many high-tech American firms, such as

"Techform." According to one employee, "If innovation is . . . the basic tenet [at Techform], then expertise that leads to technical and scientific innovation is [Techform's] capital. The numerous patents for processes and applications are tangible assets. The intangible assets from which these come are the people: experts in their various disciplines."

Young engineers in many high-tech firms are recruited like professional athletes. As is the case with many of these athletes, the young engineers soon become less valuable, in their case because they lose touch with the rapidly changing knowledge base they acquired in college or graduate school. Similarly, young accountants and product designers often have more credibility than their older, more experienced—but dated—co-workers. Physicians retain considerable respect and power among their colleagues at an East Coast suburban hospital. However, the hospital has recently been purchased by a major investment firm and is now being run in a more "businesslike" manner. The physicians now have to compete with the fiscal expertise of this hospital's new financial administrator and auditor.

A lawyer in a successful law firm confides that "the best lawyers are actually the largest threat to the firm and while this is well understood it is largely unspoken. [Our best lawyer] alone generates over $2 milllion in revenues each year and is a top producer of new business. This gives him the ability to 'call the shots,' and while he does not abuse this power he has exercised it in some important ways." The new capital in many postmodern organizations—at least as defined by influence in the company and the ability to "call the shots"—is determined not by ownership of the company or even by one's formal position or tenure in the company but rather by one's possession of knowledge and skills relevant to the immediate needs of the organization.

Cleveland (1982) noted ten years ago that information is expandable without any obvious limits; it is also compressible (to fit on rapidly shrinking silicon chips), transportable, substitutable (replacing capital, labor, or physical materials), diffusive (leaking out everywhere), and, most important, shareable. All of this amounts to a growing recognition that our increasing reliance on information changes the very nature of the workplace and of the men and women who occupy this workplace. Knowledge workers can readily take their expertise elsewhere, and corporate lawyers have yet to find a way to effectively patent or somehow legally claim ownership of the mind and ideas of employees. Thus, knowledge workers claim a form of capital that remains with them and that is always renewable, even after being spent in the generation of a new idea. The only hazard the knowledge worker encounters is becoming out-of-date, a fear particularly relevant for knowledge workers in scientific and technological fields. Financial wealth in the modern era was usually a less stable form of capital than was property as the primary form of capital in the premodern era. The new knowledge capital of the postmodern era is even less stable and more elusive.

Internalized Control: Autonomy and Shame

Sennett (1981) suggests that this new postmodern knowledge-based capital is closely associated with psychological approval and its inverse, psychological shame. While Sennett agrees with Bell and Drucker that "technical expertise and innovation have become the [new] forms of capital," he suggests that autonomous character structure rather than skill may be the central commodity of exchange in contemporary organizations.

> Autonomous character structure means a person has the ability to be a good judge of others because he or she is not desperate for their approval. . . . When a person is needed by others more than he needs them, he can afford to be indifferent to them. . . . [A]utonomy removes the necessity of dealing with other people openly and mutually. There is an imbalance; they show their need for you more than you show your need for them. This puts you in control. . . . The fear and awe of experts is a familiar sentiment, most notably as it concerns doctors. . . . Someone who is indifferent arouses our desire to be recognized; we want this person to feel we matter enough to be noticed [1981, pp. 85–86].

Thus, autonomy—the desired state of the new worker—builds on acquired and highly valued knowledge and expertise. It is fueled, in turn, by the desire to avoid shame. "The shame an autonomous person can arouse in subordinates is an implicit control. Rather than the employer explicitly saying 'You are dirt' or 'Look how much better I am,' all he needs to do is his job—exercise his skill or deploy his calm and indifference. His powers are fixed in his position, they are static attributes, qualities of what he is" (Sennett, 1981, p. 95).

Sennett describes the controlling force of shame as subtle and even elusive.

> It is not so much abrupt moments of humiliation as month after month of disregarding his employees, of not taking them seriously, which establishes his domination. The feelings he has about them, they about him, need never be stated. The grinding down of his employees' sense of self-worth is not part of his discourse with them; it is a silent erosion of their sense of self-worth which will wear them down. This, rather than open abuse, is how he bends them to his will. When shame is silent, implicit, it becomes a patent tool of bringing people to heel [1981, p. 95].

While Sennett's analysis may be overdrawn and perhaps melodramatic, the role of shame as a means of control is prevalent, yet subtle, in many contemporary organizations. The leaders of a high-technology firm on the West Coast exemplify the interplay between knowledge and shame in their management of risk inside their organization. According to one of this organization's leaders:

> The decision-making process [in this organization] varies depending on the decision to be made; its visibility and potential impact on our customer. It is possible, if you are willing to take the risk, to make very visible and high-impact decisions. If you are successful, you will be acknowledged and rewarded. Should you fail, you will be punished in an indirect

way. This usually means a short time spent in the
penalty box, where you are not allowed to make any
decisions without concurrence from other members of
the senior staff.

   This penalty box is not widely announced in
the corporation. This allows you to still influence decisions indirectly and maintain your positional power.
During any number of crises, you can be removed from
the penalty box due to the needs of the company. All
is forgiven and you are placed at the apex of an organization or issue to lead again.

Though "all is forgiven" in this organization, one wonders
about the residual humiliation associated with the penalty box and
the accompanying loss of influence in the organization. This same
manager later speaks of this organization as being a spiritual waste-
land in which there is no animating vision of the future or expression of courage. Shame, as Sennett observes, is not something that
has an immediate and explicit impact on an organization. Rather
it wears down those working in the organization and drains the
organization of its spirit, especially under the turbulent conditions
of a postmodern world.

   In essence, the new capital (knowledge, autonomy, shame)
identified by Drucker, Bell, and Sennett belongs to the employee,
and not to the organization, though the organization may honor
knowledge, encourage autonomy, and induce shame. These forms
of capital belong to the employee and are carried by her to her next
job.

   Knowledge, in addition to being highly portable, is not easily controlled by those who own and run organizations. Administra-
trators and managers must rely on the information given to them
by staff members and information specialists (computer programmers, program auditors, engineers). They often have to compete with other organizations for these highly paid custodians of
their organization's information. Thus, the only power many leaders of postmodern organizations hold over their key employees is
psychological (rather than economic or positional) in nature. They
give approval and encouragement, withhold approval, or even at-

tempt to shame their employees (through indifference or indirect public exposure), since they can't control or hold their employees in any other way.

Organization and Commitment

How do postmodern organizations effectively confront these problems of knowledge and shame? In part, the answer resides in a simple recommitment to employees. Some postmodern organizations, such as Techform, place great value on their employees and devote considerable time and money to their technological updating rather than replacing them with newly recruited employees. "As [Techform] prides itself in its scientific and technical innovation, so too it comes to foster sociological innovation. Courses for employees include not only the technical skills needed to perform their jobs, but also communication skills, managing professional growth, and other subjects that develop the whole person. . . . When the climate is one of innovation, experts in nontechnical areas are nurtured for their innovations too. On the one hand they are recognized for their unique talents, on the other their human worth and value as developing members of a developing team."

Techform is not alone in this endeavor. A contemporary "fairy story" from *Fortune* magazine (Perry, 1991, p. 68) tells the tale.

Once upon a time, in the profit-minded kingdom of Corporate America, an anonymous copywriter came up with a slogan that fast became the phrase of the land. It read, simply: "People are our most important asset." Companies loved it. Soon the line appeared in annual reports everywhere. The only problem was, companies didn't really value their employees that much. The slogan, says Jerome M. Rosow, president of Work in America Institute, "was pure bull."

Then one day foreigners invaded the kingdom. These international companies were flexible, quick, and responsive to customers. Searching for ways to compete with the invaders, a few American companies discovered that, given a little freedom and the proper training, workers could do things that machines could not. People could grow, invent, solve problems. The kingdom was rocked by a new thought: that people truly are its most important asset.

This revelation has led to a human resources revolution. Corporate training programs are proliferating as companies seek to help workers adapt to rapidly changing technology and work processes. Personnel departments are scrambling to create improved benefit programs to attract and retain the best people. And finally, to make sure the next generation of workers is as well educated as possible, companies are forming partnerships with schools and colleges.

What is the nature of the commitments that must be made by the postmodern organization? I suggest they include a commitment to continuity and to learning.

Commitment to Continuity

Without some sense of continuity and a commitment by the organization to the welfare of its employees and to some greater good or value, members of an organization are left standing on the edge of the postmodern world, viewing the blank space in front of them as an abyss. Nelson (1991, p. 105) suggests, as I do throughout this book, that economic development has religious underpinnings and that postmodern organizations must catch the "moral imagination" of its employees, a decidely premodern notion: "Tremendous material progress did take place [during the modern era], lifting most of the human race far above the subsistence level where it had stagnated throughout most of human history. But material progress didn't bring hoped-for spiritual progress. It brought the Holocaust and conspicuous consumption and wars instead. . . . Good-bye, then, to the old idea of progress as a universally accepted goal. . . . [In nineteenth-century America] progress was valued not for its own sake or because it would put more meat on people's tables, but because it would bring about spiritual salvation."

Nelson further suggests that it is essential that the free market and Western capitalism be brought back into accord with the deeply embedded religious values and ideals that undergirded earlier American entrepreneurship: "So capitalism needs new moral arguments and spiritual dimensions if it is to endure; efficiency is no longer defense enough. This is more a task for the theologian than for the economists. If no such spiritual endorsement is forthcoming, capitalism could end up winning the war with communism, but losing the peace" (p. 107).

While I disagree with excluding economists from the dialogue on new corporate values—since in the postmodern world all disciplines must be brought to bear on the complex and fragmented problems being faced—I do agree that capitalism and free market economies have been shown to be relatively successful mechanisms for generating economic growth and stability. They have been unsuccessful, however, in engendering a sense of purpose or commitment among postmodern workers and leaders.

The malaise of which Nelson speaks is true whether the employee is working within the chaotic environment of an urban governmental office or within the seemingly more sedate confines of an established American bank. It is not the level of confusion in the daily life of men and women who work in organizations that creates the pervasive sense of edginess. Rather it is the frequent shifts that occur between different systems and subsystems. Each of these systems and subsystems has its own distinctive character and culture. None of them are bound together by any common purpose or sustaining vision (Bellah and others, 1985).

Many twentieth-century intellectuals (for example, Rollo May, Erich Fromm, Jean Paul Sartre, Teilhard de Chardin) see the primary source of the modern individual's anxiety and accompanying sense of alienation as the evolution of reflection and consciousness. We look around us at the enormous continuum of time and space and wonder what our role is—or should be—in this world. The modern question was: can we really make a difference? This question was posed (and answered) by the protagonist, George Bailey, in the Frank Capra film classic *It's a Wonderful Life*. George, like most of us, wondered if anyone's life would have been different—if the world would really have been worse off (or better off, for that matter)—if he had never existed. With the help of an angel-in-training, George discovered that his life did make a difference. Capra, no doubt, wanted the filmgoers of his day (late 1930s and early 1940s) to also be assured that they made a difference. Unfortunately, in the 1990s we have no Frank Capra to tell us we are important.

Our postmodern world has become much too complicated and our communities much too large and impersonal for many of us to feel much reassurance about our place in the universe. We have very few guardian angels to point out our importance. I suggest that modern-day anxiety is compounded and transformed into edginess by the size and complexity of our postmodern organizations, by the profound individualism of contemporary Western society, and by the unpredictability and seeming randomness of events and forces (both internal and external) we face on a daily basis. Modernistic individualism, which was promoted by the Protestant emphasis on personal relationships with God and the acquisition of personal wealth, must give way to a new form of community awareness and commitment (Bellah and others, 1985) if people are to avoid spiritual starvation. The administrator of a moderately large manufacturing firm spoke of these matters, when analyzing her own company.

> [There is a] lack of a visible spiritual anchor accepted across the company. Each individual is fulfilling their particular spiritual need and the organization in general is starving. We are on an annuity program. We stay because of the unique opportunity and the potential for great wealth. Many of us are doing the same things we have done all our careers. There is no growth, no fulfillment. In this desert land we cannot find large groups banded together, instead, we have small groups all going in a different direction. . . . We are fearful and unsure that we can provide our personnel a better life. Even I . . . continue to focus on the bad things that happen. I explain everything in the negative. My glass is half empty and not half full. . . .
> In all the key areas I see [my company] moving

toward a postmodern organization. I believe that this is caused by the diversity of people at [my company] and a lack of leadership in many key areas of the company. When I speak of leadership, I am not speaking of the "great man," but a clear statement of purpose. We are doing great at doing the specific task required to make a product and develop a market. We are, still, lacking an entire human orientation at the top. This approach allows our personnel to develop their own approaches, adding chaos at one level and order to another, but never in sync. Everyone and anyone can have a butterfly effect on the company.

This is the essence of postmodern edginess. One is poised on the edge of a cliff. The transition is not just from one world to another world but from one world of nothingness, sustained by ambiguous or contradictory values, to another world of nothingness. We experience the abyss as uncomprehendible. An organization's (and employee's) commitment to a central set of values with a spiritual base and a commitment to the continuation of a relationship are essential if this edginess is to be addressed in a satisfactory manner.

Commitment to Learning

A commitment to learning associated with change is also essential—by both the organization and the employee. Any contemporary organization doing its job with regard to public relations will include in its promotional piece a statement about education and training. Dusting off Alvin Toffler (1971; 1980), the brochure will speak about the great demands being placed on employees of the organization to master new technologies and cope with accelerating change. In the postmodern world, however, a commitment to learning must move far beyond what was promoted (and usually not acted on) in the modern world. The postmodern condition requires that an organization include a commitment to learning in its mission statement and that this organization prepare its employees for a new kind of learning to accommodate second-order changes.

A successful postmodern organization must have a clear mission statement, and I suggest that it also must have a commitment to organizational learning. At the heart of any organization (in its mission statement) should be a twofold commitment: (1) to inquiry and reflective action, based on a continuing search for new meaning and experiences within the organizational context and (2) to discussing and teaching what was learned from this inquiry and reflection.

The skills of reflection and inquiry are particularly important in a world filled with unpredictability and change. We are likely to make many mistakes while negotiating the turbulent waters of postmodernism. It is critical, therefore, that we are particularly skillful in learning from our mistakes. This type of learning is very difficult and demanding; we tend to become quite defensive when we make mistakes, and we are typically involved in real-time problem solving after making a mistake and rarely feel in the mood for either reflection or inquiry. Argyris (1982) suggests that we often learn while being defensive. Perhaps in our new postmodern organizations recognition will finally be given to the essential role of reflection and inquiry in all aspects of one's job and to the critical need for this type of learning immediately following any mistake (or success).

Leaving the Age of Anxiety

I end this analysis of capital and worker values by examining the modern and premodern eras and identifying the lingering elements from these previous eras in our current notions about capital and labor. The remnants of these earlier eras can serve either as barriers or as gateways to the solution of contemporary problems. I will linger longer in the premodern and modern eras than in previous chapters because an understanding of the capital and worker-related values that underlie our present world is critical to the transformation of contemporary organizations. Furthermore, the modern membrane that separates us from our premodern origins is particularly thin with reference to our notions about capital and worker values. We confront very old assumptions and values when exploring the ways worth is assigned to our contemporary organizations and the work performed by those within these organizations.

The uneasiness of the modern individual has been closely related to a search for some form of stability and tangible capital that can be used to help fend off the anxiety associated with the recognition of a finite, never fully satisfying world. In the latter days of the modern era, employees were mostly concerned about finding a way to create and sustain meaningful work at a time when technology was eliminating many jobs. The continuity of the working culture was disrupted by machines and bureaucracy. The context for assigning value to work was called into question. A search for continuity and support led neither to a wise man nor to a spoken agreement or handshake. Stories about the founding values of the organization were rarely told. Rather, there were systems and procedures, a formal letter of agreement and a visually pleasing, though often vacuous, annual report. During this era, emphasis was placed first on the written (rather than spoken) word, as exemplified by the omnipresent memorandum (used primarily for CMA—cover my ass—purposes). As organizations became modern, they became consumers of enormous volumes of written and and printed words. While most premodern organizations had little use for written words, modern organizations thrived on these words and on the new forms of capital and worker values that underlay and gave meaning to these words.

While the premodern world was built on land and reputation, with a strong parallel emphasis on service and community, the modern world was built on a different form of capital: money. Reputation and ancestry became much less important in a rapidly changing world in which democratic values and the myth (or reality) of upward social mobility were dominant. New wealth—and the new bourgeoisie—were much more fluid and volatile than was old wealth. Rich men came and went in the modern world. In essence, the modern era produced a shift from direct sources of personal meaning in life (through one's work and family) to more indirect sources (one's wealth and consumption). Whereas the premodern man and woman were able to take pride in the cultivation of crops or the production of crafts and in providing food and shelter for members of the family, modern-day men and women became alienated from the products of their work and from owner-ship of the means of production. Since our products could not be admired by our neighbors, then we needed to use the money we obtained from our work to buy things we could display to obtain our neighbors' admiration.

Jameson (1991, p. 316)—like Fromm and many other social critics—proposes that modern-day consumption served as a substi-tute for meaning in life and "as compensation for an economic impotence which [was] . . . an utter lack of any political power." This alienation from the direct sources of meaning in our work was joined with the alienation that comes with the loss of personal voice and connectedness among people working in small or relatively small premodern organizations. This dual form of alienation pro-duced the anxiety so closely associated with the modern era.

The Protestant reformation is at the heart of the modern emphasis on money and (in distorted form) consumption, as doc-umented by Max Weber (1958) in his classic study of the Protestant ethic and the rise of the spirit of capitalism following the Protestant reformation. Partially in response to Marx's proposition that reli-gious beliefs are based ultimately on economic considerations and that the church is primarily used for repressive purposes, Weber wanted to show that economics and religion work hand in hand. Marx was unable to explain why the acquisition of wealth had become such a dominant concern in Western society. Weber sug-gested that we must look to religious domains to find the driving force behind the secular concerns for money and capitalism.

It is becoming increasingly clear, as I have noted throughout this book, that organizations are inherently sacred in nature. They are not only directly influenced by religious beliefs but also by the impact religion has on other critical sectors of society (Boulding, 1952). Thus, as we look specifically at the role religion has played in forming contemporary attitudes about capital and worker values, we look to Protestantism. Whereas the Catholic church, as the pri-mary source of premodern values associated with capital and work, tended to emphasize service and good works as the primary criteria for salvation, John Calvin and other Protestant reformers argued that an all-powerful and all-knowing God would have already de-termined the state of an individual's salvation before that person was ever born. Exhibiting his training as a lawyer and his overriding concern for order and structure, John Calvin envisioned a world in which personal futures were predetermined (predestination) and in which spontaneous acts of charity and good work would have little bearing on the clockwise precision of a well-ordered society and universe.

If good works do not have much bearing on personal salvation and if one's own salvation is predetermined, then how does one know what will be his or her eternal state? John Calvin suggested that an orderly and consistent God would structure a world for us on earth that would parallel the ones in heaven (or hell). Thus, worldly prosperity is a sign of impending salvation, whereas a life on this earth of poverty, manual labor, or crime is suggestive of a hellish eternal life to come. While the wealthy person, in Calvin's world, should never flaunt his wealth and should be kind and considerate to those in need, the world will not be altered, in any substantial manner, by any personal act of charity or any social legislation or collective actions. The world is simply to be endured by those who have not been chosen and God is to be continuously praised by those who have.

The primary effect of this Protestant ethic was to liberate the capitalistic and entrepreneurial energies of the emerging middle class. Whereas the Catholic church forbade the use of money to make money, the Protestant churches indirectly encouraged investment of money through the equation of personal financial prosperity with personal salvation. John Calvin himself, as Weber noted, did not encourage obsession with financial wealth and conspicuous consumption. His advocacy of predestination, however, removed the religious onus from the acquisition of money (rather than just land) and set the stage for the later emphasis on financial wealth as the primary means of defining personal achievement and worth for many men and women.

Given Weber's thesis, what are the modern-day effects of this Protestant ethic? First, this ethic changed the nature of power in Western society. One's power and status were defined by money in the modern world, rather than by either land or reputation (as in the premodern world). As the English social analyst R. H. Tawney (1921, p. 57) noted more than a half century ago:

The characteristic fact, which differentiates most
modern property from that of the pre-industrial age,
and which turn against it the very reasoning by which
formerly it was supported, is that in modern economic
conditions ownership is not active, but passive, that to
most of those who own property today it is not a
means of work but an instrument for the acquisition
of gain or the exercise of power. . . . In modern industrial societies the great mass of property consists . . .
neither of personal acquisitions, such as household
furniture, nor of the owner's stock-in-trade, but of
rights of various kinds, such as royalties, ground-
rents, and, above all, of course, shares in industrial
undertakings, which yield an income irrespective of
any personal service rendered by their owners.

In the modern era, individuals could not measure their accomplishments in this world, let alone their eligibility for higher
status in an afterlife, by property holdings or even by personal productivity in a craft or trade. Rather, accomplishments and ultimately salvation were defined by the much more abstract notion of
financial independence and wealth—and by more tangible criteria
associated with conspicuous consumption. Donald Trump recently
was asked why he was so concerned with acquiring money and
exhibiting his financial wealth in such public ways. He proposed
that this is the scorecard by which one's success in life is measured.
Mr. Trump (and many other corporate leaders) have not moved
much beyond John Calvin. Personal achievement and consumption
are still considered the modern-day, secular signs of salvation.

A second side to Weber's analysis of the Protestant reformation concerns the contributions of Martin Luther to our modern
emphasis on individualism and personal conscience. Luther broke
with the Catholic church over the right of individual believers to
communicate directly with God rather than through an interme-
diary institution such as the Catholic Church or its representatives
(priests, bishops, the pope). Luther argued that God spoke directly
to his believers and that they should be guided by this inner voice
rather than by the all-too-human dictates of the church. With the

success of Luther's perspective in many parts of Europe and, in particular, the United States, we see the emergence of a profound and at times isolating individualism. According to Luther, we must look inward for God's grace and guidance rather than to any external authority. In modern organizations we find a parallel emphasis on individual rights and the formulation of individual solutions to organizational problems by isolated problem solvers. We look for the brilliant analyst and creative problem solver, while retaining the right to question any form of authority. While Martin Luther had wanted his vision to be restricted to religious life, he lived (as did John Calvin) to see his vision transformed into a highly secular conception of an individualistic, antiauthoritarian, and economically oriented employee.

Most modern perspectives on the motivation to work have focused on economic factors and on individual accomplishments. While many of these perspectives are distinctly anti-Marxist, they share with Marxism an assumption that worker values are primarily determined by secular economic factors. Eric Fromm (1955) noted more than three decades ago that an emphasis on economic man is readily transformed into the model of man as consumer and to the marketing orientation that seemingly replaced the religious orientation of modern individuals. We derive meaning in the modern world not from our religious beliefs or from the institutions that sustain and interpret these beliefs but from the individualistic pursuit of wealth and acquisition of goods that convey our personal identities and offer the promise (through advertisement) of happiness and personal esteem.

When Reputation and Service Counted for Something

During the Middle Ages, when the Catholic church dominated Western civilization, capital and property were defined primarily in terms of land, for members of the church were forbidden (under penalty of excommunication) from charging interest on money lent to other people. This was defined as usury and was a cardinal sin. Only Jewish people were allowed to charge interest, for they were already outside the purview of the church. Thus, the major financial houses of Europe were primarily developed by those who were outside the dominant Catholic church. Christians could accumulate wealth only by acquiring land or by establishing a solid trade with a strong reputation.

This emphasis on land and reputation was reinforced by laws regarding property. Added to the divine right of kings were newly emerging rights (in Western societies) of the common man to own property and pass property on to his descendants. While numerous non-Western societies (such as many Native American cultures) embraced the notion that property (land, home, livestock) belonged to the entire group, or to the gods, or to nature, our ancestors in the Western world created a society in which personal acquisition was allowed and highly valued.

For those in the premodern era who could not acquire land or own a small business, there was nothing much to hope for except a secure life in a highly paternalistic setting: as a servant, as a laborer in a small business or on a farm, or as an apprentice who eventually might become a master craftsman with some independence. In these settings, conformity to rigid codes was critical. These workers relied on paternal care and asked for little in return.

McGregor (1960) provided a vivid and highly influential description of this world of work more than twenty years ago when he described his Theory X model of management. This model was based on the assumptions that most people are inherently lazy and lack self-discipline (hence the need for external motivation) and that personal and organizational goals are inevitably incompatible (hence the need for external controls). McGregor proposed that the Theory X form of management, which was dominant in premodern times, was no longer appropriate in contemporary organizations. In making this point, he overlooked the positive aspects of the paternalism associated with premodern management. An employer (usually the head of a family) was expected to take care of his employees much as he took care of other family members. We still find this orientation in many businesses started in non-Western countries. I recently worked, for instance, with a company owned by a man who had emigrated from Asia fifteen years ago. He would have been offended if anyone asked him to lay off an employee, for he considered each member of his firm to be a member of his family. He often spoke of his employees as nieces and nephews, even though there were no formal family ties. A similar commitment is, of course, legendary in many other Chinese and Japanese firms.

In the premodern era of Western civilization, as in contemporary Chinese and Japanese cultures, one was expected to take care of those less fortunate, largely as a result of the Catholic church's emphasis on good works as a means to obtain salvation. Successful members of society were expected to donate money to the poor and various charitable organizations (usually associated with the church) and were to be available on specific days of the year (often holidays) to give conspicuous attention to those in need. While these forms of charity helped preserve class distinctions and highly conservative and repressive forms of government, they also encouraged the growth of community and interaction among all segments of society. With the modern emphasis on public funds and public policy to ameliorate the problems of poverty and injustice, the sense of community and contact broke down—ironically, in the name of greater social justice and equity.

The premodern reliance on institutional life—in particular, the church and community—for guidance is still seen in many Eastern European and Asian cultures. It has become unacceptable, however, for most constituencies in the corporate sector of Western society to look to institutions for daily guidance, especially since the Protestant reformation. Individual initiative and entrepreneurship are prevalent.

We do find major remnants of premodern institutional life in contemporary Western (particularly American) societies, particularly in the human service sector. Public health agencies, schools and colleges, social activist groups, and hospitals borrow their notions about institutional life and organizational functioning from the Catholic church. A strong commitment to service in these institutions is coupled with a Catholic-oriented emphasis on institutional clarity of procedures and lines of authority. Unlike corporations, which often allow much more flexibility in institutional form (if this form will yield greater productivity and profit), human service organizations are usually quite resistant to structural or procedural innovations. While bureaucracy is often equated with the emergence of modern-day corporations, it is actually much more dominant in governmental agencies (its birthplace) and other nonprofit human service organizations. Innovative structures (such as matrix organizations) or procedures (such as management by objectives) that have become commonplace or "old hat" in corporations are still considered radical and unacceptable in most human service settings.

People (most often women) are expected to dedicate their lives to human service organizations, often at low pay and with long hours of work. Members of these organizations perform services as if they were nuns or priests, the legacy of the Catholic church's initial emphasis on service to the underserved. Men and women working in these organizations are expected to do their jobs for the inherent worth of the services provided, rather than for money or public recognition. Like nuns, the women who work in human service agencies are often expected to forsake family or even friendships for late night or early morning service to others. Unionization of these agencies is unthinkable. When it does occur (for example, in school systems), the general public is rarely supportive, even though the working conditions for these men and women are often much worse than for factory workers, who usually are supported by the general public in their efforts to improve working conditions.

We also find remnants of the premodern emphasis on integrating work and service in the emerging emphasis on volunteerism in our society. Many people find their most meaningful work not in the corporate or governmental sectors of society but rather in the contributions they make on their free evenings or weekends through churches, community service organizations, and community action programs. In the second in their extraordinary studies of American society, Robert Bellah and his colleagues (Bellah and others, 1992, p. 50) comment that "American culture has focused relentlessly on the idea that individuals are self-interest maximizers and that private accumulation and private pleasures are the only measurable public goods. We have been blind to the way that institutions enable or cripple our capacity to be persons we most want to be. We need to understand historically that institutions stand in the way of our freedom. We need to understand how we failed to see that the virtue of autonomy, in the sense of personal freedom, can be realized only along with other virtues, such as care and responsibility."

As Bellah and his colleagues have observed, many Americans have become disenchanted with governmental agencies in their efforts to ameliorate major social problems. Peter Drucker (1989, p. 59) notes that "For almost two centuries, we hotly discussed what government *should* do. We almost never asked what government CAN do. Now increasingly the limits and function of government will be the issue."

The slogan "Think globally; act locally" speaks to the need for broad-based thinking about social problems. It also speaks to the need for committed and sustained action on a specific problem, in a specific location, serving a specific population, within a community context. These new commitments and concerns have led to the creation of the so-called third sector of our society: the world of volunteer action. The leaders of this sector have much to learn from the premodern emphasis on community and service to others. While the modern era has provided us with extraordinary tools to "think globally" and has enabled us to escape the parochial perspectives of premodern man, it has not prepared us to "act locally." To do this, we must reexamine the premodern communities or create our own distinctive postmodern communities, a very difficult task indeed.

The disillusionment with government, the desired return to community, and an emphasis on concrete service are particularly prevalent among middle-class men who have spent most of their lives pursuing individualistic career goals; now in their forties and early fifties, they find a growing need for more tangible, service-oriented work, particularly in a community setting. A recent informal survey of volunteer services in the San Francisco Bay Area revealed that many of the women who volunteer for public service seek out membership on the board of directors of an agency or assist with administrative functions. By contrast, men tend to seek out opportunities to provide direct services to clients. Rather than serving on a board, they want to counsel a young delinquent or help clean up a freeway. Many psychologists (for example, Levinson and others, 1978; Gilligan, 1982; Bergquist, Greenberg, and Klaum, 1993) have written about shifts in the lives of many mid-life men toward community and service and away from corporate pursuits and, by contrast, the shift among mid-life women toward more individualistic pursuits and positions of leadership and responsibility.

We are likely to see the Catholic church's emphasis on service as a vehicle for salvation and, more immediately, as a vehicle for finding meaning in life as particularly appealing to successful middle-class males in our society. This premodern concern for service and community is interwoven with a modern concern for individual achievement and a newly emerging concern for the integration of personal and professional growth—thus helping to produce the complex, often contradictory world we have defined as postmodern.

Part Three

Organizational
Models
for
Meeting
Postmodern
Challenges

Chapter 8

The Hybrid
Organization:
Linking Diverse
Forms and
Dynamics

Postmodern management can be about choice. . . . [T]he
choices that are available are not unimportant with respect
to management of many of the particulars of most people's
everyday worklife, matters of the capacity for skill formation, for community, for control. There are no guarantees,
however. Postmodernity may well turn out in ways which
serve to cramp rather than enhance capacities. Postmodernity is not a prognosis nor a prediction but it does seem to
index some human possibilities. Against the rationalizing
tendencies of recent modernity such small consideration
may not go amiss.

Stewart R. Clegg, *Modern Organizations*

The concept of postmodernism is
valuable because it provides a series of descriptive tools for captur-
ing the essence of a newly emerging era and also conceptual tools
for reinterpreting the nature and dynamics of various phenomena,
including human organizations. In these final four chapters, I apply
a postmodern perspective to the domain of organizational life, specifically to four different (though interrelated) models of contemporary organizations: the hybrid organization, the cyclical organization,
the intersect organization, and the turbulent organization.

The first of these models—the hybrid organization—speaks
directly to postmodern themes of complexity and fragmentation.

Contemporary organizations are described as strange mixtures of diverse forms and processes, incorporating premodern, modern, and postmodern elements. The second model—the cyclical organization—encompasses the theme of complexity. In this instance, complexity is described in terms of both predictable and unpredictable shifts that occur in organizations as a function of their stage of development, the season in which the organization is operating, and the specific perspective from which the organization is being assessed. The third model—the intersect organization—also speaks to the theme of complexity, as well as the postmodern theme of ambiguity. Organizations are described in terms of an interplay between public and private, profit and nonprofit, and large and small forms and functions. The fourth model—the turbulent organization—specifically addresses the complexity of the variable rates and scope of change within most postmodern organizations.

The underlying concepts in these chapters are taken from contemporary theories of postmodernism and chaos, as well as from the exceptional interdisciplinary perspectives of Gregory Bateson and Teilhard de Chardin. In many instances, the theorists from whom I borrow have never applied their ideas or models to organizational life—and may, in fact, be troubled by such an application. The organizational applications, therefore, in most instances are of my own creation. The original postmodern theorists should not be blamed for any misjudgments about the applicability of their notions to organizations, though they should be credited, at least in part, with any insights one might gain from these perspectives. In each of these four chapters, I attempt not only to provide new perspectives on organizational life but also to offer tentative solutions to the problems inherent in these organizational forms. I will also identify several of the conditions I think essential for a successful confrontation with our postmodern world.

I do not examine specific solutions in any detail, for this is premature and inappropriate, given the inconsistent and fragmented nature of our contemporary world. I instead examine several processes of reflection, inquiry, and learning that seem relevant to the identification of solutions to emerging postmodern problems; in doing this, I begin to build a postmodern model of organizational life. These reflective processes are necessarily gentle in nature, rather than being confrontational or mechanistic, for they involve the tending of postmodern phenomena that are complex and often irreversible, more like fires than pendulums. Much as in tending a fire, we can neither predict nor control the exact effect of our tending. We can move the logs closer to one another or stir the coals, but we can never be sure where the coals will burst into flames. By abrupt or overly assertive actions or by our inactions, we can also snuff out a fire, though it may smolder and begin again at a later point (perhaps when we are not watching).

Our Hybrid Society

All around us we find ample evidence of three different eras: the premodern era of our parents and grandparents, the modern era in which most of us were reared, and the postmodern era, which our children and grandchildren will lead. Recently, I was listening to the radio as I drove through the central valley in California. As I grazed through the AM and FM radio stations, I heard a wide range of music. Country music and classical music. Music of the late 60s and early 70s (Crosby, Stills, Nash, and Young singing "Four Dead in Ohio") evokes images of the Vietnam War and student protests. Then music from the 90s (hard rock and rap), then music of the 30s (Judy Garland singing "Somewhere over the Rainbow"), then on to the 40s (Artie Shaw playing "Summit Ridge Drive") and 50s (the Four Aces singing "Love Is a Many Splendored Thing"). It is remarkable that music from each of these eras is still being played on the radio. Music from the 30s and 40s isn't just being played on National Public Radio for historical purposes or on a Sunday afternoon program that features the "quaint old music of the past." This music is being played on regular, commercial radio stations that appeal to many middle-aged, elderly, and even youthful listeners.

The range of tastes in our hybrid society is amazing. When we talk about "popular music" today, we must include music that is more than fifty years old, for this music is still being heard on commercial stations. Back in 1940 or 1950, this never would have occurred; we never would have found a radio station that featured songs from fifty to sixty years earlier—that is, music of the 1880s and

1890s! We would have had to tune into programs of an academic
bent: programs on American folk music or special retrospective
programs on turn-of-the-century music halls. Yet, in the 1990s, we
live easily with this diversity of musical taste and rich mixture of
differing popular music formats and tastes. We are not, in other
words, entering a "new" world. Rather, we are entering a "new"
world, an "old" world, and a world still in transition. These worlds
live side by side in our hybrid society.

At the heart of the matter is our passing modern-day disdain
for anything old or outmoded. We tended to devalue that which was
premodern, unless it was in a museum or existed in a place we
visited as a tourist. Everything of value was new and different, innovative, better than what came before: the "new model" of automobile each fall, the "improved" soap product, the latest generation
of stereo receivers (remember when those things were called "hi-fi").
In each of these cases, we discover an emphasis on change in style,
as well as, perhaps, technical improvement. The newness, in other
words, had to be visible to the Joneses next door as well as to
ourselves. If it didn't look bright and new, then it certainly wasn't
considered much of an improvement. So we stuck some fins on it
one year and then removed the fins the next year, while adding a
two-tone paint job to the "new and improved" model. We had a
utopian vision of the twenty-first century that differed entirely from
either the premodern or the early modern era, though it was a log-
ical systematic extension of the trends of the late modern era. These
visions included free-flowing overarching freeways above clean cities composed of identical high-rise buildings intermingled with
manicured city parks.

The postmodern era calls into question this emphasis on
newness and challenges the assumption that "progress" is always
an important and constructive product. We are now skeptical about
claims of technological breakthroughs. The "new deal" probably
would not fly today, nor would the "great society"—with its utopian vision of uniformity and systematic obliteration of old communities and neighborhoods. There is now deep-seated suspicion of
claims that politicians, social engineers, or fashion experts know
how things are going to be better or how a new way is somehow
superior to the old way. The old Greek adage about how the more

things change, the more they remain the same is now widely accepted as essentially true, especially regarding seemingly intractable societal problems.

The old is often in fashion today. An emphasis on enduring materials and long-lasting styles has replaced a fascination with disposability and rapid style changes. That which has remained in place over many periods of change is now more often venerated, perhaps because we ourselves hope to be able to survive multiple changes and are ourselves now exhausted by change. We long for that which has not changed and has endured. Diversity of styles is now accepted, leaving us with the freedom to wear old as well as new garments—and to embrace organizational elements from the premodern and modern eras, as well as new elements from the postmodern era. In a typical contemporary organization, one will now find a variety of different (and often contradictory) processes and functions, as well as diverse forms and structures of premodern, modern, and postmodern origins, some of which are temporary and others permanent.

A Mixture of Premodern, Modern, and Postmodern

We seem to be entering a postmodern era, but our sight is as much backward as it is forward. We long for the good old days. Everything seems to be in flux, and we look back with a distorted (almost reverential) perspective on a seemingly simpler world, one conducive to strong, visionary leadership. It was a world in which men and women found gratification in the work they performed and found community in the people with whom they affiliated. We often forget the alienation of premodern sweatshops, the stifling conformity and stagnation of premodern towns, and the depressing poverty associated with tenant farming and small family-owned businesses. Instead, we meander down the main street of a small Iowa town or the replication of such a street at Disney World. We collect antiques and memorabilia. We look forward to watching movies and television programs about living on Walton mountain or living in a Frank Capra world of virtue, values, and family commitments. Is this all a dream—an attempt to escape from the vagaries and complexities of contemporary life? Certainly when I come home after a long and difficult day of shifting gears between five different projects and four different constituencies, each with its own agenda and perspectives, I often seek out the reassurance of a novel from or about a premodern world or listen to music from an earlier era.

Yet, there is realism in our search for premodernism and in our wistful yearnings for a return to this era, in part because the premodern still exists in our society. This is a central message in postmodernism: the premodern and modern continue to exist side by side with newly emerging forms, perspectives, and attitudes. The postmodern organization incorporates diverse elements from many different times and places. We look around us every day and see vital signs of premodernism: the small bakery that specializes in pies and birthday cakes; the small town square created in the new housing project; the urban green filled each morning with retired men and women talking about the previous day's news; the small city park that draws together Asian-American men and women performing tai chi. Christmas pageants and President's Day celebrations are still offered at local elementary schools and churches.

Fortune magazine (Sellers, 1991b) recently reported that many of the old brands (Cheerios, Betty Crocker, even Hamburger Helper) are making a comeback. In part, this is because new brands are expensive to launch, while old, established brands need only an occasional boost. The old brands give us a sense of assurance. We have been told (and as young children believed) that Cheerios are "good for us"; now we find out this is true, given the current emphasis on oats as a nutritional grain and on the elimination of refined sugar from our diets. We can't believe modern (let alone postmodern) combinations of truths and lies; hence we look back to older times for enduring truths.

As a society, we are only a moment away from the premodern era. American culture was predominantly premodern less than one hundred years ago. In a recent article, Frank Rose (1991, p. 92) writes of a shift in American values away from the "licentiousness of the Seventies and the materialism of the Eighties" to a new emphasis on premodern morality: "if it feels good, it must be bad." Campaigns against smoking, drinking, and excessive eating all have a Victorian consciousness about them. They are being waged to rescue the bodies and minds of postmodern man, rather than his soul. Nevertheless, they are based on the negative ("just say no") moralistic foundation of premodern Western civilization.

There is clearly only a thin veneer of modernism covering the deeply rooted premodernism of Western European society. The willingness and capacity of seemingly hedonistic American consumers to so easily abandon some of their pet vices provide impressive evidence of the lingering presence of premodern morality and perspectives in our world. While we have not yet chosen to deny our greatest "sin" (our love affair with the American automobile), one wonders how far off a successful "just say no" campaign to reduce the use of private automobiles may be.

We also see premodern values in our renewed emphasis on family and children. Not only are young couples having more children than was true several decades ago, they also now demand that work life be integrated with family life. In some areas of the United States, new building permits for corporations are approved only if these corporations start a day-care center. Other corporations now provide maternity leaves for both mothers and fathers and encourage men (not just women) to stay at home with their sick children. In part, this new level of support for integrating work and family is possible because of new communication technology. Many working men and women can now work out of their home (with the help of computers, modems, and facsimile machines) just as easily as they can work at the office. This shift is a result of the new worker values I described in Chapter Seven and a longer-term perspective on the value of child raising. "Without doubt, helping improve child care is in the best interest of business—today's children, after all, are tomorrow's labor pool" (Labich, 1991). This emerging concern, however, also comes from a growing recognition that premodern parents were correct in their assessment that children need parents around if they are to mature in a healthy manner. Latchkey children simply are not getting enough attention, even if dual-career parents are able to provide superb child care, education, and material possessions (Labich, 1991).

Unfortunately, this premodern concern with the quality of child raising, like many reemerging premodern concerns, does not match the apparent postmodern structures of our society. Both men and women must work in this postmodern world, and insufficient public dollars are available to support adequate child-care facilities or to assist men or women in staying home with their children. Job sharing is on the rise, and various forms of part-time employment are certainly coming to the fore. However, they may not be adequate, given the need for two full-time incomes in most families and the continuing reticence of many organizations to provide equivalent pay to part-time employees. In many instances, premodern remnants in our society continue to demand reexamination of modern-day values but do not provide us with the mechanisms for enactment of the older values. As I have noted throughout this book, we cannot simply return to premodern forms but must instead invent new forms that incorporate aspects of both the premodern and modern. This new hybrid will in many instances be based on the values of a premodern world, while incorporating many of the mechanisms and structures of the modern and postmodern worlds.

As we welcome to our shores many people from other cultures (Asian, African, Near Eastern) that in many ways are still premodern, we will find that modernism holds an increasingly tenuous position in our society and that we face an even more challenging task of integrating premodern, modern, and postmodern elements from various cultures into our hybrid society. Men and women with whom I work from various Asian countries (Taiwan, the Philippines, Thailand, Indonesia, China) often speak of the major revolutions now taking place in their countries, as they leapfrog over the premodern era into the postmodern. It is quite clear that the world cannot afford major energy consuming expansion of the modern industrial sector in these societies, yet they are unprepared (just as Americans are unprepared) for the values, structures, and styles of the postmodern world. Several of the most prosperous Asian countries, such as Japan, try to restrict the intrusion of other cultures into their own basically premodern world. Other countries, such as Taiwan, that rely heavily on Western trade are already an amalgamation of Eastern and Western cultures and premodern, modern, and even postmodern forms and structures. In this new global village, we must all find ways to blend varying perspectives in a new postmodern manner.

A Mixture of Processes and Functions

We have learned in our postmodern world that we can't solve the problem of integration, which is inherent in growth, simply by devoting more resources to integration as we grow larger. The integration of functions in large-scale organizations may no longer be possible, or if it is possible, it will require too large a proportion of the total resources of the organization for the organization to survive. A new emphasis has thus emerged in postmodern organizations on the value of being small—or at least flexible in one's attitude about appropriate size. This began with the small-is-beautiful theme of the early 1970s. One of the most widely read proponents of this perspective, E. F. Schumacher (1973, pp. 64–65), observed:

> Even today, we are generally told that gigantic organizations are inescapably necessary; but when we look closely we can notice that as soon as great size has been created there is often a strenuous attempt to attain smallness within bigness. The great achievement of Mr. Sloan of General Motors was to structure this gigantic firm in such a manner that it became, in fact, a federation of fairly reasonably sized firms. . . . While many theoreticians—who may not be too closely in touch with real life—are still engaging in the idolatry of large size, with practical people in the actual world there is a tremendous longing and striving to profit, if at all possible, from the convenience, humanity, and manageability of smallness.

Since 1973, Schumacher's vision of a world filled with large organizations that have been broken down into smaller semiautonomous units has partially been realized. Smallness within bigness is now a common theme in the writing of many management theorists and consultants. Kanter (1983) and Peters (Peters and Waterman, 1982; Peters, 1987) both encourage the use of small, highly flexible work teams and speak to the problems inherent in large cumbersome organizations. Small autonomous businesses also are in vogue. McCarroll (1992) writes in *Time* magazine about jobless Americans who have launched small businesses (some with government assistance). According to McCarroll, "an estimated 1.3 million new businesses opened their doors in 1991, up nearly 9% from 1980. . . . More than half the new enterprises are sole proprietorships or microbusinesses with no more than two employees, typically operating out of a garage, basement or spare room" (p. 62).

Schumacher goes on to emphasize the role of diversity in institutional size and scale. While some of Schumacher's critics portrayed him as always favoring small-sized organizations, he actually advocated the selection of an appropriate size for organizations, not just small size. He wrote, "For every activity there is a certain appropriate scale, and the more active and intimate the activity, the smaller the number of people that can take part, [and] the greater is the number of such relationship arrangements that need to be established. . . . What scale is appropriate? It depends on what we are trying to do. The question of scale is extremely crucial today, in political, social and economic affairs just as in almost everything else" (1973, p. 66).

Many enterprises simply cannot be run as small businesses because of the volume of sales needed to sustain the business. In many instances, small businesses are undercapitalized and never get off the ground. The recent recession has led to a cutback in credit for small businesses (Light, 1991), while the internationalization of many business sectors has required the presence of rather large organizational structures (or even consortia involving several large corporations) in order to compete effectively with the complex legal, financial, and political forces operating in international arenas. Small organizations, in general, are most successful if they serve specific marketing niches, pioneer new technologies, or supply parts (or second sources) to larger corporations (Stewart, 1991, p. 18).

This emphasis on appropriate-sized organizations is reinforced by the findings of the studies on growth commissioned by the Club of Rome (Meadows and others, 1972; Mesarovic and Pestel, 1974) during the mid 1970s. As both reports concluded, societies can be created and maintained on earth in which people can live indefinitely. However, to do so, we must impose limits on ourselves, on our production of material goods, and on the use of nonrenewable or slowly renewable resources. We must concentrate on growth in those domains of life (the arts, scientific knowledge, personal development) that do not consume the world's resources, and we must find ways to bring population and reproduction under control if we are to achieve a state of global equilibrium. Furthermore, we must make use of renewable, highly portable resources (information) rather than nonrenewable, immobile resources (energy). We can best do so by keeping many of our organizations small and highly flexible.

Organizations—or nations, for that matter—that are large and centrally controlled are inclined to incur large energy costs because of the need to ship goods from one production facility to another or to move people (via airplane, train, car) from one location to another for planning meetings, coordination of production, and so forth. In the Soviet Union, for instance, coal was mined in one of the republics and then shipped to another republic for use in the production of steel, which in turn was shipped to a third location for the manufacturing of automobiles or tanks. A similar pattern of distributed production was common in the United States until very recently. Modern-day America saw the production of coal in one location, the use of this coal to produce steel in a second location, and the production of automobiles from this steel in a third location. In general, transportation in both the Soviet Union and United States was extensive during the modern era. There was minimal concern for cost containment in such industries as automobile manufacturing or the production of military weapons, in part because transportation costs (and environmental concerns) were minimal during the modern era. In the postmodern world, this form of distributive production has become prohibitively expensive, as well as ecologically unsound. Smaller organizations that produce goods using local resources are much more likely to survive this turbulent and energy-conscious era.

Modern organizations tend to be much more complex than premodern organizations in large part because of size and population density (Durkheim, [1893] 1933); the postmodern organization is distinguished from the modern organization in that it is often a hybrid of many different organizational forms and dynamics. We find premodern elements in many contemporary organizations. A postmodern perspective on organizational communication, for instance, is particularly likely to include the premodern characteristic of the oral storytelling traditions of organizations. While the modern organization seemingly was held together by the ubiquitous memorandum and organizational chart, premodern and postmodern organizations rely heavily on the spoken word (gossip, stories, and other forms of informal communication). A postmodern perspective, in fact, pushes us even further with regard to communications within organizations. It suggests—as I noted in Chapter Six—that organizations are nothing more than—or at least primarily composed of—extended conversations between members of the organization.

Premodern elements often show up in postmodern organizations in the form of corporate celebrations, ceremonies, and retreats. These elements are premodern in either their origins or their use of tools and techniques rarely associated with modern-day management practices. Members of an organization are brought together, as in premodern times, for recognition of accomplishments, reflection on organizational learning, food, recreation, and other activities not usually considered work. Company-sponsored baseball teams, chili cook offs, and wilderness programs (for example, the highly successful "Ropes" program) build corporate support and team spirit by using premodern organizational forms in a postmodern context. Men and women who participate in these activities are faced with very elemental tasks of premodern origins: their hands (and hearts) are being used for the first time in interaction with their work life colleagues.

Examples of the intermingling of modern and postmodern elements are even more prevalent in our emerging postmodern organizations. We find both moderately large and very large organizations existing as independent, autonomous institutions that are very modern in nature and also as interdependent collaborating members of complex postmodern consortia and partnerships. Within the high-tech field, research consortia are now abundant. The National Center for Manufacturing Sciences, for instance, is an $80 million operation involved in collaborative interinstitutional improvement of machine tools and software. The Microelectronics and Computer Technology Corporation similarly encourages cooperation between corporations in the areas of advanced computing, software, computer-aided design, and semiconductor packaging (Faltermayer, 1991, p. 49).

Even inside many contemporary corporations, traditional modern bureaucracies exist alongside postmodern ad hoc task forces. Small project teams ("skunk works") are integrated with formal hierarchically organized departments. The new "adhocracy," as Toffler (1970) labeled it thirty years ago, typically makes extensive use of teams that "are assembled to solve specific short-term problems. Then, exactly like . . . mobile playgrounds, they are disassembled and their human components reassigned. Sometimes these teams are thrown together to serve only for a few days. Sometimes they are intended to last a few years. But, unlike the functional departments or divisions of a traditional bureaucratic organization, which are presumed to be permanent, the project or task force team is temporary by design" (Toffler quoted in Best, 1973, p. 70). Toffler's comments exemplify the mixture of modern emphases on assembly and automation (the description of human components on teams) and the postmodern emphasis on flexibility and product-focused design of work teams.

Postmodern organizations are particularly hybrid with regard to policies and procedures. There is very little uniformity. Personnel manuals that reflect the values and priorities of the modern era are found in many contemporary organizations. These manuals are highly detailed and often legalistic. They are based on the assumption that specific jobs are unlikely to change on a daily basis and that the skills and knowledge required to perform these jobs in a satisfactory manner can be clearly and consistently identified.

These same organizations, however, have embraced postmodern incentive programs and joint union-management problem-solving groups not particularly compatible with a uniform set of policies and procedures. Incentive programs may motivate workers to test new ways of doing their jobs, as might the joint union-management groups. Self-governing task forces need to create their own performance criteria, while managers often ask employees to learn new skills not anticipated when the personnel manual was prepared. Organizations face turbulent and unpredictable changes in the near future that may make lists of desired knowledge, skills, and attitudes obsolete.

A major source of the hybrid forms found in many contemporary organizations is the powerful, but often invisible, move from primary reliance on formal lines of authority to reliance on staff roles and informal lines of authority. Staff members (secretaries, administrative assistants, legislative analysts) rarely take over from the boss. Their advancement through the organization is dependent on their relationship with—and the fleeting whims of—their boss (Kanter, 1977). This is a throwback to premodern conditions. The movies *Nine to Five* and *Working Girl* offer sometimes humorous and often painful visions of the role of staff members as serfs. The blending of line and staff relationships exemplifies the mixture of modes in the postmodern organization. Premodern quasi-serf relationships exist alongside postmodern and modern policies and procedures. We have a modern-day affirmative action policy to govern the personnel procedures of the line staff, yet we set this policy aside when it comes to the treatment and review of staff members.

On the one hand, staff members have very little formal power and are beholden to their bosses. On the other hand, they often have a great deal of informal power. It is not unusual for staff to assume too much authority in postmodern organizations. For example, the president of a large national association in Washington, D.C., had a staff assistant who falsified reports from the president to outsides (actually offering his own opinions rather than the president's) and screened information sent to the president (including complaints from other members of the organization about this assistant's behavior). All of this reduced the credibility of the president and led to his eventual departure from the organization. The staff member felt he was being absolutely loyal to the president and was simply protecting him from distracting and confounding input from the outside. This phenomenon is repeated in many different forms and in many different organizations throughout the United States every day. It was especially dramatic in the Johnson, Nixon, and Reagan administrations.

In the words of the evil witch in the musical *The Wiz*, most of us "don't want no bad news," hence we appreciate and indirectly collude with our staff in their screening and distortion of information. Under conditions of high stress and complexity (the prevalent postmodern condition), we are particularly attracted to the attentive staff member's screening and filtering of information into and out of our office. As Peters (1987, p. 514) notes, "In the office, whether you are chief of a big organization or a small one, you are shielded from the truth by a bewildering array of devices, prudent or malicious, all designed to 'save' you from trivia and complexity so that your mind can be clear as you confront the 'big picture' decisions. Instead, your mind is all too likely to be empty of all but prepackaged data, leading you to make uninformed decisions." Perhaps this is one of the reasons why Tom Peters's suggestion that we get out of our offices and wander about the organization was such good advice in the 1980s. We need to get out of our offices in order to bypass our staff assistants.

A final source of the hybrid character of structures and processes in postmodern organizations is the changing nature of the problems being faced. Senge (1990, pp. 71–72) identifies an older form of complexity that he calls "detail complexity." This form exists when many variables are present in a situation. By contrast, Senge identifies a newer form of complexity—"dynamic complexity"—that exists when there is subtlety of cause and effect and when it is difficult to assess the impact of any specific intervention. Detail complexity can be addressed by simply adding more people, more tools, and more money to the analysis of a problem—the growth strategy used in many modern organizations. We assume, for instance, that an accurate census of the United States population could be obtained if we had sufficient staff, sophisticated computers, and a substantial budget. Yet, is this the case? Aren't some of the problems associated with the census related to problems that are less easily solved, for example, counting people without homes, without legal passports, or without a compelling reason to participate in such a data gathering process? These problems are not solved simply by more people or money, for in many instances— as I noted in Chapter Three—they primarily concern scope and measurement. They require a different kind of solution and are often exacerbated rather than resolved by large-scale interventions.

A Mixture of Permanent and Temporary Systems

As we ask men and women to lead our hybrid organizations, they must be prepared to face both dynamic and detail complexity, as well as the unique problems of both staff and line relationships and the intermingling of many different premodern, modern, and postmodern elements. To add a further challenge, these leaders must also live with both permanent and temporary structures. Recent analyses of organizational dynamics have emphasized the role played by temporary systems. The emerging dominant structure for communication in postmodern organizations is the short-term task force or the five-minute meeting. The emerging employment contract is one that requires short-term or contracted services.

As far back as the late 1960s and early 1970s, Warren Bennis spoke of the "end of bureaucracy," Alvin Toffler wrote about "adhocracy" as the new form of organizational life in America, and Donald Schön described "self-destructing organizations" (Best, 1973). At about this time in the United States, we came to realize that Americans (and members of many other Western societies) were living in a world of temporary arrangements, one characterized by temporary groups and temporary (though intense) face-to-face or electronically mediated relationships. Toffler (in Best, 1973, p. 77) spoke of "the emergence of a new kind of organization man—a man who, despite his many affiliations, remains basically uncommitted to any organization. He is willing to employ his skills and creative energies to solve problems with equipment provided by the organization and within temporary groups established by it. But he does so only so long as the problem interests him."

Bennis and Slater (1968, pp. 73–74) predicted an even more accelerated movement toward temporary structures:

> The social structure of organizations of the future will have some unique characteristics. The key word will be "temporary." There will be adaptive, rapidly changing *temporary* systems. These will be task forces organized around problems to be solved by groups of relative strangers with diverse professional skills. The group will be arranged on an organic rather than me-

chanical model; it will evolve in response to a problem
rather than to programmed role expectations. The
executive thus becomes coordinator or "linking pin"
between various task forces. He must be a man [or
woman] who can speak the polyglot jargon of research, with skills to relay information and to mediate
between groups. People will be evaluated not according to rank but according to skill and professional
training. Organization charts will consist of project
groups rather than stratified functional groups.

Bennis and Slater went on to note that this movement had
already begun in the aerospace and construction industries. Today
we can readily observe such systems in many different businesses,
ranging from conservative banking and insurance companies to
much more free-ranging high-tech and communication industries
(Kanter, 1983; Peters and Waterman, 1982). Many contemporary
organizations are composed of both permanent and temporary systems, yielding a complex mixed mode of organizational functioning. Edgar Schein (1969) spoke of the new postmodern organization
encompassing three kinds of groups: permanent systems (such as
production units and sales forces), temporary systems (such as task
forces and ad hoc problem-solving groups), and coordinating systems that may or may not be permanent (such as coordinating bodies and committees).

Several assumptions were made during the modern era about
the permanent nature of the work force. Emphasis was placed on
full-time employment and on the employee's absolute dedication to
the organization in which he or she was employed (a comparable
long-term commitment on the part of the organization—at least in
American and European companies—was not assumed). Today, as
we enter the postmodern era, this is changing. Many companies
now rely on part-time employees, temporary employees, and contracted services for a large portion of their work force. Chief executive officers and directors of companies that lay out hundreds of
millions of dollars each year for data processing find that outsourc-
ing of computer services to other companies or to individually con-

tracted computer specialists "has powerful appeal" (Kirkpatrick, 1991, p. 103).

Colleges and universities rely on part-time instructors to reduce overall instructional costs and to infuse stagnant institutions with new life and more realistic perspectives. Mental health systems, health management organizations, and accounting firms hire professionals on a per-client or per-hour basis in order to not only reduce costs but to also increase accountability. Temporary secretarial, clerical, accounting, and mechanical services are available everywhere and are widely advertised. A recent San Francisco newspaper article (Burdman, 1992) indicated that almost twenty million individuals (one out of five civilian workers) put in fewer than thirty-five hours a week in 1991 (a 70 percent increase over the past two decades). The number of temporary workers hired by American companies more than tripled between 1982 and 1990 to about one million workers per day. At least ten million Americans contract with other organizations as consultants, technical experts, and members of third-party firms.

This reliance on part-time, temporary, and external workers yields not only cost and quality benefits for the employer but also creates new independence and, in many ways, a more influential role for those providing the services. We are now entering an era of knowledge workers and of new forms of capital, which build on this knowledge. These new workers and new forms of capital, along with the temporary systems in which they best fit, demand new forms of communication. Temporary workers must be able to make fast connections with one another and with their short-term employer, and then break these connections as they move on to another assignment. The problems associated with truth and lies are exacerbated in such settings; typically, even greater reliance is placed on verbal and informal modes of communication since the temporary worker rarely has enough time (let alone interest) to peruse the modern-day written documentation (policies, procedures, rules) still found in most organizations.

Temporary systems breed quick familiarity and disengagement. The central issue is: are we, as human beings fresh out of the modern era and not very far removed from the premodern era, prepared to adapt to the hybrid organizations we seem to be creating?

What will be the new forms of communication that ensure sincerity and commitment, be they ever so short in duration? These questions are universal; they are equally as applicable to our marriages, our friendships, and even to our role as parents. As we enter the post-modern era, we must be prepared to face a hybrid society, which requires flexibility, an openness to learning, interpersonal sensitivity, and in particular a tolerance for pervasive troubling ambiguity.

Chapter 9

The Cyclical Organization: Managing the Interplay Between Order and Chaos

My current image . . . is almost a cartoon which many post-modern companies will reenact. It is Wiley Coyote back-pedaling madly clawing at the ground trying to stop as his inertia carries him to the precipice. There, the great cosmic roadrunner hovers in midair with a silly grin on its face. The coyote goes over and down silently, and with a look of utter chagrin. "Beep! Beep!" is the only communication heard.

—mid-level manager in a large corporation

In this postmodern era, men and women look for order in the midst of chaos, as they stand, like Wiley Coyote, poised on the edge—or already over the edge—of a psychological and organizational abyss. Given the complex, hybrid society in which we now live, the search for the layer of order is often of highest priority in contemporary organizations, at times disrupting those processes of the organization (planning, coordination, and supervision) that actually help to bring about order. A middle-aged corporate executive stated this point quite eloquently in his description of a moderately large corporation that he helped to found.

Our people spend their time looking for the insignif-
icant events; the events at the margin that can add
order or stability to the complexities they live in. This
reduces our effectiveness as an organization and ultimately limits our ability to survive in a very competitive marketplace. They are constantly looking for
ways to reduce their frustrations and uncertainty by
seeking and challenging the vision and leadership of
the company. While we the senior management focus
on growth and largeness, they focus on transitions.

Our continuous play between chaos and order
is reflected [in] our need to constantly be in meetings.
Someone finds a chaotic situation and quickly calls the
group together for resolution. Instead of making clear
and concise decisions that are communicated to the
organization we tend to increase the ambiguity in the
company and clarify only the smallest of issues. We do
not address with clarity the process required to make
uncertainty easier to resolve for the organization.

What then is the nature of this interplay between order and
chaos in contemporary organizations, and how do leaders help to
discover and maintain the orderly aspects of their institutions? A
key concept is the notion of cycles. Organizations go through
changes that appear to be chaotic. Yet, at another level, order can
be observed in the midst of change. In most organizations, order is
found in three areas. First, we find that chaos becomes more orderly
and meaningful when the institution is described in terms of cycles
associated with life stages. Second, the seemingly chaotic organizational changes can be seen as orderly and cyclical when seasonal
alterations that occur in the lives of many organizations are taken
into account. Third, organizations are defined as orderly or chaotic
depending on which perspective is used to assess the organization.
A shift in perspective can readily lead to a move from chaos to order
in any organizational setting. Thus, we may find that our own
personal periodic shifts in mood and attitude affect our perspectives
on organization, which, in turn, yield either order or chaos.

Organizational Life Stages

The notion that organizations pass through life stages has become more popular in recent years, particularly through the work of Sarason (1972), Kimberly, Miles, and Associates (1980), and Adizes (1988). According to Adizes, "Organizations have lifecycles just as living organisms do; they go through the normal struggles and difficulties accompanying each stage of the Organizational Lifecycle and are faced with the transitional problems of moving to the next phase of development. Organizations learn to deal with these problems by themselves or they develop abnormal 'diseases' which stymie growth. . . . Because the stages in the organization's lifecycle are predictable and repetitive, knowing where the organization [i]s in the lifecycle enable[s] management to take proactive, preventive measures and deal with future problems earlier or avoid them altogether" (1988, pp. xiii–xiv).

The notion of organizational life stages or cycles has great implications for each of the dimensions we have explored in this book, ranging from an understanding of cycles of growth and decline in size and complexity to cycles of change and stabilization. First of all, virtually all of the organizational life stage theorists describe an early stage that is decidedly premodern in terms of unclear boundaries, simplicity of form and structure, and small size. Most of the resources of the newly formed organization are devoted to direct services (production, sales, service). In some cases, the new organization has a clear mission. In other instances, it is more premodern, in terms of unclear goals and even minimal concern for mission. As organizations grow larger and older, their boundaries become clearer and an increasing proportion of their total resources are devoted to integrative administrative functions.

Organizational life cycle theorists also describe the eventual decline in the capacity of virtually all organizations to produce in an efficient manner (because of extensive integrative functions) and to respond flexibly to changing environmental conditions. Kenneth Boulding (1973) writes about the genetic code for death found in all biological organisms but missing in human organizations. Unfortunately, many organizations continue to exist long after they stop contributing in a positive manner to the welfare of either their employees or society. Organizational life stage theories suggest that organizational leaders must confront the prospect of someday choosing to bring their organization (and their own job) to an end or step aside for new leaders to participate in a radical restructuring or rebirth of the organization.

With regard to life stages and styles of leadership, we can look to the situational leadership models of Hershey and Blanchard (1977), who related leadership styles to levels of maturation in a group or organization. The relation of organizational life stages to leadership is also important when considering the movement of a single institution from a premodern (paternalistic) to modern (bureaucratic) style of appropriate leadership, or the movement of a modern-day organization to a more postmodern, flexible style of leadership as the organization grows, matures, and seeks to delay inevitable decline. A West Coast manager described a shift that had occurred among leaders in his own technology firm: "So we seek an evolution in leadership style. From the entrepreneurial father taking care of his children [paternalism], to the autonomous bureaucrats following company policy, to the reflective leader seeking to develop the human potential of all with whom he is involved."

In outgrowing paternalism, this organization underwent stress and turmoil. "When the company had grown from the original 'garage' to 'Fortune 500' status, something changed." The founder of this organization no longer even knew the name of all his employees, much less was able to "take care of them." At this point, the organization shifted from a premodern to a modern assumption about the proper role of leadership in the organization. In the past, the founder of the organization was central to this organization. His philosophy was accepted as the company's philosophy; his vision was the predominant vision for the entire company. However, "for all his genius, for all his caring, it was time for [the founder] to retire, regardless of age."

If the founder of this organization was the premodern, paternalistic father, then his successor came in as a postmodern butterfly, bypassing the usual move to a more managerial-type leader. The new leader's purpose is to bring about change. His life as a leader, like that of a butterfly, is likely to be short; the change is overdue, but the costs associated with this change apparently are great. "Four days after [the successor] took over, he implemented a dramatic reorganization. . . . Much was done to flatten the organization. Many of the layoffs . . . were of midlevel managers/supervisors. With this level removed, it seemed that the company was freer to experiment with new ways of doing business, with new ways of managing."

Unless leaders in postmodern organizations are ready to acknowledge the changes required for them to remain effective, they are likely to become victims rather than champions of change in their own organization's life stages. The founder of this organization properly acknowledged the need for a shift in style of leadership in his company. The new leader was able to introduce a needed change that the founder either could not or wished not to initiate.

Organizational Seasons

Another approach using the concept of cycles has been given much less attention than life stages has received. This is the seasonal cycle found in the yearly history of many organizations. The whole notion of organizational seasons is a decidedly premodern notion. Just as there are winter, spring, summer, and fall in most temperate climates, so there are seasons in the lives of many organizations. These seasons are most obvious in organizations that have a beginning and ending point each year. Schools, for example, begin anew each fall and come to an end each spring. Similarly, many merchandising firms have a "heavy season" (usually Christmastime), as do agriculture-based businesses geared toward specific products and specific growing seasons. Sports teams obviously have seasons, as do most performing arts organizations and recreational facilities. With obvious seasons, an organization can automatically renew itself: "wait till next year," "we screwed up this time, but next time we'll learn from our mistakes and do much better," "Jim didn't do very well this time around, but will do much better, I'm sure, when we start up again."

Many other organizations are not so fortunate. They either had seasons but no longer do or they have never had new years to start up. The automobile industry is one of the corporate sectors that recently lost its season, partly as a result of its efforts to obtain a competitive edge in response to foreign competition and partly in an effort to be less "premodern" in its emphasis on seasons. While the fiscal years of most corporations formally start a new seasonal cycle, this is rarely treated as a time for reflection back on the old year, as a time for forgiveness, or as a time for renewed hope ("wait till next year"). Rather, corporate leaders are inclined to say: "Great! But what have you done for me lately?" In our postmodern world, we must find a way to return to seasons. The new year becomes an excellent time for organizational reflection and learning and for telling stories about past triumphs and failures. The new year also provides us with a sense of order and predictability, which is particularly important in a world that often seems to defy prediction, let alone control.

Organizational Perspectives

A popular song recorded by Bette Midler in the early 1990s speaks of the world looking quite beautiful and free "from a distance." At a distance, according to the song's lyrics, there are no national boundaries nor are there any wars or evidence of human despair. However, when looked at from a close, personal perspective, our world is filled with both nationalistic fervor and despair—it all depends on one's perspective. One of the central features of any large system, according to chaos theorists, concerns vantage point. A system is perceived as chaotic or orderly in part as a function of how the system is studied. Teilhard de Chardin anticipated this fluctuation between chaos and order as a function of perspective. He described the universe as "passing from State A, characterized by a very large number of very simple material elements . . . to State B, defined by a smaller number of very complex groupings" (1955, p. 61). According to Teilhard, State A is defined by entities that "are extremely numerous and extremely loose at the same time." These entities "only reveal themselves by overall effects which are subject to the laws of statistics. Collectively, that is, they obey the laws of mathematics" (1955, p. 61).

This way of viewing the universe is labeled "nomothetic" by the American psychologist Gordon Allport (1937). It is a mode of analysis typified by statistics and large-scale surveys. Allport speaks of a nomothetic science that emphasizes the study of a large number of subjects, primarily through quantitative means, to determine what they have in common. The purely nomothetic sciences (traditional physics and chemistry) are prevalent today and serve as models for virtually all the other sciences. Typically, when viewed from this very broad nomothetic perspective, everything in our world looks quite orderly and well behaved. A certain number and percentage of Americans will buy Grape Nuts on any given day, regardless of what any of us individually thinks about Grape Nuts. A certain proportion of the American public will be living below the poverty level and local human service agencies can plan for increases or decreases in the use of their facilities, based on statistics regarding rates of unemployment, rates at which tax dollars are being received by the local government, and so forth.

Teilhard also speaks of a second, more immediate and chaotic state (State B) that involves the inspection of a smaller number of entities in much greater depth. "[These] more highly individualized elements gradually escape from the slavery of large numbers. They allow their basic non-measurable spontaneity to break through and reveal itself. We can begin to see them and follow them one by one, and in so doing we have access to the world of biology" (1955, p. 61).

Allport would describe State B as "idiographic." The idiographic sciences tend to encourage study of the single case, primarily through qualitative means, to determine what is distinctive about that case. This approach involves attention to the unique setting in which an individual entity is being studied. This in turn often leads one away from order into chaos. An ideographic or State B analysis might involve a study of the individual consumer who may decide on a whim to either purchase or not purchase a box of Grape Nuts on any particular day. State B might involve the in-depth study of a particular person or family living below the poverty level unable to find adequate human services because of location, bureaucratic red tape, or personal motivation.

We can readily produce scientific laws and build public policy on the basis of the nomethetic approach. We are much less successful in building either science or government on the basis of idiographic analyses. Yet, postmodern conditions and the repeated failure of nomothetically produced modernist truths and policies to adequately inform our knowledge of the world make a new appreciation of idiographic perspectives imperative.

A midlevel administrator in a governmental security agency recently expressed this viewpoint when commenting on the inadequacy of many governmental strategies for downsizing defense-related operations. He observed that governmentwide, macropolicies regarding the closing of military bases and reductions in force typically are thought out in a reasonable manner and are understood by most men and women both within and outside the military. There is order and coherence at this macrolevel. When these policies, however, are moved to a more microlevel and a specific percentage of staff is eliminated in each unit of the military, we find chaos and absurdity. The loss of a quarter of the staff at a small office differs greatly from the loss of a quarter of the staff at a large office. In many cases, the small office simply cannot function without some of these staff members, whereas the larger offices often can shift remaining staff into the understaffed areas. Consistency in the application of policies across diverse settings thus leads to order at one level (the macrolevel) and to disorder and chaos at another level (the microlevel).

This same principle applies in many different organizational arenas, ranging from the application of affirmative action policies to the formulation and application of standards regarding academic or mental health services. The best of intentions can lead to unintended and even disastrous results. When planning for change or invoking new policies, we must look at the problems to be solved from multiple perspectives—both macro and micro. We must prepare scenarios that describe the impact of the proposed changes on both the overall organization and on subunits within the organization. We must rely not only on large-scale organizational statistics but also on the individual case studies obtained through direct contact with members of the organization.

Cycles and Subsystem Mirroring

Both order and chaos reign in organizations not only because of organizational stages and seasons or differences in the realities derived from nomothetic (macro) and idiographic (micro) perspectives, but also because of different realities obtained by looking at both repetitive and distinctive elements in organizations. On the one hand, organizations consist of many replicated elements and processes, thus providing the organization with order and stability. "The entire universe," Teilhard noted, "is to be found in every grain of sand." In this brief statement, Teilhard has set the stage for a new way of thinking about the interplay between order and chaos in organizations (and in other systems).

This new concept, called "subsystem mirroring" by British organizational theorists (Colman and Bexton, 1975), is one of the potentially most useful principles in postmodern theory, especially as applied to large and complex organizations. This concept also helps us further understand the orderly and cyclical nature of organizations, even in the face of seemingly chaotic conditions. The principle of subsystem mirroring is based on the premise that there are a few basic structures and dynamics within any system that are replicated again and again and from cycle to cycle in all of the system's subsystems, as well as in its overall structure and dynamics. If we can clearly observe and truly understand the nature of any one unit of an organization, then in some basic way we can accurately understand and predict something about the essence of the overall organization.

If, for instance, I can observe and understand the interaction between a single physician in a hospital or clinic and several of her patients, then I can discover something that is valid and of critical importance about the entire hospital or clinic—or even about the medical enterprise in general. Similarly, if I can figure out what is happening when the manager of a high-tech production unit fails to motivate his subordinates, then I may have discovered something that is problematic throughout the company, at least at this level of interaction. Each subsystem of an organization mirrors the overall structure and dynamics of the organization, as well as all the other subsystems. In this way, the single-case idiographic study is reintegrated with the systemwide nomethetic analysis.

The concept of subsystem mirroring is often attractive to organizational theorists confronted with the unpredictability and complexity of postmodern organizations. By viewing subsystems as mirrors of the dynamics of all other subsystems and of the overall system within any organization, we regain the hope of finding order in what appears to be disorder and of finding simplicity in a very complex world. Recently, for instance, I was asked to consult with a very large bank regarding the values exhibited and expressed in this organization. At first, I was overwhelmed and couldn't figure out where to begin in terms of observing and analyzing the values of this complex institution. However, once I applied the hypothesis of subsystem mirroring, I realized that I could start at any place in the organization and discover specific values that would, in turn, be enacted in all other subsystems of the bank.

Typically, when looking for the most obvious, richest source of subsystem dynamics, one looks at the points of interface between the system and the outside world. In the case of the bank, I chose to focus on the interaction between bank tellers and customers and between loan officers and potential borrowers. In these basic transactions, which are repeated many times each day in every bank in this corporation, one should be able to find one or more essential system dynamics. This realization reduced the task to human scale for me and enabled me to plunge into the large, but manageable, project of observing and interviewing bank tellers, customers, loan officers, and potential borrowers.

Most organizations are inclined to be particularly resistant to change in their style and manner of operations (what system theorists call *homeorhesis*). The informal and "invisible" style of operations in an organization is typically much more important, ultimately, to members of the organization than is the particular status of the organization with regard to resources, products, customers, or goals (what system theorists call the *homeostasis* of the organization). For example, members of an organization are likely to sacrifice profits, position, and power if they can retain their accustomed way of doing things. These ways of doing things, in turn, are the basic elements that Teilhard suggested are built into a system or organization at or near the time of its birth. "Life on earth," according to Teilhard, "is not replicable. It is a onetime phenomenon" (1955, p. 71). Similarly, the birth of an organization is a onetime thing. It can never be replicated or undone. In this sense, any organizational change effort will always be limited by these deeply ingrained founding conditions and patterns ("rhesis") of the organization. There is, in other words, nothing new under the sun, at least with regard to the initial styles of management, leadership, and work within an organization. First-order changes don't alter these initial styles. Second-order changes may alter them—but often at great cost to the organization and in the face of massive organizational and cultural resistance.

Teilhard goes on to suggest that even when something new does enter a system after its birth, it typically is very difficult to perceive, let alone understand: "when anything really new begins to germinate around us, we cannot distinguish it—for the very good reason that it could only be recognized in the light of what it is going to be. Yet, if, when it has reached full growth, we look back to find its starting point, we only find that the starting point itself is now hidden from our view, destroyed or forgotten" (1955, p. 121). Furthermore, according to Teilhard, what may appear to be new in a system—what Thomas Kuhn (1962) calls an anomaly—is usually found to have always been there in some small form. This suggests something about the essential role played by the remnant in any system.

A remnant is composed of the people, traditions, policies, and values in an organization that were once prominent (or at least a major force) but that now play a marginal or even invisible role. The long-term employee who is now out-of-step or the story of the "good old days" told by a loyal, long-suffering member of the secretarial staff are all part of an organization's remnant. These old, seemingly nonfunctional elements of a system should never be eliminated, for they cannot readily be recreated if the system should again need them. Teilhard suggests that all elements in a system must be present from the start; they cannot be added later. We must be careful, therefore, about completely eliminating any existing element of an organization, given the difficulty of finding it again when change does take place. As we look at the appropriate role of the premodern era in our current organizations, we can see the importance of premodern remnants, as well as the replication of founding premodern elements, in the organizations in which we currently live. While most individual organizations may be products of the modern era, the basic assumptions we make about living and working in these organizations—and the basic culture of many of these organizations—are likely to be premodern in origin.

If Teilhard's notion is extended to organizational theory, all central elements of an organization must have existed within the boundaries of this organization at the point when it began. These central elements are replicated again and again as the organization grows and becomes more finely differentiated. Thus, when Bill Hewlett and David Packard began building oscillators in their garage, all of the central dynamics of the Hewlett-Packard Company must have already been in existence: all of the major points of both promise and struggle, all of the major strengths and weaknesses, all of the principal modes of operating (planning, problem solving, decision making, communication). The "H-P way" would have already been established and was replicated many times over as Bill and Dave moved to bigger quarters and hired more people to meet the needs of their growing company. Similarly, in the case of the bank I studied, the basic style of interaction between teller or loan officer and customer would have been established when the first branch of this bank opened more than seventy years ago.

Returning to Teilhard's biological world, we find an excellent example of subsystem mirroring in his analysis of the similarities in the fauna and flora of Africa and South America (which apparently split off from Africa many years ago). Teilhard suggests that animals and plants growing on the new South American continent replicated on a smaller scale the same biological designs and evolutionary process found among the animals and plants that continued to live on the African continent. The South American environment produced its own "pseudo-elephants, its pseudo-rodents, its pseudo-horses and its pseudo-monkeys. . . . A complete biota in miniature, a sub-biota within the original [African] one" (1955, pp. 125–126). Building on this analysis, I predict that companies that spun off from Hewlett-Packard carried the basic dynamics of Bill and Dave's original shop into the new organization(s) and that banks that spun off from the one I studied (as well as new branches of the existing bank) retained the same basic style of interaction between bank employees and customers. Thus, subsystem mirroring refers not just to the replication of structure and dynamics within the existing organization but also to its replication within other new units of the organization or other organizations that spin off from the parent company.

While organizations do tend to be orderly in their replication of elements and processes through subsystem mirroring, they also are chaotic in the distinctiveness found among organizational elements and processes. Teilhard offers insights that suggest caution in the application of subsystem mirroring at *all* levels of an organization. He proposes that elements of a system do not necessarily replicate themselves at all levels of a system or organization. However, they do tend to replicate themselves at the same level throughout the system. According to Teilhard, at each level of a system or organization, the structure and dynamics operate quite differently. At each level of an organization or system, there are subsystems that operate in quite different ways from other subsystems at the same level and, in particular, at other levels. Thus, we find yet another reason why large, postmodern organizations become very complex and fragmented.

In the case of Hewlett-Packard, we might find some basic dynamic in the relationship between Bill and Dave replicated in some of the units of the company, but not in others. Furthermore, we might find this same dynamic at the highest executive level of the company or at the level of concrete problem solving between an H-P representative and customer. In the bank I studied, we might expect the employee-customer style of interaction to be replicated in other employee-customer interactions, but not in the interactions between auditors and corporate executives or between the bank's public relations department and local government officials. With each additional level of the organization there are greater possibilities of differences in the character and dynamics of each of the subsystems in the organization, whether these subsystems exist at the same or at different levels.

The Birth of Organizational Forms and Structures

What does the interplay between order and chaos tell us about the nature of the organizations in which we work? Most important, it tells us that the character and structure of an organization are determined at its origins. Bateson (1979) suggests that organizations take on specific forms from their very beginning. Initial organizational forms (much like the forms of all living beings) have a profound impact on the subsequent functions and achievements of the organization, for the birth of an organization always requires some initial defining marker of difference. Without a marker event there will be no differentiation of the organization, hence no growth. An embryo, for instance, will mature only if some external object penetrates its membrane and in doing so establishes an orientation for the embryo in terms of head and feet (or tail). Bateson (1979, p. 163) concludes that "nothing can come from nothing." Whatever the nature of this initial marker event, it defines the entire orientation for this organization throughout its life. Thus, once an organization is started—with distinctive form and characteristics— it is very hard to change in any substantial manner.

In many ways, the resistance of organizations to change strongly resembles the resistant characteristics of many other organic roots, in particular, certain kinds of trees, with their deep roots, gradual growth, and long life. Bateson (1979) identifies the maple tree as one of the major prototypes for systems of all sizes and characteristics in our world. The maple tree has deep roots. Organizations similarly have strong traditions, abundant reserves, and a solid base of community (or market) support and understanding. Organizations, like maple trees, also have their own predictable seasonal cycles. In organizations, growth is slow, for change in one part of the organization (in one "limb" of the tree) requires changes in all other parts of the system. The growth of a small outer limb, for instance, requires growth of the supporting branch and the main trunk. Even limbs on the other side of the tree must grow at a corresponding rate to keep the tree in balance.

All of the elements (roots, trunk, branches, leaves) of the maple tree were there when it was a very small tree.. Each of these elements is replicated again and again as the tree grows larger; in this way, the maple tree (and "maple tree organization") are very orderly. However, these replicated elements remain distinctly different; a maple tree leaf would never be mistaken for a maple tree root. In this way, the maple tree and maple tree organization are diverse and, in some sense, chaotic. Maple tree organizations gradually change their structure as they grow, another sign of chaos. They move through rejuvenating and predictable cycles of birth, death, and rebirth, however, in response to seasonal changes in the weather; in this way they remain orderly. They remain viable for long periods of time, though they are vulnerable to major short-term changes because they lack the flexibility to bend in the wind. Yet, even with a windstorm, roots rarely pull out; hence, even though limbs may break off, the basic root systems and trunk remain intact: the tree (or organization) survives.

On the surface, many modern organizations resembled maple trees. However, many modern organizations (unlike those from the premodern era) grew very fast and had insubstantial root systems. These organizations were quite vulnerable to short-term changes in customer needs or shifts in public funding or policy. Other modern-day organizations tended to lack coherence, having been formed with little sense of purpose or mission. These organizations might be said to lack a trunk or roots. They operate more like a set of branches stuck haphazardly in the ground, soon to wither away. As we enter the postmodern era, fewer organizations are likely to resemble maple trees. If organizations are to survive, other forms and structures will have to be invented. There are already many organizations, for instance, that resemble palm trees more than maple trees.

Palm trees, like maple trees, preserve and build on their own founding structures and processes. A "palm tree organization" differs from a maple tree organization in that growth occurs rapidly. This happens because growth of a palm tree—or palm tree organization—primarily involves the repeated replication of one specific unit, this element being a segment of the trunk. While the palm tree does have roots and is topped by branches and leaves, most of its mass consists of a long trunk simple in organic structure that remains essentially the same diameter from base to crown. Rather than replicating several differentiated elements (for example, roots and branches), as in the case of the maple tree, the palm tree's energy is focused on one element (the trunk). This replication is even more visible in the bamboo tree (a sister of the palm tree), where each segment of the trunk or stem replicates every other segment.

Organizations that grow by replication of a specific function die as a result of their own growth and success or are artificially supported beyond the point where they are of value to the environment. Many contemporary organizations (especially high-tech ones) personify the palm tree organization. They exhibit fast growth and can weather short-term changes. The palm tree can bend in the wind and can even survive a hurricane. It has a relatively short life span, however, and lacks the capacity to weather long-term changes (for example, a drought) due to a shallow root system. In a palm tree organization, the mission must be very clear, for it will be replicated again and again by means of growth.

Franchises exemplify the palm tree organization. They are extensively employed to rapidly replicate successful organizational models (such as fast-food restaurants). A recent *Fortune* magazine article (Caminiti, 1991, p. 126) pointed to the development of franchises in more than sixty different industries in the United States and reported that the International Franchise Association in Washington, D.C., "devotes 139 pages to franchise listings as diverse as accounting and tax services, pet care centers, and vitamin and mineral stores." More than nine thousand franchised companies have been opened by McDonald's (fast food) and more than three thousand by 7-Eleven Stores (convenience shopping). We can also point to the tendency of many high-technology firms to spin off new ventures that replicate the same structure and manufacturing processes of the parent company.

The palm tree organization can be very successful for a short period of time. It is a type of organization, however, that tends to have a very short organizational memory. It lives in the present and finds little need to understand the past or future, given that it is simply replicating past history again and again, and that it probably will not have much of a future. The founder of one of these organizations—a high-tech company—recently reflected on the experience of working in this type of organization. He suggested that the conflict-oriented, high-stress environment in which he works

> is caused in part by too great a vision; too large an
> opportunity. We are looking at being a billion-dollar
> corporation in just three years. This means everyone
> is thinking big. It also means we do not focus on our
> relationships today, but constantly project them into

the future with all its complexities. . . . We have
avoided creating and recognizing culture. Instead we
talk in ambiguous terms about what we want it to be
in the future. This approach adds chaos to the twenty
new people we are adding every week. These people
then create their own small autonomous group.

We may find in the postmodern era that organizational prototypes other than the maple or palm tree will become prevalent.
Perhaps we will find banyan tree organizations that are very big and
very old, yet can set down new trunks and new roots as they spread
out. The premodern Catholic church and many contemporary international organizations have been successful in part because, like
banyan trees, they possess the ability to expand and grow by establishing deep, culturally sensitive roots in a variety of cultures and
socioeconomic settings. Other postmodern organizations may resemble grasses rather than trees. In some ways, these organizations
will resemble unsuccessful modern organizations that operated like
maple tree branches stuck in the ground. The new postmodern
organizations, hopefully, will take root and proliferate in small
clusters or consortia. They will be temporary in nature, with short
growing seasons. However, each year (or several times each year),
these organizations will reappear (like county fairs or Christmas
tree lots) with full vitality.

Some organizations begin and stay in balance through the
limitation of growth by accretion and death. Palm trees and grass
exemplify this type of system. Other organizations—like maple trees
or banyan trees—remain relatively stable and live for many years.
The shape of an organization is determined by its origins, whether
the organization resembles a palm tree or a maple tree. A maple tree
organization's structure and dynamics are determined by its previous growth. The founding of a maple tree organization is extremely important, defining (in a highly resistant manner) the
future culture, processes, structures, and purposes of this organization. The initial definition of form and characteristics of the palm
tree organization is just as important because the basic, founding
mission and structure of this organization is replicated again and
again as the organization grows in a rapid manner. Thus, regardless

of the organizational form, basic founding structures and processes remain intact.

Even as the organization grows in size and scope and becomes more finely differentiated (with an increasing number of subsystems and increased hierarchy and specialization), the various subsystems continue to replicate or mirror the major features and dynamics of the whole system and (most important) of the original system. As Bateson (1979) noted, there is a profound difference between changing the form or character of an organization and trying to change the specific actions of that organization. The latter is relatively easy; the former is very difficult, whether that organization is like a maple tree, a palm tree, a banyan tree, or the grass under our feet.

Several important lessons can be derived from this cyclical perspective. First, we must be very careful in starting new organizations, for the structures and processes that are initially established will be very resistant to later change. Second, we should recognize that while the deeply embedded patterns (subsystem mirroring) of an organization provide one type of order, short-term (seasonal) and long-term (stage) changes inevitably result in a second type of order. These changes produce chaos over the short term but order over the long run. Seasonal and stage-level changes can only be avoided if leaders of organizations choose stagnation over vitality, thereby shortening the life of their organizations.

Finally, a cyclical model of organizational life teaches us— as do many other postmodern concepts—that organizational reality is determined, at least in part, by the perspectives one takes rather than by the organizational phenomenon being observed. In any organization there is good reason to find both order and chaos. We must choose what we want to see and why. This is one of the major challenges facing the postmodern leader.

Chapter 10

The Intersect Organization: Living with Ambiguous Boundaries

In the twentieth century many societies have witnessed the development of "peculiar" organizations which did not fall into any of the well-recognized categories. They are not quite government, although they are usually the result of some kind of government action. They are not quite business, although they perform many business functions. They are not quite educational or charitable organizations either, though they may also perform some of these functions. They frequently occupy "cracks" or interstices in the organizational structure of society. They have been named "intersects" because they have some qualities of more than one conventional type of organization.

Kenneth E. Boulding
"Intersects: The Peculiar Organizations,"
in *Challenge to Leadership*

Postmodern organizations have great potential not only because of their hybrid characteristics (1973) but also because so many of them are what Boulding calls "intersect" organizations. This new status holds out great promise for an organization's ability to solve long-standing problems in our society; yet, the intersect organization also is subject to "troubling ambiguity." In this chapter, both the promise and problems of the intersect organization are explored.

Many contemporary human service agencies in the United States exemplify Boulding's intersect organization. An innovative California community college district operates a geothermal greenhouse project (funded by the California Energy Commission) in cooperation with one of the counties in its region and owns an environmental refuge, which has been deeded with the provisos that certain structural maintenance be observed and that it also be used for instructional projects. An urban hospital in Northern California began as an elitist institution primarily serving upper-class clients. Its founding doctors remained splendidly isolated from the social changes of the 1960s and 1970s; however, as this institution enters the 1990s, the isolation can no longer hold up. The boundaries have fallen. According to one of its staff members government regulations dictate what kind of patients must be served by the hospital. The state of California mandates that certain measures be taken to make the hospital earthquake proof. The hospital has also experienced some financial problems. "When [the founding physicians] had their leather chair meeting recently, they discovered that the patients were not coming back and the bank balance was also getting low. The patients were going across the street [to another hospital that offered higher-quality service at lower costs]. . . . The word is out that we are broke and [the owners of the hospital] across the street made an offer to rescue us."

This hospital has suddenly become an intersect organization. It is now both private and public, receiving funds from both individual patients and government subsidies. It is also both a service organization and a business that must break even (if not turn a profit). Like a college in New York state that runs a roller rink or a human service agency in Illinois that provides corporate services, this hospital must find a way to generate revenues while retaining its commitment to providing quality services.

Many health insurance and health maintenance companies are intersect organizations, by Boulding's definition. They operate on behalf of the public—monitoring medical or dental costs, reviewing the performance of professionals in the field—and, as a result, often obtain not-for-profit tax status. These same companies, however, are run like for-profit businesses and often attempt to influence federal and state legislation through lobbying efforts that typify for-profit companies. These health-oriented companies also often look more like governmental regulatory agencies than either for-profit or not-for-profit organizations. They may control costs and determine the nature of appropriate licensing for the provision of certain professional services (through withholding payment for services by unqualified personnel).

Kaiser Permanente was one of the first of these intersect health organizations. Founded as a combination health delivery system and health insurance program, Kaiser has blazed the trail for many of the other health maintenance organizations (HMOs) in the United States. Kaiser is a classic intersect, being both a delivery and insurance organization, and both a human service agency and private business. The Delta Dental Insurance Companies in the United States provide yet another example of an intersect organization in the health field. Most states have a Delta Insurance plan that covers payments for dental services. Delta Dental is a nonprofit organization that makes a profit; excess funds are placed in reserve or given as bonuses to management staff. In many ways, Delta Dental operates like a private insurance company, having a very active marketing and advertising program; yet, it also operates as a quasi-governmental regulatory agency, given that it controls the cost of dental care by only reimbursing member dentists a specified amount of money for specific dental services.

Some intersect organizations (for example, regional transit districts) serve as buffers and mediators between conflicting organizations, while other intersect organizations (for example, Amtrak) serve as quasi-governmental agencies that run utility, transportation, or communication systems. The Small Projects Assistance (SPA) program fosters collaboration between the Agency for International Development (AID) and the Peace Corps, at both the field and headquarters levels. According to Jim Patterson, a former SPA manager, "This collaborative program . . . support[s] small, self-help projects occurring at the community level and [does] so with a minimum of red tape. The program supports these projects through a combination of grants and technical assistance. . . . To initiate a program, during each year the Peace Corps Country Director and the AID Mission Director negotiate an agreement which states the level of funding and details the review and evaluation process."

While the Peace Corps and AID share a similar identification with a specific country or geographic region, their operations tend to be focused on different modes of technical assistance. SPA, according to Patterson, "operates best at the intersection of sectors, such as raising fish for food, for protein, and for income." Representatives of both the Peace Corps and AID begin to conceive of the problems they face in more holistic fashion when SPA is working effectively with both agencies. In the case of SPA, not only is the agency itself an intersect organization—serving in some ways as a private, highly flexible consulting firm and in other ways as a government agency—it is also an agency that works primarily between other organizations and encourages these other organizations to spend more of their own time and resources in the intersect, where most pressing and enduring societal problems seem to exist in our postmodern world.

Another of these quasi-governmental agencies, which I will call Centrix, operates, according to manager Ed Cole, as a

joint powers agency established to provide personnel and management services to public and nonprofit organizations. It is a "cross-over" organization. It is public, but received no public funding; consequently, it is entrepreneurial. It is not in the business of profit but since its existence is not supported by statute or funding, it is highly concerned with long-term financial stability and financial health to support expansion as needed. . . . Even though public, Centrix faces similar issues to private organizations: client satisfaction, efficiency, market analysis, etc.

Centrix finds its market niche through the size and complexity of its client organizations. Some are small and unsophisticated in the area of personnel management, yet have employees, boards, publics, or simply the laws of the land which require some sophistication. Centrix can provide that. Others are large and complex and have difficulty reacting to immediate needs. Centrix is both small and uncomplicated by typical political processes, consequently can provide a nimbleness otherwise unavailable to the client.

Centrix, like SPA, works at the intersect between other organizations and the government. It is entrepreneurial and, like SPA, can provide rapid response and cut through red tape, the classic advantages of many intersect organizations. Many other joint powers administration organizations similarly operate in a flexible, intersect manner.

Privatization and the Intersect Organization

In part, the proliferation and growth of intersect organizations are indicative of the recognition that government agencies are unable to meet many of the pressing needs of our society. A multigenerational example of this can be found in a comparison between federal legislation proposed in 1955 by Albert Gore, a senator from Tennessee, for a new interstate highway system and similar legislation proposed in the 1991 U.S. Senate by his son, Albert Gore, Jr., for a new interstate "information highway" (fiber-optic cables). Whereas the first Senator Gore was able to obtain massive federal dollars for this extraordinary undertaking, the younger Senator (now Vice President) Gore requested "a dollop of federal dollars—just $2 billion over five years—to catalyze a much larger investment by a wide variety of private companies" (Coy, 1991b). There are insufficient federal funds to support such an effort. The federal money requested by Albert Gore, Jr., would be used primarily for research on ways to employ and interconnect supercomputers as well as on how to upgrade existing networks. Ironically, at the end of the modern emphasis on bigness, we have gotten "too big for our britches" and can no longer solve major technical (let alone social) problems without the help of many different organizations operating out of many different sectors of society.

The turn toward private industry in support of public projects has also been precipitated by a growing disenchantment with the ways business is done in the public sector. New solutions are being sought to old, unrelenting organizational problems in public agencies. The demands of citizens—for affordable health care and housing, for safe streets and efficient courts—are becoming clearer and more persistent; yet these demands are often contradictory and cannot be readily addressed by one large, bureaucratic agency.

Furthermore, public institutions rarely have sufficient resources or expertise to address the need for health care, housing, and safety, and current employees in these bureaucratized organizations often resist and have acquired few skills that are relevant to these needs. Government administrators are asked to become more collaborative in dealings with their employees and with various public interest groups. College faculty are asked to begin marketing their services. Elected officials are asked to justify their personal expenses.

Often it is because governmental agencies are unwilling or unable to provide adequate services that new intersect organizations have emerged. These organizations are small, highly flexible, and efficient. City governments are now contracting with private organizations for fire protection, criminal detention facilities, waste disposal, education—and even, potentially, energy.

> The Public Utility Regulatory Policies Act of 1978 opened up the utility industry to competition from nonutility generating companies—cogenerators, alternative energy producers. But that was only half the matter. Unless Congress also opened electric power transmission lines to outside competition, the independent producers were still limited in how freely they could compete for markets.
>
> What many independent power producers wanted was the right to sell their output not just to the utility in whose territory they operated, but also to other customers on other systems beyond.
>
> Early this year President Bush made open transmission access a part of his national energy strategy. It would break up the monopoly once and for all and make the electrical transmission industry fully competitive for the first time in its history [Cook, 1991b, p. 122].

As early as 1969, Drucker predicted the coming "privatization" of governmental agencies. Twenty years later, he (1989, pp. 63, 65) observed that

> A government activity can work only if it is a monopoly. It cannot function if there are other ways to do the job, that is, if there is competition. . . . [If] there are alternative ways to provide the same service, government flounders.
>
> Government can do well only if there are no political pressures. The Post Office and the railroads did well as long as they had a simple purpose. But very soon, perhaps inevitably, the pressure builds to misuse such services to create employment, and especially employment for people who otherwise would find it hard to get jobs. . . . And as soon as a government activity has more than one purpose, it degenerates.

Thus, there is an increasing need for new kinds of organizations that blend the governmental mandates for the provision of public services with the private capacity to offer these services in a cost-effective manner. These organizations hold the potential for major change in our society, yet they are going to be difficult to establish, especially if they are created out of the existing modern-day organizations of our society. Resistance to change is likely to be great as we address the substantial problems associated with the unclear boundaries of the intersect organization and as we attempt to address the complex forms this type of organization is likely to engender.

Working in the Intersect Organization

Intersect organizations require new modes of communication and leadership. A bottom-line mentality is typically not appropriate in the intersect organization. Conversations must be held about other matters, and the conversations themselves (across traditional organizational boundaries) often are the only forms of influence that exist when moving across the intersect (as in the efforts of one sovereign nation to influence the internal politics of another). Organizations no longer (if they ever did) exist simply to make money for their owners or stockholders. This is an inadequate mission for any organization, especially one with diffuse or highly flexible boundaries. In essence, a bottom-line mentality tends to hide or distort the founding or driving purpose of the institution and leaves it directionless in a rapidly changing world. Drucker (1989, p. 230) concludes that "neither the quantity of output nor the 'bottom line' is by itself an adequate measure of the performance of management and enterprise." Senge (1990, pp. 147–148) similarly notes that a primary emphasis on profit in an organization diminishes the vision of the organization and leads to a focus on means rather than ends.

> Many senior executives . . . choose "high market share" as part of their vision. But why? "Because I want our company to be profitable." Now, you might think that high profits is an intrinsic result in and of itself, and indeed it is for some. But for surprisingly many other leaders, profits too are a means toward a still more important result. Why choose high annual profit? "Because I want us to remain an independent company, to keep from being taken over." Why do you want that? "Because I want to keep our integrity and our capacity to be true to our purpose in starting the organization." While all the goals mentioned are legitimate, the last—being true to our purpose—has the greatest intrinsic significance to this executive. All the rest are means to the end, means which might change in particular circumstances.

The natural gas division of a large oil company exemplifies this issue. The company moved during the past decade into the business of producing not only gasoline and motor oil but also natural gas. Its natural gas division addressed the issue of diffuse boundaries and potentially unclear mission by focusing on the needs of its customers and by emphasizing the processes of the organization—specifically, employee involvement and teamwork. This division connects with the parent corporation and its emphasis on oil production and profit by looking behind short-term and limited visions to the underlying founding vision of the corporation, which the division believes has to do with service to the customer and the preservation of quality.

Whether or not this admirable attempt to uncover and recommit to the founding mission of the corporation is successful must await further developments in this division. One manager summarized her sense of the company's future in a postmodern world in the following way:

> As we move into the twenty-second century, [this] corporation will work hard to keep its place near the top of the Fortune 500 list of biggest companies in the United States. For the last two years we have been working under a . . . slogan that says we will be "Better than the Best." The slogan has been the source of some derision since no one but the Nifty Fifty top executives in the company are sure what "Better than the Best" might look like. One thing that happens in BIG companies: it is very hard to communicate throughout the organization. Most thoughts, ideas, passions, concerns get caught somewhere in the middle. And there are a lot of "middles" in a corporation of 50,000 plus employees.

She goes on to suggest that as a strategy getting bigger may not make the company "Better than the Best." The "Nifty Fifty" must be able to handle the ambiguity inherent in an intersect organization, as well as be certain that their mission is clear to all employees. They must be prepared for change and not just react to it when it happens.

Boulding indicates that the problems of measurement and evaluation associated with the intersect organization will become even more common in the future. When these problems of measurement in intersects are compounded with measurement problems induced by size, it is not hard to understand the postmodern emphasis on relativistic social and organizational values and its skepticism regarding clearly perceived and measured "realities." The new "reality" in the intersect organization is the communication that occurs among members of the various constituencies incorporated within and served by the organization.

Boulding suggests that the "peculiar" intersect organizations must be led and managed in ways somewhat different from those of their more traditional modern counterparts. This holds further implications for the nature and function of communication that occurs in these organizations. First, the managers of intersects typically have one or more governing boards to contend with and a set of competing values and visions for the organization. The United States Post Office, for instance, was set free in 1970 by the Postal Reorganization Act and was to start operating more like a business, that is, becoming increasingly efficient and cost conscious. Yet, the Post Office is not like other businesses, in that the 1970 law "is loaded with protections designed to keep the service from abusing its monopoly position. . . . [The Postal Reorganization Act] made it difficult to respond to competitive threats from newer forms of telecommunications. Postal executives have neither the freedom nor the accountability of private sector managers. 'I'm the only CEO of a major corporation in America who doesn't have control over his own prices,' [Postmaster] Frank notes. Rate changes must be approved first by the President-appointed Postal Rate Commission, then by the Board of Governors" (Lewyn, 1991, p. 56).

While Postmaster Frank is in the same boat as many utility CEOs, he experiences the unique pressures of many intersect leaders in that he must be responsive to public concerns about prices while also trying to compete in a field with private sector industries with much more freedom to invest in research and development and to explore alternative modes of communication. As Frank himself admits, the Post Office is affected by many different constituencies and the turmoil of conflicting public interests, the typical environment for intersect organizations.

If postmodern organizations must have clear missions yet are also likely to have unclear boundaries, then leaders of intersect organizations must devote a considerable amount of time to communicating about the mission and to building a consensus regarding mission and goals among diverse constituencies and governing board members. According to Boulding, this means that intersect managers need mediation and negotiation skills; traditional decision-making and problem-solving processes of a rational or linear nature will not be of much use. New modes of mediation and compromise must be used by Postmaster Frank and his intersect compatriots if they are to find ways to make the post office and other intersect organizations responsive to changing communication technologies and changing public demands for accountability.

Goodman and Loveman (1991) suggest yet another central issue in the management of intersect organizations—or more precisely, in their case, public functions that have been privatized. There must be a blending of public interest and private benefit. They note that "neither public nor private managers will always act in the best interests of their shareholders. Privatization will be effective only if private managers have incentives to act in the public interest, which includes, but is not limited to, efficiency" (p. 28). Thus, if an intersect leader is to be effective, he or she must be given the freedom (found in private sector organizations) to manipulate the reward systems within the organization to achieve results.

Goodman and Loveman also suggest that "profits and the public interest overlap best when the privatized service or asset is in a competitive market. It takes competition from other companies to discipline managerial behavior" (1991, p. 28). In the case of the United States Post Office, the competition comes not from competing post offices but from companies that sell other modes of communication. Unfortunately, the Post Office can't compete in these other communication domains, hence it doesn't really have either direct competitors to keep it honest and disciplined or the freedom to increase effectiveness by moving into related fields (as in the case of Clorox, Wells Fargo, or the Keystone Valve Company). Goodman and Loveman seem to anticipate the problems encountered by the Post Office when they go on to suggest that "when these conditions [incentives and competition] are not met, continued governmental involvement will likely be necessary. The simple transfer of ownership from public to private hands will not necessarily reduce the cost or enhance the quality of services" (p. 28).

Many intersect organizations other than the United States Post Office are likely to face the challenges posed by Boulding and Goodman and Loveman. As one of the earliest health management organizations and intersect organizations, Kaiser Permanente struggles with the ongoing problems of complex and conflicting societal demands and the related problems of appropriate employee incentives and disciplined management. According to one Kaiser manager:

> Kaiser is a very fragmented institution in that there is no common goal throughout its distinctly different areas. It is as if it is two different organizations, holding together in a symbiotic relationship for profit, while pretending to be a nonprofit organization. The two different halves of the whole are the doctors and hospitals and the health plan which sells the memberships and generates the revenue which supports the hospitals. The two sides are constantly battling with each other for control of the organization and for the financial backing of expenditures from the common budget. This power struggle is at the crux of all important decisions.

The dual functions of Kaiser are not easily reconciled. On the one hand, the public image of this organization is critical. Television commercials portray caring physicians and personal service. Customer service education classes are offered for all employees. On the other hand, according to this same manager, "doctors have quotas of patients that they must see daily in order for the organization to remain viable financially. The focus is on quantity rather than quality. Ultimately the member is bound to be disillusioned when the effort is placed on public relations rather than improved personal service."

Another health maintenance (and intersect) organization—U.S. Healthcare—has taken a somewhat different approach by emphasizing disease prevention and detection programs and cost controls rather than marketing and patient volume (as seems to be the case with Kaiser Permanente). "According to Ken Abramowitz of Sanford C. Bernstein in New York City, medical costs eat up 82% of the premium income for a typical publicly held HMO. But U.S. Healthcare has squeezed its ratio down to 78%, freeing up millions of dollars for expansion—new offices, more marketing. . . . The premium they pay per insured employee has gone up a mere 13%

annually since 1986, compared with 20% for traditional insurance plans" (Rice, 1991b, p. 94).

U.S. Healthcare has been a leader in sponsoring cholesterol screening and breast cancer risk assessment, thereby increasing the possibility of early detection of illness (and reducing attendant medical expenses). It also has been structured with more diffuse boundaries than Kaiser Permanente, with primary care physicians being hired as independent contracters who treat patients for a flat annual charge per person. U.S. Healthcare closely monitors the practices of their member physicians (thereby breaking down another traditional barrier) in order to keep down costs and increase quality and provides bonuses to doctors with high patient ratings. As Goodman and Loveman suggest, this intersect organization is successful in part because of its incentives and the disciplined management that comes with competition. While U.S. Healthcare acts like other insurance companies in providing its members with assurance that their health care needs will be met, regardless of the nature and extent of the illness, it—like Kaiser Permanente—participates actively in the ongoing medical practices for which the insurance pays, thereby ensuring quality care. Unlike Kaiser, U.S. Healthcare has adopted the postmodern strategy of dropping traditional boundaries in medical care and has, as a result, produced a high-quality, low-cost health care program.

In addition to the ongoing problems of management associated with an intersect organization, Boulding proposes that intersect managers are likely to experience the problem of measurement with regard to program outcomes. The outcomes of intersect organizations are inherently complex and ambiguous: "Almost every human activity produces both goods and bads, and whether the activity itself is justified depends on whether the goods outweigh the bads. Thus, if an organization increases the GNP, which is good up to a point, but increases pollution, which is bad, or if it diminishes conflicts, which is good, but makes income more inequal, which may be good or bad depending on where one puts the optimum, how are we to add all these up in a final evaluation?" (Boulding, 1973, p. 192).

At the heart of this complexity and ambiguity of outcomes is the tendency of most intersect organizations to be primarily in the business of producing services—and, at an even more basic level, communication—rather than widgets or automobiles. While all postmodern organizations are likely to be in the business of providing some services—even manufacturing firms now realize they will only be successful if they can provide follow-up services (information, consultation, maintenance, and repair)—the intersect organization is particularly directed toward service. The traditional barriers in an organization are usually lowered not because an organization can't manufacture some product but because this product must be linked to other products. Intersects work primarily through the provision of information, which is in essence a service function. Such functions cannot easily be measured. As noted in a recent *Business Week* (Armstrong and Symonds, 1991, p. 100) article, "In many cases, the hard part in improving quality in services is the fleeting nature of the product. 'You can't use the traditional manufacturing tools to measure it or inspect it before you deliver it,' says James A. McEleny, vice-president for corporate quality improvement at Chicago & North Western Transportation Company. 'Our employees create it, and then it disappears.' "

In addition to the problem of measurement associated with the nature of customer service, Armstrong and Symonds point to another key feature of service-oriented businesses that brings us immediately back to the issue of management in an intersect organization: "The word 'employees' is key here. 'What management needs to understand is that it isn't in charge of customer satisfaction,' says Gunneson President Stanley M. Cherkasky. 'It's the employee who talks to the customer.' This has alarming implications. It means that employees have to like their jobs, probably a lot more than they do now. They'll also need more authority. . . . Making this work means hiring, training, and keeping the right employees—not exactly hallmarks of most . . . companies" (Armstrong and Symonds, 1991, p. 100).

The intersect organization demands not only that its leaders be able to negotiate across traditional boundaries and to measure and live with ambiguous signs of success; they must also work effectively with and empower those men and women they supervise. This, in turn, requires a new way of thinking of organizations: new definitions of leadership, new modes of communication in the organization, and, in particular, a new level of tolerance for the many ambiguities inherent in the intersect organization.

Commitment, Faith, and Doubt in the Intersect Organization

The postmodern world—and, in particular, the intersect organization—is one that demands a relativistic perspective. The days of good and bad, right and wrong, are behind us. We are now living with the troubling ambiguity of organizations that are partially public and partially private—that are simultaneously for-profit and not-for-profit. Who knows if these were ever appropriate perspectives. All that we do know is that they no longer work. We have no ground on which to stand that is firm and familiar. We need faith, yet find cause for doubt everywhere. We know that leadership requires faith and some sense of confidence, yet we also know that it would be naive and destructive to pretend certitude about that which is constantly changing and unpredictable.

What are the implications of constructivist thinking and postmodern theory for taking action in an intersect organization—or, more generally, in a world that is fluid and in which ethics are situational and elusive? William Perry's (1970) description of the movement from relativism to a commitment in relativism offers us some insight into this process. Perry suggests that many mature men and women move from a way of thinking ("dualism") in which everything is either black or white, good or bad, right or wrong, clear or unclear to a way of thinking ("relativism") in which there are rights and wrongs, goods and bads, that exist within a specific framework or community of belief and that are not universal. Thus, within a specific scientific community, certain postulates are accepted as valid and are subject to rules of verification that have been formulated by that specific community. Yet, in another scientific community a different set of postulates is accepted and a different set of rules is followed in efforts to verify these hypotheses. Thus, in each of these communities there are "truths" but in neither can truth be claimed as universal or all encompassing.

What are the appropriate responses to this condition? Perry suggests that the typical response is a turning to "multiplicity," in which we conclude that since there is no one right way or moral way to do things, then any old way is acceptable as long as we don't get caught. A skeptical or cynical posture provides some shelter against the postmodern storm. At least we will never be fooled or made to believe in something that is ultimately found to be inadequate or dead wrong.

Multiplistic thinking is certainly compatible with life in an intersect world. It is based on the assumption of multiple truths and multiple realities, each of which is equally valid. The dominance of one truth or reality over another depends not on the extent to which any one of them is more compatible in some sense with some ultimate truth or reality—for there is no ultimate anything. Rather, truth and reality are defined by less rational forces involving governments, political pressure, social and economic power, and subtle media-based coercion. We need not worry, therefore, about who is right; rather we must worry about who is in charge and what they believe is the truth and reality. A new "golden rule" applies for the multiplist: "he who has the gold makes the rule (and defines reality)!"

Perry suggests another response to the problems of a relativistic world. This is the response he calls "commitment in relativism." This response requires the willingness to take a risk and make a commitment to something, despite the fact that there are alternative truths and realities that can make viable claims on our sense of the world. At this point, Perry moves beyond the line of argument found among most constructionists. He writes of the need for mature men and women to make decisions and take stands in the face of this relativism. We must make commitments while living in a relativistic world. In order to be able to do this, Perry suggests that we need courage and the capacity for self-reflection. Courage is needed because both dualism and relativism without commitment enable one to avoid anxiety.

Dualism, as Fromm (1941) noted years ago, enables us to "escape from freedom," whereas relativism without commitment allows us to float above the fray (Kundera's, 1984, "lightness of being") and avoid making the tough decisions. If we can simplify the world by embracing dualism and sorting things into goods and bads, then we can avoid ambiguity and the difficulty of making decisions with incomplete knowledge and unclear guidelines. If we can hold a relativistic stance, then we need never make decisions or commitments. We are breathtaking in our clever and often cynical social analyses. We are brilliant Monday morning quarterbacks regarding politics, corporate decision making, and our parents' child-raising strategies. Because we ourselves never have to make decisions, we can successfully criticize those who do.

When we face the complex and changing conditions of living and working in an intersect organization—more generally, when we face the postmodern edge of order and chaos—and when we are willing to make decisions and commitments within the context of these postmodern conditions, then we have made an "existential leap" of faith (Kierkegaard, 1980) and have found what Merleau-Ponty (quoted in Prigogine and Stengers, 1984, p. 299) has described as a "truth within the situation":

> So long as I keep before me the ideal of an absolute observer, of knowledge in the absence of any viewpoint, I can only see my situation as being a source of error. But once I have acknowledged that through it I am geared to all actions and all knowledge that are meaningful to me, and that it is gradually filled with everything that may *be* for me, then my contact with the social in the finitude of my situation is revealed to me as the starting point of all truth . . . and, since we have some idea of the truth, since we are inside truth and cannot get outside it, all that I can do is define a truth within the situation.

The movement to commitment—to a truth within the situation—requires courage and a willingness to encounter an unknown and unknowable world in order to do the best job possible with the information and perspectives that we do have.

Once this first difficult commitment is made, a bit of increased self-knowledge often comes along. We find a new level of appreciation for our parents, our bosses, and even our national leaders when we first discover how difficult it is to make good choices in a relativistic world. With increased self-knowledge, we become somewhat more comfortable about making commitments and adopting a style of operating that leaves options open for an appropriate period of time and that moves the intersect decision maker to commitment. Even after the decision is made, the committed relativist remains open to alternative perspectives that could lead to a modification in this decision and follows up the decision with feedback on the effects of this decision. Chris Argyris and Donald Schön (1974) propose that the most effective decision makers are not men and women who avoid making mistakes but men and women who learn from their mistakes and do not continue to repeat them. By assuming the role of learner, the committed relativist effectively confronts the ambiguity and often immobilizing anxiety associated with the postmodern, constructionist view of reality essential in virtually any intersect organization.

What then becomes the nature of certainty and commitment within an intersect organization, given this relativistic framework? The key seems to lie in an emphasis on the process of knowing and inquiring rather than on the outcome or product of the search for knowledge or inquiry. Alfred North Whitehead first spoke of such an orientation in his portrayal of a theology of process; in this sense, he was one of the first postmodernists. According to Whitehead, God is changing along with everything else—much as some scientists are now hypothesizing that the basic laws of the universe may themselves be changing over time. Anderson (1990, p. 210) suggests that in Whitehead's universe "there is no ultimate reality to which things happen, and consequently we don't need—in fact should be on guard against—the absolutes we make up to describe ultimate reality. Whitehead, agreeing with the American pragmatist philosophers such as William James, with whom he had made common cause, thought that the 'intolerant use of abstractions is the major vice of the intellect.'"

For Whitehead, James, and many contemporary feminist philosophers and psychologists (for example, Gilligan, 1982; Belenky and others, 1986), truth must always be viewed within its particular context and with regard to its purpose and use. Thus, one must examine not only the outcomes of one's deliberations but also the methods and purposes that defined this deliberation. The postmodern deconstructionists encourage us to look at the words and sequencing of words as well as the message conveyed by the words. Whitehead and his process-oriented colleagues similarly encourage us to look past the outcomes of thought to the thought process itself.

In essence, an intersect world of relativity and process requires that we find and manifest courage. We must confront the issues of faith and doubt in such a way as to lead to commitment. Courage, in turn, is to be found only when we have found some understanding of and have properly nurtured our own inner life. Courage comes when we have been successful in integrating the disparate elements of our selves. John Sanford (1977) suggests that the successful man is not someone who is able to achieve perfection (or who thinks he has achieved perfection by repressing aspects of himself). Rather he is someone who has acknowledged and integrated all aspects of himself, including those parts that are not very mature or even acceptable to our personal sense of the ideal self.

Chapter 11

The Turbulent
Organization:
Navigating
the Warped
Plane

> Ask not that events should happen as you will, but let your
> will be that events should happen as they do, and you shall
> have peace.
>
> —Epictetus

Premodern organizations typically experienced gradual, simple growth, which could be readily anticipated and incorporated within the already existing structures and processes of the organization—perhaps with the help of an expanding family (additional children, sons-in-law, daughters-in-law, grandchildren). Many premodern organizations had an agricultural base; hence, changes in their operations were seasonal. In general, formal paternal authority was the only ingredient needed to bring about a desired change in premodern times. Employees (usually children, spouse, or hired hand) did what they were told to do, rather than what they might personally have liked to do. The chains of external constraint were dominant in the premodern era (Foucault, 1965).

In the premodern world of little change, minimal planning was required. Operations continued in the same manner for many years. The needs of customers changed very slowly and were readily understood and predicted by the leaders of the organization. In those instances when the external environment was not kind to the premodern organization (droughts, insects, military invasion), the response was typically one of endurance and persistence. To the extent that these catastrophic events could be anticipated or prophesied (as in the case of the biblical figure Joseph), then the response was typically one of building a reserve (food storage, inventory of goods) to help the organization weather the difficult times. This "reserve mentality" is still with us today as a remnant of premodern planning (Galbraith, 1977). In some instances, it works very effectively. Yet as contemporary American farmers are painfully aware, the policy of reserve can also create many problems and is rarely adequate to meet the demands being placed on organizations by the turbulent external environments we now face.

While change in the premodern world was nonexistent or gradual, change in the modern world often could be planned and "managed." Even change that was not planned tended to be predictable and was typically understood by those who managed the organization. The rate of change accelerated during the modern era, as Toffler (1971) told us two decades ago. He warned that many men and women in our society have not yet acknowledged the exceptional changes that have taken place since the 1930s. We are like sleepwalkers who are not cognizant of large and obvious shifts in the very core of our existence. Toffler believed that the later stages of the modern era have been among the most exciting periods in human history; yet he acknowledged that the accelerating rate of change during this period of time was quite threatening to many people. According to Toffler, people simply were unable to internalize the implications of the rapid change they saw occurring all around them. They did not see how it would influence their own life goals and living conditions.

Toffler suggested that much of the modern-day acceleration of change was initially driven by new technologies, though like many futurists of the later stages of the modern era, he believed that enduring changes come not from the technology, per se, but rather from the ways in which new technology alters our way of perceiving and acting in the world. Anticipating the more relativistic perspectives of the postmodern era, Toffler proposed that our basic ways of conceiving our society and our organizations—and our role in social institutions—were unalterably changed. These changes, in turn, have set the stage for a new, more diverse image of society, which serves as a foundation for the emerging postmodern era.

At about the same time, Donald Schön (1971) described a similar state with regard to modern society. According to Schön, most members of modern society believed that a stable state existed and that critical aspects of their lives would be constant and not subject to radical change. They also assumed that modern society could attain such a state of constancy. Schön suggested that this belief is strong and deep within us and that this belief is deeply embedded in every aspect of our society. We may talk a good game about change, but we still define our world in terms that are modern or even premodern in nature. Schön indicated that this belief is central because it protects us against uncertainty and the threats inherent in change. According to Schön, the later stages of the modern era loosened the anchors of personal and societal identity. These anchors have been pulled loose and our sense of self is now often unstable and, in the words of Christopher Lasch (1984), diminished in size. With all the anxiety associated with accelerated change and with our resistance to the undoing of a stable state, the rate of acceleration in the modern world has generally been rather steady and predictable. As both Toffler and Schön suggest, we could prepare for this accelerating change and make it work for us rather than against us.

Hovering on the brink of the postmodern era, our contemporary organizations have, as both Toffler and Schön noted, experienced remarkable changes. A hospital administrator at a suburban, west coast facility, for instance, describes an acceleration in the rate of change in her organization: "our rate of change . . . is consistent in that we're 'always' changing, adding, growing. Long-term planning used to be three years; now it's six months to one year." Another manager uses more poetic terms in describing the rate of change in his military unit: "Since the fall of the Berlin Wall in November 1989, there was talk by elements within DOD [Department of Defense] . . . that future changes had to be made. The changes which were meant to occur had to do with budget cuts, reduction in civilian as well as military personnel, and reduction of equipment as well. Flexibility was definitely an asset during 1990—especially in Europe, where the rapid changes ricocheted off the crumbling East-West political barriers like laser beams in a light show."

This midlevel military manager goes on to note that this accelerating rate of change is not specific to his unit: "The changes are still being ricocheted from the highest to the lowest levels of every organization in the military, and also, to a large extent in other organizations which are nonmilitary. . . . [T]he current trends indicate that the [military] must be prepared to respond to a broad range of potential scenarios, from short contingency operations to large-scale, high-intensity wars, over the next several years."

Modern processes of organizational change are distinguished from premodern (and postmodern) not only by the accelerated rates of change but also by the very nature of the change itself. Premodern growth was usually simple, involving an expansion in the size or number of elements in the organization. Modern organizational growth, on the other hand, tends to be structural in nature, involving not just an expansion in size but also a change in the way things are done in the organization. As Toffler noted, modern technology not only increases productivity (first-order change) but also changes the way in which we perceive the organization and the basic ways in which we manage the work force in the organization (second-order structural change). As a result of this emphasis on structural change, considerable attention is given in books on management and in the work of organizational consulting to such structural domains as reporting relationships, role descriptions, the design of physical plants, and new technologies.

In keeping with this structural emphasis, modern organizations and modern society in general moved to a legalistic mode, wherein most efforts at reform took place in legislative chambers (for example, new disability acts) or courtrooms (for example, school busing)—with mixed results. Structural properties were also prominent in the modern-day emphasis on linear planning. Making extensive use of trend analyses, corporate managers were able to accurately project into the near future market shifts, changing client needs, organizational resource needs, and anticipated technological breakthroughs. The future could be reasonably predicted based on the direction and speed at which change was occurring inside the organization and the environment in which this organization was situated. Linear causality could be assumed when the leaders of a modern organization were solving problems and planning for change.

The engineering-based problem-analysis tools of Kepner and Tregoe (1981) were widely accepted for solving the structural problems of modern organizations. Scientific methods were widely employed in newly formed management information systems, which provided for systematic diagnoses of the organization's needs based on research and development. These analyses could in turn be employed in the formulation of an overall plan for structural change in the organization. The later stages of the modern era have been filled with reorganization plans, new accounting systems, modifications in personnel policies based on new governmental affirmative action guidelines, the proliferation of program auditors, and the emerging influence of legal counsels in corporate decision-making bodies.

A Turbulent World

While the modern era was characterized by accelerating change, the postmodern era is typified by a mixture of accelerated and unpredictable change, on the one hand, and gradual or nonexistent change on the other hand. We can use the metaphor of a turbulent river—with its swirling eddies, rapidly flowing water, and quiet pools—to describe the postmodern era. As we move into the postmodern era, change ceases to be predictable, either in terms of direction or speed. Change is also usually unplanned and inconsistent with regard either to direction or rate of acceleration or deceleration. Postmodern organizations are hybrids of varying forms and functions, including varying rates of change. In many instances, change is rampant; in other settings (often within the same organization), we are likely to find stagnation or even tranquility.

The Bell companies certainly can be offered as a prime example of rapidly changing organizations that have had to face and cope with a host of changes since the 1984 breakup of AT&T. Yet the Bell companies have not changed very much in certain respects. Many of the dramatic changes that were anticipated in 1984 have not taken place. Upper-level managers still make decisions in a traditional top-down manner. Many of the projects that were initiated when the Bell companies began competing against other phone companies have moved along very slowly, despite the efforts of upper management and the general public. According to a Bell manager, "We have much work ahead of us. The work will involve dividing and redoing all the systems and technologies that have been going on for some time. . . . [It will take some time before] the resources of people and technology will [be available.] We are changing, but some of these changes will take time. [Some] changes are happening fast. Others are . . . slow."

Thus in a setting in which several different changes exist side by side, we are likely to find pockets of slow change or nonchange. After the 1989 earthquake in San Francisco, for instance, many damaged buildings were immediately repaired, torn down, or even remodeled with the assistance of federal and state financial aid. Efforts to deal with other damaged structures, such as the freeway system in the Bay Area, however, have been much less successful. Environmental concerns, political pressure groups, a lack of funds, and insufficient knowledge about structural resistance to major earthquakes all have contributed to the slow movement of freeway construction in Northern California (though a recent mayoral election suddenly began to accelerate this stagnant process).

In turbulent postmodern organizations, one is faced not just with new things and new ways of doing things but with an emptiness or void. The current ways we construct our social reality (Berger and Luckmann, 1967) are no longer appropriate. We must face new ways of looking at the world (second-order change), and this usually begins by seeing nothing more than a blank wall or impenetrable haze in front of us, which can leave us terribly confused. At the heart of this demand for a profound reorientation of our perspectives on change is the need to reexamine the ways in which we understand and measure the nature and output of our organizations.

A leader at the Tensfield Corporation (a fictitious name) describes the turbulence in his organization:

> We are in the midst of turbulent changes of a social, political and economic nature. The pace of change has accelerated in the last years so much that almost nothing can be taken for granted, neither by our customers nor by our sales people who are serving them. To top it all, what [Tensfield Dynamics] is trying to do is introduce yet another change into the customers' operations and way of thinking. Like all change, the [Tensfield] one is evoking a lot of fear in our customers because of the perceived risks associated with all new things.
>
> At [the Tensfield] headquarters . . . we are involved in change. The changes are due to the torrid pace of technology developments in [our field] and our determination to remain a leader. It is also a cultural one as a freewheeling startup is struggling to bring structure to its organization. We realize that the rules we had as a twenty person company no longer work now that we are a five hundred person corporation.

On the surface, Tensfield seems like a classic case of accelerating change. Our Tensfield manager, however, observes efforts to slow down or even freeze change and defines this as a means of grappling with the turbulence and resulting chaos associated with accelerating movement in any system. "Product management by its very charter is trying to bring a layer of order into this chaos. It does this by trying to 'freeze' technology at a certain moment and conceive a product which 'meets the challenges of the marketplace by recognizing the customers' needs and desires far enough ahead of time to have the right product designed and produced.' Product management has to balance the trends in requirements with the many compromises which are necessary to make the final product both reliable, performing well and selling at a competitive, afford-able price."

This description of change at Tensfield seems to move us beyond the typical modern emphasis on structure and calls into question the adequacy of this approach, at least for turbulent orga-nizations entering the postmodern era. In the later stages of the modern era, the structural approach to organizational change has been shown to be inadequate in addressing the problems of many organizations, not just Tensfield.

Efforts to bring about change in postmodern organizations typically focus on the domains of process and attitude. Authority is not available or appropriate for most of this change, often because the change is unauthorized and takes place through the informal communication channels of the organization. This emphasis on process and attitude is a product, in part, of the accelerating and unpredictable changes that occur in most contemporary organiza-tions. This emphasis shows in the observations of west coast man-ager John Wood:

> Organizational charts are everywhere but are given lit-tle attention except when dealing with customers who seem to require those types of things. Oftentimes these charts are created, or at least the structures and title changed, to meet a particular situation. It just doesn't seem to matter too much.
>
> The "big picture," if it exists at all, must be in the [company] auditorium, behind the theater screen. I imagine that on the large wall there is a three-story-tall collage—some sections drafted on CAD systems—others drawn in crayon on lunch napkins—"lines of authority" done in yarn. All of this pinned and taped to a large felt-board so it can be easily rearranged.

Contemporary systems theorists (for example, Senge, 1990) suggest that processes (such as delay in the flow of information or resources) are just as critical to the understanding and prediction of systems behavior as are structural properties. They often prove to be more critical to improvement in the performance of an organization than are the structural properties of the feedback systems in the organization. We must also look beyond both structure and process to the domain of attitudes (Watson and Johnson, 1972) if we are to fully comprehend the dynamics of human systems and the best ways in which to influence these systems (Bergquist, 1992). Attitudes are not embedded in the structures of an organization or even in the ongoing processes of the people who work within these structures. Rather, they are embedded primarily in the culture and the climate of the organization. Modern strategies for change are ineffective in shifting either culture or attitudes (Burke, 1987). Change is likely to be quite precipitous when a shift in attitude is required of men and women in the organization. As we look to the postmodern era—and its unique challenges—attitudinal and cultural components of change must be more fully understood and addressed.

The modern emphasis on planned change—whether of structure, process, or attitude—is also subject to criticism because of its failure to recognize and plan for an equally important dimension of organizations: stabilization (Bergquist, 1992). This dimension requires an attention to organizational processes that are usually not as exciting as those associated with organizational change. These processes include reflecting on, learning from, and honoring past accomplishments. Stabilization encourages learning from past mistakes. Perhaps most important, stabilization frequently provides time and space for the essential questioning and testing of a host of implicitly held assumptions about change. This, in turn, requires the presence of temporary systems and sanctuaries where such learning, reflection, and renewal can take place. Often, change is assumed to be inherently a good thing and those who oppose the change (the remnants of the organization) are seen as necessarily off base or misinformed. This is clearly not always the case. It is often the remnant that provides the pathway to the culture and attitudes of an organization. Temporary systems and sanctuaries become even more valuable as we move into a postmodern era in which change takes on a different shape and often a different function.

Planning for change has shifted in the postmodern world toward contingency models. In place of trend analysis and linear causality, we are moving to nonlinear models of causality and to models of simultaneous interevent causality and interdependence. The clearly articulated strategies for change prevalent during the modern era become much less clear in the postmodern world, for there are now multiple changes, each influencing the other and leading to turbulent backwashes. These backwashes often represent a return to previous states of the organization, a backlash in political terms or a strange attractor in chaos theory. These multiple interacting changes also lead to a strange mixture of order ("meadows of tranquility and predictability" in the words of the ecologist Robert May) and chaos (highly complex, confusing, and unpredictable states of being). Instead of planned change and an emphasis on the structural properties of change (for example, the goals of the change effort and the overall change strategy), we are left with an emphasis on the processes of change and on attitudes about change. These, in turn, lead us to processes of trial-and-error learning or groping, organizational processes to which I now turn my attention.

Navigating a Warped Plane: Groping and Bifurcation

An adequate postmodern model of organizational life must describe the complex and often elusive processes of irreversible change that typify contemporary organizations. One of the most important (and sometimes overlooked) concepts to come out of chaos theory is the observed tendency of all fluid systems to bifurcate (split into two or more pathways). In essence, when fluid systems begin to break up (as a function of the speed at which the fluid is moving or as a result of the introduction of a foreign, intrusive element), parts of the system tend to move in different directions and to form into two or more coherent subsystems, which may later subdivide again. Thus, if I pour a small glass of water on a smooth surface (such as a table or countertop), it will tend not to flow in one direction as one coherent mass; rather, it will soon break into two or more substreams that flow in different directions across the surface of the table or countertop.

The noted biologist Conrad Waddington (1977) describes this tendency toward bifurcation in his model of *chreods,* warped planes on which objects move in an unpredictable manner. Waddington describes placing a ball at the top of a sloping plane (thin sheet of metal or plastic). If the plane is even, the ball will simply roll from the top edge to the bottom edge, roughly in a straight line. However, if we bend and warp the plane, ridges and valleys are formed (see Figure 11.1). When the ball is placed at the upper end of the warped plane, the inherent dynamics of the plane become evident. The ball will begin to roll straight down the plane until it encounters one of the ridges. At this point a series of oscillations occurs. The ball moves back and forth before it eventually begins to roll down one of the valleys and pick up speed again.

If several balls are rolling down the plane at the same time, this first ridge becomes a point of bifurcation for the entire system. Some balls will move in one direction (depending on the pattern of

Figure 11.1. A Warped Plane.

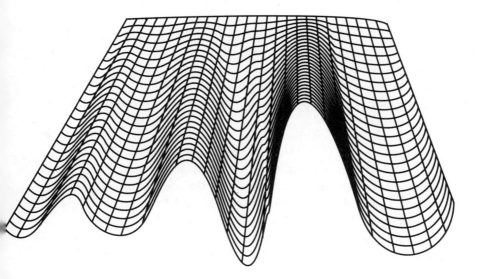

oscillation) and roll down one valley, while other balls will move in a different direction, rolling down one or more of the other valleys. A ball may gain enough momentum to roll over the top of one ridge into a second valley. If there is not sufficient momentum, the ball will remain in the current valley. Thus, a few critical moments in the life of the ball's movement down the tilted plane yield a major difference in the outcome of the ball's movement. The pattern of oscillation determines which valley is chosen and whether or not the momentum is sufficient for the ball to shift to another valley. There is a cluster of conditions (in the form of valleys and ridges) that define the specific alternative courses available to the ball.

Waddington's warped plane relates directly to the alternating patterns of chaos and order identified by chaos theorists. The tendency toward order is evident in the movement of the ball down a specific valley. Once we know which valley is chosen, we can predict the movement of the ball back and forth down this valley. In this way, the movement of the ball resembles the movement of a pendulum. Teilhard notes, in keeping with Waddington's warped plane, that there is a "predilection for what is rhythmic in events" (1955, p. 101). Events tend to occur in repetitive and cyclical form (as in the oscillation of the ball rolling down the valley). On the other hand, while there are predictable cycles that are played out in (and help to define) time, there are also random elements in any change process—the groping process that occurs in any major organizational change.

Groping refers directly to the process of oscillation that occurs immediately before the balls bifurcate and begin rolling down one of the specific valleys. Groping is a trial-and-error (oscillating) process in which many different options are examined and even tested. Teilhard (1955), Bateson (1979), and Prigogine (Prigogine and Stengers, 1984) all speak about evolution, change, and learning as a groping process, a series of binary (bifurcation) choices. Successful adaptation of any type—whether individual or organizational, reactive or creative—must always contain a random component. In essence, an organism seeking to adapt to a changing condition or environment begins by trying out a variety of behaviors. It will fluctuate in its behavior and become temporarily unpredictable, as in the case of the ball's oscillating back and forth at the top of the warped plane.

Oscillation tends to occur at a point immediately prior to an organism's transition from a stable to chaotic state and its ultimate commitment to a specific, irreversible course of action (a bifurcation). Many of these oscillating behaviors—these trial-and-error efforts—are not effective. One or two do work, however, leading the organism to expand its repertoire and to shift its regular mode of functioning to accommodate these changes. The exploratory processes—the endless trial and error of mental progress—can achieve a new state only by embarking on pathways randomly presented, some of which when tried are selected for the survival of an individual or organization. Prigogine (Prigogine and Stengers, 1984, pp. 177–178) describes this stochastic, self-organizing process as "order through fluctuation."

Toffler offers a clear summary statement regarding this model of fluctuation and bifurcation in his introduction to Prigogine and Stenger's *Order Out of Chaos* (1984, p. xv):

> In Prigoginian terms, all systems contain subsystems, which are continually "fluctuating." At times, a single fluctuation or a combination of them may become so powerful, as a result of positive feedback, that it shatters the preexisting organization. At this revolutionary moment—the authors call it a "singular moment" or a "bifurcation point"—it is inherently impossible to determine in advance which direction change will take: whether the system will disintegrate into "chaos" or leap to a new, more differentiated, higher level of "order" or organization. . . . One of the key controversies surrounding this concept has to do with Prigogine's insistence that order and organization can actually arise "spontaneously" out of disorder and chaos through a process of "self-organization."

There is increasing evidence in the few years since Toffler wrote this introduction that "self-organization" does take place and is a central feature in the understanding of any dynamic system. Fluctuation, bifurcation, and self-organization are illustrated in such macrosystems as avalanches and social revolutions, as well as in smaller systems, such as Bak and Chen's sandpile and Waddington's warped plane. These processes also occur at a microlevel. They often are unobserved, yet play a central role in defining the characteristics of any system in a state of change (Prigogine and Stengers, 1984). Fluctuations, bifurcations, and subsequent processes of self-organization help to create and define new situations, as well as providing system stability and order.

Prigogine proposes that irreversibility brings order out of chaos—that fire (not the pendulum) is the ultimate source of pattern and stability in our world. In essence, he suggests that any system is filled with random fluctuations. On occasion, usually with the introduction of some change in the external environment, one of these fluctuations is accepted as a new form or order in the system. The new order is, in turn, solidified. The process of change that just occurred is not reversible (operating more like fire than a pendulum). Branching has taken place, and the system can never return to its former state.

How does the metaphor of a ball rolling down a warped, tilted plane relate to our understanding of turbulent postmodern organizations? First, as I have noted throughout this book, I believe that organizations are best conceived not as static structures but as complex, ongoing processes. A ball rolling down a tilted and warped plane represents a complex, ongoing process. Second, Waddington's warped plane effectively illustrates the process of bifurcation and groping I believe is central to understanding the processes of change and learning in any organization. Third, the unpredictability and seeming randomness or chaos of the ball's movement on the warped plane parallels the seeming randomness and chaos that operate in contemporary organizations (and perhaps organizations throughout history).

The warped plane metaphor, however, does have several major limitations. First, there is not one ball rolling down a plane in a complex, contemporary organization. Rather there are many balls, all moving at the same time, that are not only influenced by the warped plane but also by the movement of the other balls as they bounce against one another. As we begin to conceive of many balls moving over a warped plane, we return to our central metaphor in this chapter: the turbulent river. Each ball represents one drop of water moving across the riverbed with its many valleys, boulders, and flat sandy sections. Second, an organization is composed of living beings, not inanimate balls or drops of water. Thus, when people bump into each other they don't interact in a mechanistic cause-and-effect manner but in a highly interactive way that incorporates mutual causality. Our warped plane model, therefore, may lead us in a preliminary manner from the simplistic, mechanistic organizational models of the modern era. It should not, however, be considered adequate in portraying the complexities of the postmodern organizations in which we now work.

Given these precautionary notes, what can be learned from Waddington's warped plane—if we wish to get a better sense of how the dynamic ordering processes of bifurcation and groping work? I begin by equating the ball to a specific organizational process: a major change in the compensation program offered by a hypothetical corporation I will call Renfield. At the start, when the new compensation program is initially proposed (when the ball begins to roll down the warped plane), it encounters the first choice point (the first warp or ridge between two adjacent valleys). This choice point might be the selection of a spokesperson to make the initial presentation of the compensation program, or it might be the initial wording of the compensation proposal. This initial choice point can have a major impact on the future course of this proposal in the Renfield Corporation. Furthermore, this initial choice can never be reversed. While there can be later statements of support for the proposal and rewording of the proposal, the initial conditions set the stage.

At this choice point, those people who are in charge of presenting the proposal will tend to oscillate—much as the ball oscillates at the edge of the first valley. Bifurcation—that is, a choice point—tends to be preceded by oscillations. Those responsible for the proposal will shift back and forth in their opinion about who would be the most effective presenter. The president of Renfield could present the proposal. She has credibility and people will listen to her. However, some of the Renfield employees don't trust her and will assume she has some hidden agenda. The vice president of personnel could present the proposal. He would be an appropriate spokesman; however, he is not very convincing and has little credibility. What about the chair of the board or a member of the quality circle group that first identified the need for this change in compensation policies? The compensation program proponents will also shift back and forth regarding the wording of the proposal: should we be sure that the proposal covers all of the legal requirements, or should we write it in a clear and simple manner?

Once the decision is made—once the ball ceases to oscillate—the proposal is presented and has its initial impact. The ball begins to move down one of the adjacent valleys. At this point, an irreversible decision has been made. Second-order change has occurred, and in the real world, second-order learning must take place if proponents of the program are to be successful in their presentation of the proposal (in their movement into the initial valley). As the Renfield Corporation begins to move in the new valley, new forces come into play that were not present before the presentation of the proposal (entrance into the valley). Old forms and styles will have to be readjusted or abandoned.

The inherent resistance to change in any organization will be evident in Renfield at this point. The proposal, like the ball, experiences friction while moving down the new valley. Members of the organization line up on various sides of the issue. Organizational resistance builds up if the new compensation program challenges older forms and styles. Some of the old compensation programs at Renfield still exist as remnants; the new proposal must, after all, address issues that have existed in various forms throughout the life of the organization. The proposal hopefully addresses these long-standing issues in new and better ways. The ball is rolling in a new way down this valley. No two proposals are ever identical (even if the only difference is the shifts that have occurred in the organization's environment since the proposal was previously presented). No two balls rolling down a valley take exactly the same path.

When the ball begins to move down one of the valleys, it usually doesn't move directly down the center of the valley. Rather, because it entered the valley at an angle (having oscillated between several options before entering the valley), it rolls up the side of one of the valley's ridges and then corrects itself (like a pendulum) by rolling back across the floor of the valley and up the other ridge of the valley—while continuing to roll down the valley. Similarly, the new compensation proposal never affects the organization in the way it was originally conceived. It begins to run its own distinctive course. Members of the corporation who were thought to be probable supporters turn out to be detractors; anticipated enemies become improbable friends. Rogue events occur that influence both the amount of attention given to the proposal and the context within which the proposal is being evaluated.

At this point, the Renfield Corporation will tend to act like a pendulum: making orderly, first-order changes and operating in a self-correcting fashion. Proponents of the new compensation proposal will adjust their message to make it more appealing to the hourly employees or to the senior executives. Members of the marketing division will be given extensive attention. First-order learning will also be critical in determining the success of the proposal. Workshops will be offered to proponents of the proposal on how to be more effective in influencing their fellow employees, or senior executives will meet with the proposal leaders to review and modify the strategy used to present the proposal. The Renfield Corporation is moving toward a specific goal (acceptance of the new plan—the bottom of the valley) regarding the compensation program, and its leaders usually can clearly articulate the skills, knowledge, and attitudes needed among the men and women working in the organization if this new program is to be successful. This intermediate stage in the life of the new program is an evolutionary process, whereas the initial decision point—the movement into this particular valley—was much more revolutionary in nature.

The proposal leaders, however, may not yet be done with second-order change. At times, the ball may swing too far and actually roll up over the top of the ridge into the adjacent valley. First-order changes in the first valley have become too great, usually as a function of the speed of the ball's movement (the faster the speed, the wider the swings). The problems encountered by the compensation proposal may be too great for the proposal as written to remain intact or for the initial strategy for gaining acceptance for the proposal to remain in effect. As in the case of the oscillations that preceded the initial decision point (the ball's movement into the first valley), the movement to a revised proposal or to a new strategy (the second valley) is preceded by shifts back and forth with regard to the revisions, though in this case the oscillations are often much larger and more public than was true at the initial decision point. Everyone knows that things are in disarray and that something is about to happen.

One can only speculate on what will happen under these circumstances, for when the proposal or strategy is unraveling— when the ball is swinging widely from one ridge to the other—it is just as likely that changes in the proposal will move the organization in one direction as it is likely to move the proposal in another direction. Rumors abound. Anything is possible. The ball has as great a chance of moving over the top of the left ridge into the adjacent valley as it does of moving over the top of the right ridge into that valley. Most of the members of an organization don't really know much about any of the alternative proposals or strategies. Typically, there is even greater resistance to alternative proposals than there was to the original proposal. The adjacent valleys are just as alien as the one in which the ball is now moving, and there is always hope that the ball will continue to roll down the current valley and never really go over the top. Many members of the Renfield Corporation are likely to be suddenly wistful about the original proposal (after it is too late to go back to the proposal as originally written) or even about the world at Renfield prior to the introduction of this new compensation proposal.

If the proposal is substantially modified or if a new promotional strategy is implemented—if the ball does move over the top of one of the ridges—then a second revolution will take place. A choice has once again been made that is irreversible. The ball will roll down the side of the second valley. A whole new set of parameters will be in effect. Renfield needs to make some immediate adjustments when it enters the new valley. The ball will not be at the top of the valley when it rolls over the top of the ridge. Hence, it is not like a ball that is starting at the top of the valley and has had ample opportunity to learn from its mistakes. Members of the Renfield Corporation who are supporting the revised proposal must "hit the ground running" in this new valley. It will never be the same as if this revised proposal or strategy were selected at the first choice point, when the organization was poised at the top of the valley.

Those who are arguing for the revised proposal must employ a distinctive style that would probably not have been needed at the early choice point. Democracy in Russia, for instance, will never be the same as democracy in countries such as the United States that have already been working in this valley for two hundred years. A large company that downsizes will never be the same as a smaller company that was never large in the first place. A reformed alcoholic will never be the same as a lifelong teetotaler. The wounds caused by downsizing will never really heal, and the Russians will inevitably develop a governance system that will incorporate elements or "ghosts" of both their years of communism and their years of premodern czarist rule. Renfield's future compensation programs will never be the same as they were several years ago, given the success or failure of the current proposal.

The ball enters the second valley at an angle and at the peak of one of the second valley's ridges. Therefore, it tends to roll high up on the opposite ridge of this second valley. It may even roll over the top of this second valley into yet another valley. Regardless of the valley in which it settles, the ball will swing back and forth wildly from one ridge to the other before settling into a more stable pattern of slowly oscillating, self-correcting movement down the floor of this valley. The Renfield Corporation is likely to produce a variety of other compensation proposals, and many suggestions regarding better ways to sell the proposals will appear. There will be many prophets, visionaries, and kibitzers, each with a different idea of the best route to take. The outcomes of the proposal review process are likely to be unpredictable at this point. First-order changes and pendulum corrections are required of this organization, yet these changes must somehow be reconciled with the second-order change processes that have just taken place (and that may take place again).

What determines the nature and outcome of the movement of the organization or ball down the warped plane? We have already mentioned speed as an important determinant. The faster the ball is moving—the more quickly an organizational change is introduced—the more likely it is to jump to an adjacent valley. The amount of oscillation is also dependent on the height of the ridges. Adjacent valleys (and organizational types) with low ridges (highly permeable boundaries) are conducive to second-order movements between valleys. Thus, in a postmodern world with highly permeable boundaries, we are likely to find more second-order, revolutionary changes in organizations—more shifting between valleys. The amount of oscillation within a specific valley is also dependent in part on the amount of friction between the ball and the plane on which it is rolling. High levels of friction in a valley tend to slow down the roll of the ball, hence reduce the height of the movement up the side of either ridge of the valley. Organizational valleys exhibit friction to the extent that they have strong cultural resistance to change, as is often found in organizations that resemble maple trees rather than palm trees.

Maple tree organizations and others with dominant, stable cultures tend to slow down oscillations as well as the movement of the organization down the valley. Maple tree organizations are likely to be less efficient and responsive to change but are more often stable. They need first-order (rarely second-order) change and learning, whereas proposals presented in palm tree organizations are more likely to shift valleys and, as a result, elicit second-order change. Given the emergence of many palm tree organizations in our world, we are likely in the near future to see organizational change portrayed as an irreversible traverse of many different warped planes. These processes more closely resemble the flickering of a flame than the systematic movement of a pendulum.

In previous chapters I have spoken of the central role that narration and conversation play in the life of an organization. Narratives and conversations, in general, follow the same path down a warped plane as the rolling ball. Narratives involve a series of decisions about which direction to take in forming and telling a story. A set of bifurcations occurs. The story moves in one direction and can never return to another narrative valley without taking into account the first choice made. We speak the truth or a lie, we converse with other people, and we tell our stories—then we must live with the consequences. This warped plane cannot be traversed again. We must learn from our successes and our failures at communication and begin again, crossing yet another warped organizational plane.

How Do We Cope with the Turbulence?

How do we work in turbulent postmodern organizations? How do we live on the edge of order and chaos? How does one survive on a warped plane? What occurs when one is oscillating back and forth through a valley or rolling across the top of a ridge into a new and foreign valley? Both the first-order changes that occur within a single valley and the second-order changes that accompany movement to a new valley leave one with the sense of edginess, the common malady of the postmodern era. While there are no remedies for this edginess, in terms of modern medical or mental health models (which tend to emphasize the pathological rather than adaptive aspects of edginess), there are premodern and modern remedies that have been available to us for many years, though we have tended to look elsewhere during the secular years of the modern era. There are also newly emerging strategies that may provide partial relief.

To begin with, we must identify and nurture quite different attitudes about organizational life and leadership, given that change is neither predictable nor consistent from place to place in the organization. We can look to Teilhard de Chardin for guidance in this matter. Teilhard proposes that effectiveness in such a setting builds on the process of synthesis: of ideas and of people. Given the emphasis in modern society on analysis (breaking things down into their constituent parts) and the control of discrete entities, the notion of synthesis is truly radical, though the seeds for such an approach are found in many contemporary organizations.

A woman who heads a successful gourmet coffee company talks about sitting in her office and knowing exactly what is happening throughout the company as a function of the sounds she hears through the wall and the smell of the coffee being produced. She doesn't know exactly how she is able to gain this overall sense of the company's health at any one point in time, but she firmly believes that this unifying sense of her company is essential to this organization. Another leader suggests that in his role as teacher, he gains a clear sense of the overall, coherent mission and dynamics of the school he heads. Like the coffee maker, he can sense or "smell" the quality of education in his school by participating in the educational process as a teacher/learner. When he is not teaching, the school often seems to lose its unity for him, and he feels out of touch with its essential properties.

Second, we must develop a new sense of community within our postmodern organizations. We must establish strong commitments and partnerships among those working in these organizations. Love is a key word for Teilhard (1955, p. 264-265) in examining the relationship between the individual and the collective: "considered in its full biological reality, love—that is to say, the affinity of being with being—is not peculiar to man. It is a general property of all life and as such it embraces, in its varieties and degrees, all the forms successively adopted by organized matter." He goes on to state:

> Love alone is capable of uniting living beings in such a way as to complete and fulfill them, for it alone takes them and joins them by what is deepest in themselves. This is a fact of daily experience. At what moment do lovers come into the most complete possession of themselves if not when they say they are lost in each other? In truth, does not love every instant achieve all around us, in the couple or the team, the magic feat, the feat reputed to be contradictory, of "personalizing" by totalizing? And if that is what it can achieve daily on a small scale, why should it not repeat this one day on world-wide dimensions?

Eisler (1987) offers a similar emphasis on relationship and partnership. She dramatically documents the destructive consequences of a world that fails to value the feminine characteristics of collaboration and colleagueship, valuing and rewarding instead the more masculine traits of hierarchy and the use of force to establish status. Drawing on a wide range of previously ignored studies of very old (pre-Christian) European cultures, Eisler proposes two different forms in which societies can be structured: "The first, designated the partnership or gylanic model . . . is characterized by 'soft' or stereotypically feminine values such as mutual accommodation, cooperation, and nonviolence. The second model is the dominator or androcratic model . . . with a characterizing value and social guidance system idealizing 'hard' or so-called masculine values such as conquest, mastery, and force" (Loye and Eisler, 1987, p. 63).

We find a parallel analysis to Teilhard's and Eisler's notions of lover and partner in Robert Greenleaf's (1970, pp. 3–4) description of leaders as servants:

> A fresh critical look is being taken at the issues of power and authority, and people are beginning to learn, however haltingly, to relate to one another in less coercive and more creatively supporting ways. A new moral principle is emerging which holds that the only authority deserving one's allegiance is that which is freely and knowingly granted by the led to the leader in response to, and in proportion to, the clearly evident servant stature of the leader. Those who choose to follow this principle will not casually accept the authority of existing institutions. Rather, they will freely respond only to individuals who are chosen as leaders because they are proven and trusted as servants. To the extent that this principle prevails in the future, the only truly viable institutions will be those that are predominantly servant-led.

Perhaps the early paternalistic leaders of the modern era who assumed the role of surrogate parent forgot (or ignored) one of the principal tasks of the premodern parent/leader: that of loving and sacrificing for one's children. It is in the role of lover and servant that a parent first creates the lifelong bond of commitment to—and commitment from—his or her children. Without this bond, leadership by means of paternalism (or autonomy, for that matter) must ultimately rely on coercive control, whether overt or covert.

As encouraging and inspiring as Teilhard, Eisler, and Greenleaf are, one may be inclined to dismiss their portrayals as hope-

lessly out-of-date or out of touch with reality. Yet all three visionaries speak to the necessity for such a shift, given the critical condition of our world and the ingredients needed for such a change.
According to Teilhard (1955, p. 266), "[if] a universal love is impossible, how can we account for the irresistible instinct in our hearts
which leads us towards unity whenever and in whatever direction
our passions are stirred: A sense of the universe, a sense of the all,
the nostalgia which seizes us when confronted by nature, beauty,
music—these seem to be an expectation and awareness of a Great
Presence."

Eisler (1987) proposes that the seeds have already been sown
for the movement of our society from a highly individualistic and
competitive dominator model to a collaborative and more feminine
model of partnership. She comments extensively on the reexamination of cultural history now occurring, which shows that our world
has known many eras when highly advanced civilizations have been
based on partnerships rather than on domination. "The peak of
ourselves," Teilhard tells us, "[and] the acme of our originality, is
not our individuality but our person; and according to the evolutionary structure of the world, we can only find our person by
uniting together. There is no mind without synthesis" (1955,
p. 263). At the heart of this new model is a sense of turbulent organizations as those most in need of a synthesis based on love,
dedication, and collaboration.

Third, at a personal level, the turbulence of postmodernism
can only be successfully confronted when we find a place in our
own being that provides sanctuary—a safe place for reflection and
renewal. In the beautifully poignant song "And So It Goes" recorded in 1983 by the popular singer Billy Joel, a sanctuary is described that exists in every person's heart. This part of our heart will
always be "safe and strong." It is where we heal our wounds from
the past and prepare for new ventures. Such sanctuaries hopefully
are supported by our organizations and society as a means of healing other wounds and providing space and time for needed reflection and inquiry. In confronting a world of turbulence, chaos, and
unclear boundaries—a world in which clarity of mission and purpose seems critical—there is great need for Billy Joel's "safe and
strong" sanctuary.

Back in the 1930s, with World War II looming in the near future and the world limping its way out of a major recession, there was a strong need for sanctuary, as captured in the popular film *Lost Horizon*. Ronald Colman played the role of a very successful British statesman who is kidnapped and taken to a remote land called Shangri-La. For Colman, this location held great attraction. It was free of pain and strife. Shangri-La also provided an opportunity for reflection on the complex and turbulent world outside, while giving those who entered its cloistered walls (in this case, a hidden valley) the opportunity for personal growth and renewal. Colman, like many of us who have created or stumbled into Shangri-La, found that the hardest part is leaving and returning to a world we don't necessarily enjoy. However, Shangri-La—like all sanctuaries—exists precisely because of our need to remain engaged in an "active life" (Palmer, 1990) in which we address the critical needs and concerns of our family, our organization, and our community.

The sanctuary may be a physical location: a retreat, a "grail castle" (Sanford, 1977), a "safe place" within or outside the organization. Some Japanese firms provide private rooms where employees can go to let loose their frustrations and anger. However, sanctuaries (almost by definition) usually exist outside of an organizational context. Wealthy men and women can escape, like Robinson Crusoe, to a remote spot on the map, like St. Simons Island off the Georgia Sea Islands, where (unlike Robinson Crusoe) they are lavished with attention and superb cuisine while they reflect on their own life and work. Alternatively, as Billy Joel suggests, sanctuary is most often found within one's own heart or head.

In one of his warm, embracing stories from "The Prairie Home Companion" radio program about life in a small Minnesota town ("Lake Wobegon"), Garrison Keillor (1983) speaks about the "storm home" assigned to him by his school when he was a small boy. Keillor lived in the country and went to school by bus. Consequently, to prepare for the possibility that he might be stranded in town as a result of a snow blizzard, the school gave him (and the other children living in the country) an alternative home to go to located in town. Keillor never had to use this home; however, he often walked by his "storm home" and reflected on the loving, supportive nature of the couple who were his "storm parents." He often thought of this man and woman and their house when things were going bad or when he was discouraged. He fantasized that this couple had specifically picked him out as their "storm child" and that they would welcome him with open arms during difficult times.

We have similar need for a "storm home" as adults working in organizations. The "storm home" of the mind may be created through a technique or a ritual that provides internal support and encouragement for our difficult decisions and risk-taking behavior. In essence, we pat ourselves on the back or find a way (through meditation, daydreaming, or quiet reflection) to calm ourselves down and gain a sense of reassurance. A colleague of mine who presides over a graduate institution found that he could gently touch his forehead when under stress and evoke with this touch a sense of personal calmness. These moments of personal sanctuary during the day may be essential components in any postmodern survival kit. Another colleague sets aside one day each week for her writing. A third friend insists on swimming in the San Francisco Bay every day during lunchtime. In each instance, an internal sanctuary—"safe and strong"—has been created for both healing and reflection.

Thus, at the heart of survival in a turbulent, postmodern world is the capacity for synthesis, love, and sanctuary. We must be able to draw together or synthesize that which seems diverse or ambiguous in hybrid organizations. We must be able to love and build a sense of community among men and women who live with the complexities of cyclical and intersect organizations. We must be able to find personal sanctuary in a world of organizational turbulence. Those of us fortunate enough to be living in this remarkable period of transition to a new postmodern era can expect to look at many irreversible organizational changes—organizational fires if you will. We will be able to tell our children and grandchildren about the early postmodern organizations of the 1980s and 1990s as they began to move irreversibly and sometimes even quietly into a new world, with new perspectives, new realities, and new visions. It should be quite a story!

References

Adizes, I. *Corporate Lifecycles.* Englewood Cliffs, N.J.: Prentice-Hall, 1988.

Allport, G. *Personality: A Psychological Interpretation.* Troy, Mo.: Holt, Rinehart & Winston, 1937.

Alpert, M. "Office Buildings for the 1990s." *Fortune,* Nov. 18, 1991, pp. 140–150.

Anderson, W. *Reality Isn't What It Used To Be.* San Francisco: Harper San Francisco, 1990.

Argyris, C. *Reasoning, Learning, and Action: Individual and Organizational.* San Francisco: Jossey-Bass, 1982.

Argyris, C., and Schön, D. *Theory in Practice: Increasing Professional Effectiveness.* San Francisco: Jossey-Bass, 1974.

Argyris, C., and Schön, D. *Organizational Learning: A Theory of Action Perspective.* Reading, Mass: Addison-Wesley, 1978.

Armstrong, L., and Symonds, W. C. "Beyond 'May I help you?'" *Business Week,* Oct. 25, 1991, pp. 100–103.

Autry, R. "Companies to Watch: Keystone International." *Fortune,* May 6, 1991, p. 100.

Bak, P., and Chen, K. "Self-Organized Criticality." *Scientific American,* Jan. 1991, pp. 46–53.

Bateson, G. *Mind and Nature: A Necessary Unity.* New York: Dutton, 1979.

Becker, E. *The Birth and Death of Meaning.* New York: Free Press, 1971.

Becker, E. *The Denial of Death.* New York: Free Press, 1973.

Beckhard, R. *Organization Development: Strategies and Models.* Reading, Mass.: Addison-Wesley, 1969.

Belenky, M., and others. *Women's Ways of Knowing.* New York: Basic Books, 1986.

Bell, D. *Coming of Post-Industrial Society: A Venture in Social Forecasting.* New York: Basic Books, 1976.

Bellah, R., and others. *Habits of the Heart.* Berkeley: University of California Press, 1985.

Bellah, R., and others. *The Good Society.* New York: Knopf, 1992.

Bennis, W., and Slater, P. *The Temporary Society.* New York: HarperCollins, 1968.

Berger, P., and Luckmann, T. *Social Construction of Reality.* New York: Doubleday, 1967.

Bergquist, W. *The Four Cultures of the Academy: Insights and Strategies for Improving Leadership in Collegiate Organizations.* San Francisco: Jossey-Bass, 1992.

Bergquist, W., Greenberg, E., and Klaum, A. *In Our Fifties: The Voices of Men and Women Reinventing Themselves.* San Francisco: Jossey-Bass, 1993.

Best, F. (ed.). *The Future of Work.* Englewood Cliffs, N.J.: Prentice-Hall, 1973.

Bion, W. *Experiences in Groups.* New York: Basic Books, 1961.

Blake, R., and Mouton, J. *Managerial Grid III* (3rd ed.). Houston, Tex.: Gulf, 1984.

Block, P. *The Empowered Manager: Positive Political Skills at Work.* San Francisco: Jossey-Bass, 1987.

Boulding, K. "Religious Foundations of Economic Progress." *Harvard Business Review,* 1952, *30*, 33–40.

Boulding, K. "Toward a General Theory of Growth." *Canadian Journal of Economics and Political Science,* 1953, *19*, 326–340.

Boulding, K. "Intersects: The Peculiar Organizations." In The Conference Board, *Challenge to Leadership: Managing in a Changing World.* New York: Free Press, 1973.

Bremuer, B., Rebello, K., Schiller, Z. and Weber, J. "The Age of Consolidation." *Business Week,* Oct. 14, 1991, pp. 86–94.

Briggs, J., and Peat, F. D. *Turbulent Mirror.* New York: HarperCollins, 1989.

Burdman, P. " 'Flexible' Jobs on the Rise." *San Francisco Chronicle,* Aug. 10, 1992, pp. C1, C5.

Burke, W. *Organization Development: A Normative Approach.* Reading, Mass.: Addison-Wesley, 1987.

Bylinsky, G. "The Marvels of 'Virtual Reality.' " *Fortune,* Jun. 3, 1991a, pp. 138–150.

Bylinsky, G. "Saving Time with New Technology." *Fortune,* Dec. 30, 1991b, pp. 98–104.

Caminiti, S. "Look Who Likes Franchising Now." *Fortune,* Sept. 23, 1991, pp. 125–130.

Clegg, S. *Modern Organizations: Organizational Studies in the Postmodern World.* Newbury Park, Calif.: Sage, 1990.

Cleveland, H. "Information as a Resource." *The Futurist,* Dec. 1982, pp. 34–39.

Colman, A., and Bexton, W. H. (eds.) *Group Relations Reader.* Anchorage, Ky.: Grex Press, 1975.

Cook, J. "Charity Checklist." *Forbes,* Oct. 28, 1991a, pp. 180–184.

Cook, J. "Wolf in Sheep's Clothing." *Forbes,* Dec. 23, 1991b, pp. 122–124.

Coy, P. "Your New Computer: The Telephone." *Business Week,* Jun. 3, 1991a, pp. 126–129.

Coy, P. "How Do You Build an Information Highway?" *Business Week,* Sept. 16, 1991b, pp. 108–112.

Csikszentmihalyi, M. *Beyond Boredom and Anxiety: The Experience of Play in Work and Games.* San Francisco: Jossey-Bass, 1975.

Csikszentmihalyi, M. *Flow: The Psychology of Optimal Experience.* New York: HarperCollins, 1990.

Deal, T. E., and Kennedy, A. A. *Corporate Cultures: The Rites and Rituals of Corporate Life.* Reading, Mass.: Addison-Wesley, 1982.

Dews, P. *Logics of Disintegration.* New York: Verso, 1987.

Doctorow, E. L. *The Book of Daniel.* New York: Random House, 1971.

Doctorow, E. L. *Ragtime.* New York: Random House, 1975.

Drucker, P. *The Age of Discontinuity.* New York: HarperCollins, 1968.

Drucker, P. *The New Realities.* New York: HarperCollins, 1989.

Dunahee, M. H., and Wrangler, L. A. "The Psychological Contract: A Conceptual Structure for Management/Employee Relations." *Personnel Journal,* July 1974, pp. 519–526.

Durkheim, E. *The Division of Labor in Society.* New York: Free Press, 1933. (Originally published 1893.)

Edmundson, M. "Prophet of a New Postmodernism: The Greater Challenge of Salman Rushdie." *Harper's Magazine,* December 1989, pp. 62–71.

Eisler, R. *The Chalice and the Blade.* San Francisco: Harper San Francisco, 1987.

Faltermayer, E. "The Thaw in Washington." *Fortune,* Spring/Summer 1991, pp. 46–51.

Festinger, L. *A Theory of Cognitive Dissonance.* Stanford, Calif.: Stanford University Press, 1957.

Fiedler, F. *A Theory of Leadership Effectiveness.* New York: McGraw-Hill, 1967.

Flint, J. "They Don't Build 'em Like They Used To." *Forbes,* Oct. 28, 1991, pp. 196–197.

Forrester, J. *Industrial Dynamics.* Cambridge, Mass.: MIT Press, 1961.

Forrester, J. *Urban Dynamics.* Cambridge, Mass.: MIT Press, 1969.

Forrester, J. *World Dynamics.* Cambridge, Mass.: Wright-Allen Press, 1971.

Foucault, M. *Madness and Civilization.* New York: Random House, 1965.

Freud, S. *The Interpretation of Dreams.* New York: Avon, 1965. (Originally published 1900.)

Fromm, E. *Escape from Freedom.* New York: Rinehart, 1941.

Fromm, E. *The Sane Society.* New York: Fawcett, 1955.

Galbraith, J. R. *Organizational Design.* Reading, Mass.: Addison-Wesley, 1977.

Gilligan, C. *In a Different Voice.* Cambridge, Mass.: Harvard University Press, 1982.

Gitlin, T. "Hip-Deep in Post-Modernism." *New York Times Book Review,* Nov. 6, 1988, pp. 1, 35, 36.

Gleick, J. *Chaos: Making A New Science.* New York: Viking Penguin, 1987.

Goodman, J. B., and Loveman, G. W. "Does Privatization Serve the Public Interest?" *Harvard Business Review,* 1991, Nov.-Dec., pp. 26–38.

Greenleaf, R. *The Servant as Leader.* Peterborough, N.H.: Windy Row Press, 1970.

Grimes, A. J., and Berger, P. K. "Cosmopolitan-Local: Evaluation of the Concept." *Administrative Science Quarterly,* 1970, *15,* 407–416.

Halliburton, D. "The Nature of Systems." Paper presented as part of the William James Lecture Series, The Professional School of Psychology, San Francisco, California, Sept. 1987–June 1988.

Heilbruner, R. "Work and Technological Priorities: A Historical Perspective." In F. Best (ed.), *The Future of Work.* Englewood Cliffs, N.J.: Prentice-Hall, 1973.

Hershey, P., and Blanchard, K. *The Management of Organizational Behavior.* (3rd ed.) Englewood Cliffs, N.J.: Prentice-Hall, 1977.

Herzberg, F. *Work and the Nature of Man.* Cleveland, Ohio: World, 1966.

Hester, G. *Breaking the Bank.* Boston: Little, Brown, 1988.

Hochheiser, R. *How to Work for a Jerk.* New York: Random House, 1987.

Hochschild, A. *The Managed Heart.* Berkeley: University of California Press, 1983.

Huey, J. "America's Most Successful Merchant." *Fortune,* Sept. 23, 1991a, pp. 46–59.

Huey, J. "Nothing Is Impossible." *Fortune,* Sept. 23, 1991b, pp. 135–140.

Huey, J. "New Frontiers in Commuting." *Fortune,* Jan. 13, 1992, pp. 56–58.

Huyssen, A. *After the Great Divide.* Bloomington: Indiana University Press, 1987.

Jameson, F. *Postmodernism or the Cultural Logic of Late Capitalism.* Durham, N.C.: Duke University Press, 1991.

Johnston, G. S. *Beyond the Boom.* New York: Poseidon Press, 1990.

Jung, C. G. *Psychology and Religion.* New Haven, Conn.: Yale University Press, 1938.

Kanter, R. M. *Men and Women of the Corporation.* New York: Basic Books, 1977.

Kanter, R. M. *The Change Masters.* New York: Simon & Schuster, 1983.

Kauffman, S. "Antichaos and Adaptation." *Scientific American,* August, 1991, pp. 78–84.

Keillor, G. *News from Lake Wobegon: Winter.* St. Paul: Minnesota Public Radio, 1983. Audiotape.

Kellner, D. "Introduction: Jameson, Marxism and Postmodernism." In D. Kellner (ed.), *Postmodernism/Jameson/Critique.* Washington, D.C.: Maisonneuve Press, 1989.

Kepner, C. H., and Tregoe, B. B. *The New Rational Manager.* Princeton, N.J.: Kepner-Tregoe, 1981.

Kidder, T. *The Soul of a New Machine.* Boston: Little, Brown, 1981.

Kierkegaard, S. *The Sickness unto Death.* Princeton, N.J.: Princeton University Press, 1980.

Kimberly, J. R., Miles, R. H., and Associates. *The Organizational Life Cycle: Issues in the Creation, Transformation, and Decline of Organizations.* San Francisco: Jossey-Bass, 1980.

Kirkpatrick, D. "Why Not Farm Out Your Computing?" *Fortune,* Sept. 23, 1991, pp. 103–112.

Korzybski, A. *Science and Sanity.* Lancaster, Pa.: Science Press, 1933.

Kuhn, T. *The Structure of Scientific Revolutions.* Chicago: University of Chicago Press, 1962.

Kundera, M. *The Unbearable Lightness of Being.* New York: HarperCollins, 1984.

Labich, K. "Can Your Career Hurt Your Kids?" *Fortune,* May 20, 1991, pp. 38-56.

Lasch, C. *The Minimal Self: Psychic Survival in Troubled Times.* New York: Norton, 1984.

Lawler, E. *High-Involvement Management: Participative Strategies for Improving Organizational Performance.* San Francisco: Jossey-Bass, 1986.

Lawrence, P. R., and Lorsch, J. *Organization and Environment.* Boston: Harvard Business School, 1967.

Levinson, D., and others. *The Seasons of a Man's Life.* New York: Knopf, 1978.

Lewyn, M. "Pushing the Envelope at the Post Office." *Business Week,* Nov. 25, 1991, pp. 56-60.

Light, L., and others; "And the Crunch Goes On." *Business Week,* Aug. 12, 1991, pp. 20-21.

Lippitt, R., Watson, J., and Westley, B. *Dynamics of Planned Change.* Orlando, Fla.: Harcourt Brace Jovanovich, 1958.

Lopez, G. *Crow and Weasel.* New York: Farrar, Straus & Giroux, 1990.

Loye, D., and Eisler, R. "Chaos and Transformation: Implications of Nonequilibrium Theory for Social Science and Society." *Behavioral Science,* 1987, *32,* 53-65.

Lubove, S. "Don't Leave Home, Period." *Forbes,* Oct. 28, 1991, pp. 164-166.

Lyotard, J. *The Postmodern Condition.* Minneapolis: University of Minnesota Press, 1984.

McCarroll, T. "Starting Over." *Time,* Jan. 6, 1992, pp. 62-63.

McGregor, D. M. *The Professional Manager.* New York: McGraw-Hill, 1960.

McLuhan, M. *Understanding Media: The Extensions of Man.* New York: McGraw-Hill, 1964.

Marquez, G. G. *The General in His Labyrinth.* New York: Knopf, 1990.

Meadows, D., and others. *The Limits to Growth.* New York: Signet, 1972.

Mesarovic, M., and Pestel, E. *Mankind at the Turning Point: The Second Report to the Club of Rome.* New York: Dutton, 1974.

Michael, D. *Planning to Learn and Learning to Plan.* San Francisco: Jossey-Bass, 1973.

Miles, M. "On Temporary Systems." In M. Miles (ed.), *Innovation in Education.* New York: Teachers College Press, 1964.

Miller, G., Galanter, E., and Pribrum, K. *Plans and the Structure of Behavior.* Troy, Mo.: Holt, Rinehart, & Winston, 1960.

Naisbitt, J. *Megatrends.* New York: Warner, 1984.

Nelson, R. H. "Why Capitalism Hasn't Won Yet." *Forbes,* Nov. 25, 1991, pp. 104–111.

Otto, R. *The Idea of the Holy.* London: Oxford University Press, 1923.

Palmer, P. *The Active Life.* San Francisco: Harper San Francisco, 1990.

Pare, T. P. "The Fortune 500: Who May Thrive Now?" *Fortune,* Apr. 22, 1991, pp. 58–64.

Perry, N. "The Workers of the Future." *Fortune,* Spring/Summer, 1991, pp. 68–72.

Perry, W. *Form of Intellectual and Ethical Development in the College Years: A Scheme.* Troy, Mo.: Holt, Rinehart & Winston, 1970.

Peters, T. *Thriving on Chaos.* New York: HarperCollins, 1987.

Peters, T., and Waterman, R. H. *In Search of Excellence: Lessons from America's Best-Run Companies.* New York: HarperCollins, 1982.

Phillips, K. "The Balkanization of America." *Harpers Magazine,* May 1978, pp. 37–47.

Pitta, J. "Buggy Whip Marketing." *Forbes,* Nov. 25, 1991, p. 193.

Polak, F. *The Image of the Future.* San Francisco: Jossey-Bass, 1972.

Polanyi, M. *Knowing and Being.* Chicago: University of Chicago Press, 1969.

Prigogine, I., and Stengers, I. *Order Out of Chaos.* New York: Bantam Books, 1984.

Quehl, G. "The Inner World of Leadership." Unpublished essay, Orinda, California, 1991.

Reich, R. "Who Is Them?" *Harvard Business Review,* 1991, Mar.-Apr., pp. 77–88.

Rice, F. "Champions of Communication." *Fortune,* Jun. 3, 1991a, pp. 111–120.

Rice, F. "America's Hottest HMO." *Fortune,* Jul. 15, 1991b, p. 94.

Rokeach, M. *The Open and Closed Mind.* New York: Basic Books, 1960.

Rose, F. "If It Feels Good, It Must Be Bad." *Fortune,* Oct. 21, 1991, pp. 91-108.

Sanford, J. *He.* New York: HarperCollins, 1977.

Sarason, S. *The Creation of Settings and the Future Societies.* San Francisco: Jossey-Bass, 1972.

Sawaya, Z. "Cutting Out the Middle Man." *Forbes,* Jan. 6, 1992, p. 169.

Schein, E. *Process Consultation.* Reading, Mass.: Addison-Wesley, 1969.

Schein, E. *Career Dynamics.* Reading, Mass.: Addison-Wesley, 1978.

Schein, E. *Organizational Psychology.* (3rd ed.) Englewood Cliffs, N.J.: Prentice-Hall, 1980.

Schein, E. *Organizational Culture and Leadership: A Dynamic View.* San Francisco: Jossey-Bass, 1985.

Schneider, B. (ed.). *Organizational Climate and Culture.* San Francisco: Jossey-Bass, 1990.

Schön, D. *Beyond the Stable State.* New York: Random House, 1971.

Schön, D. *The Reflective Practitioner: How Professionals Think in Action.* New York: Basic Books, 1983.

Schumacher, E. F. *Small Is Beautiful.* New York: HarperCollins, 1973.

Sellers, P. "Does the CEO Really Matter?" *Fortune,* Apr. 22, 1991a, pp. 80-94.

Sellers, P. "A Boring Brand Can Be Beautiful." *Fortune,* Nov. 18, 1991b, pp. 169-179.

Senge, P. *The Fifth Discipline.* New York: Doubleday, 1990.

Sennett, R. *The Fall of Public Man.* New York: Knopf, 1976.

Sennett, R. *Authority.* New York: Random House, 1981.

Sidey, H. "The Two Sides of the Sam Walton Legacy." *Time,* Apr. 20, 1992, pp. 50-52.

Slutsker, G. "If You Can't Beat 'Em. . . ." *Forbes,* Jan. 6, 1992, p. 48.

Stewart, T. A. "The New American Century: Where We Stand." *Fortune,* Spring/Summer 1991, pp. 12-23.

Sullivan, H. S. *The Interpersonal Theory of Psychiatry*. New York: Norton, 1953.

Tawney, R. H. *The Acquisitive Society*. London: Collins, 1921.

Teilhard de Chardin, P. *The Phenomenon of Man*. New York: HarperCollins, 1955. (Originally published 1937.)

Therrien, L. "McRisky." *Business Week*, Oct. 21, 1991a, pp. 114-122.

Therrien, L. "This Marketing Effort Has L'Eggs." *Business Week*, Dec. 23, 1991b, pp. 50-51.

Tillich, P. *The Dynamics of Faith*. New York: HarperCollins, 1957.

Toffler, A. *Future Shock*. New York: Bantam Books, 1971.

Toffler, A. *The Third Wave*. New York: Morrow, 1980.

Turner, V. *The Ritual Process*. Hawthorne, N.Y.: Aldine, 1969.

Vaill, P. *Managing as a Performing Art: New Ideas for a World of Chaotic Change*. San Francisco: Jossey-Bass, 1989.

Verity, J. W. "The Big Winners in Big Blue's Breakup: Customers." *Business Week*, Dec. 23, 1991, p. 28.

Verity, J. W., Peterson, T., Depke, D., and Schwartz, E. I. "The New IBM." *Business Week*, Dec. 16, 1991, pp. 113-118.

Vroom, V. H., and Yetton, P. W. *Leadership and Decision Making*. Pittsburgh, Pa.: University of Pittsburgh Press, 1973.

Waddington, C. H. *Tools for Thought*. St. Albans, England: Basic Books, 1977.

Watson, G., and Johnson, D. *Social Psychology: Issues and Insights*. (2nd ed.) Philadelphia, Pa.: Lippincott, 1972.

Wattenburg, B. *The First Universal Nation*. New York: Free Press, 1990.

Watzlawick, P., Beavin, J. H., and Jackson, D. D. *Pragmatics of Human Communication*. New York: Norton, 1967.

Weber, M. *The Theory of Social and Economic Organization*. New York: Free Press, 1947.

Weber, M. *The Protestant Ethic and the Spirit of Capitalism*. New York: Charles Scribner's Sons, 1958.

Woods, W. "Can John Akers Save IBM?" *Fortune*, Jul. 15, 1991, pp. 40-56.

Woodward, J. *Management and Technology*. London: HMSO, 1958.

Index